THE
LONG FAREWELL

DON CHARLWOOD

ALLEN LANE

Allen Lane
A Division of Penguin Books Ltd
487 Maroondah Highway, P.O. Box 257
Ringwood, Victoria, 3134, Australia
Penguin Books Ltd,
536 Kings Road, London SW10 OUH

ISBN 07139 1428 9

Designed by Helen Semmler
Set in Helvetica and Cochin by The Dova Type Shop, Melbourne
Made and printed in Australia by Globe Press Pty Ltd

CIP

Charlwood, D. E. (Donald Ernest), 1915-
The long farewell.

Bibliography.
Includes index.
ISBN 0 7139 1428 9.

1. Sailing ships. 2. Voyages and travels.
3. Australia – Emigration and immigration. 4. Great
Britain – Emigration and immigration. I. Title.

304.8'94041

Published with the assistance of the
Literature Board of the Australia Council

For Nell
Immigrant of 1945
With Love

Contents

Preface

This book is based primarily on diaries kept by emigrants on their way to Australia during the era of sail. To provide background to the diarists' world, I have told something of their preparations for the voyage, the route their ships followed and the development of the ships themselves. The diarists' stories end as they sight their new land.

The emigrants whose diaries I have used came almost entirely from the British Isles since this was overwhelmingly the main source of Australia's population during the sailing-ship era. By 1881, when the era was near its end, the census for Australasia — Australia and New Zealand then being considered jointly — showed that a total of 980,467 people resident in the two countries had been born overseas. Of these, 912,945 had come from the British Isles: 499,922 from England and Wales; 261,996 from Ireland and 151,027 from Scotland. Second to these was the group of German birth which numbered 42,203. The 1881 census also showed 1,741,121 of the population to be 'Australasian born'.

Although my main interest has been in the diarists themselves, I was struck during my research by the contrast between conditions on the voyage to Australia and conditions on the much shorter voyage to North America — differences that played a part, I believe, in shaping differences in attitudes between the peoples of the two continents. I also became much more aware of the lessons Britain had learnt for emigration from her experience in the transportation of convicts.

The La Trobe Library, Melbourne, first drew my attention to the existence of voyage diaries, especially to those placed in their own keeping by diarists' descendants. I turned then to similar collections in the National Library and the Mitchell and J. S. Battye Libraries, reading in all over a hundred diaries. To the staff of these libraries, my warm thanks; also to the staff of the State Library of South Australia for granting me access to the magnificent Edwardes Collection of nautical photographs.

Early in my research I was helped and advised by Mrs Ellie Pullin, then director of the Royal Historical Society of Victoria, and by Dr David O'Sullivan of the Australian Medical Association Library, Melbourne. To them both, my thanks. Further afield, my thanks are due to Michael Stammers, Keeper of Maritime History in the Merseyside County Museums, Liverpool, who afforded me not only time, but accommodation in his office; and Stan Barstow of Ossett, Yorkshire, who showed me the memorial to the miners buried at the Silkstone churchyard.

The libraries, public records offices and individuals who hold the diaries I have used are acknowledged in the Chapter Notes. My thanks to them all.

Many individuals were most generous in giving me information, advice and assistance of various kinds. Particularly I wish to thank Marjorie Morgan who freely and enthusiastically shared her great store of knowledge of the field in which I was working; also Captain David Wharington, not only for the extensive nautical material with which he provided me, but for his patience in explaining some of it to a one-time RAAF navigator with limited knowledge of the sea. Also, Dr Judith Armstrong, Kelson Arnold, Peter Blackney, Susan Brown, Arthur Charlwood, Michael Dugan, Rosamund Duruz, Stewart Edwards, Cliff Green, Colleen Haigh, Captain Brett Hilder, W. B. M. Hunter, A. T. Hutchinson, Jean MacKenzie, Stan McPhee, Jean Manning, Pip Marks, John Morrison, Captain John Noble, Dr Effie Ross, Olaf Ruhen, E. A. Schurmann, S. A. E. Ström, Jean Uhl, Donald Walker and Peter Williams.

Above all, I wish to thank Nell, my wife, for bearing with my wearisome requests for re-typing and, at the end, for indexing the completed book.

Throughout the book I have retained the measurements of distances, weights etc current during the era of sail; metrication would have created an anachronism.

Although today's population of Australia has been drawn from a wide range of countries, interest in our formative years persists. Here, then, is a range of vanished men and women, two or three to become well-known, most to be remembered only by their families, all of them facing what young Thomas Sutcliffe Mort called 'a long farewell'.

Don Charlwood

PART ONE

The Voyage and the People

REGULAR LINE OF PACKET SHIP,

To Sail from Gravesend on the 15th August, and will call at Plymouth.

FOR PORT PHILLIP, DIRECT.

The Splendid River-built Clipper Ship,

ANGLESEY,

A 1, FOR 13 YEARS. (1018 TONS.)

BELONGING TO MESSRS. GREEN OF BLACKWALL,

JOSEPH N. THORNE, COMMANDER.

LOADING IN THE EAST INDIA DOCKS.

This Ship having a full Poop, offers very superior Accommodations to Chief Cabin Passengers, and her lofty 'tween Decks will be fitted with spacious and well-ventilated Cabins, for Second and Third Cabin Passengers. For the Chief Cabin Passengers an excellent table will be kept, with a liberal supply of Wines, Spirits, Beer, &c. The Second and Third Class Scales of Provisions are annexed, and care will be taken that every article supplied shall be of superior quality. A large stock of Medical Comforts will also be put on board, and be dispensed according to the directions of an experienced Medical Practitioner.

Fares in the Chief Cabin according to the size of Cabin, &c.

Second Class ... 30 Guineas each.

Third Class ... £22. each.

THE FOLLOWING SPLENDID SHIPS,

BELONGING TO MESSRS. GREEN OF BLACKWALL,

Will be dispatched at the under-mentioned dates.

NAME.	TONS.	COMMANDERS.	DESTINATION.	TO SAIL.
				15th July.
		McKERLIE	PORT PHILLIP, direct	15th August
			Do. do.	15th Sept.

1   *The Perils*

Oh, hear us when we cry to Thee
For those in peril on the sea!
William Whiting

For nearly a century following the first settlement of Australia, every immigrant, bond or free, had in common an experience none could forget: a passage under sail, lasting anything from two months to six, a passage from the old world to the new. Though nearly all had set out as strangers to the sea, they had crossed the world's most tempestuous oceans by a route not long before sailed by explorers. They had lived during the voyage in a state of limbo, out of touch with everyone but their shipmates, no longer belonging to the old world nor yet to the new. Day by day they had lived under conditions they could scarcely have imagined before their departure. When at last they had landed, they were by no means the same people who had boarded ship months before.

Of all who set out, it is ironic that those condemned to transportation as convicts had best prospect of coming safely through. Fearful though their treatment often was — especially in the earliest years — losses among them through illness at sea averaged less than four per voyage.[1] On an emigrant ship a surgeon would not have considered it untoward had losses run to five times this number. The transportation system also lost remarkably few ships. In a total of some 825 passages, only five were wrecked and on one of these there was no loss of life. In all, shipwreck cost less than 550 convict lives.[2] It is difficult to compare this record with that of emigration, since free people came on a wide variety of vessels, not only on those given solely to carriage of emigrants, but it is known that at least twenty-six

Wreck of the *British Admiral* on the west coast of King Island, 23 May 1874. Driven ashore in a gale while trying to enter Bass Strait, she lost seventy-nine of the eighty-eight persons on board. Artists' 'impressions' of wrecks struck terror into the hearts of people who were about to emigrate.

1

ships carrying emigrants failed for one reason or another to arrive. The loss of life involved in some of these is not known, but it is certain that over 2500 drowned.[3]

A ship could be wrecked without people in Britain being aware of the loss for six months or more. Those waiting in the colonies for her arrival would begin expecting her in about three months, but no real anxiety would be felt until at least another month had passed. Ships waiting in Australian ports to make the return voyage would carry back word of this anxiety to Britain, but often it proved unnecessary — the overdue ship might have suffered dismasting and be limping out under jury rig and would arrive weeks or months later. But with some there came a time when there could no longer be any reasonable doubt that the awaited vessel had been lost. Then homebound ships would carry back word of certain disaster — certain, though its cause might not be known, indeed might never be known.

This was so in the case of the *Guiding Star*. A large ship, sailing on her first voyage with 'the Golden Line of Australian Packets', she was advertised as 'about to make the quickest passage on record'. The last ship to sight her read a signal from her master: he was going as far south as possible — to shorten his route and gain the most favourable winds. Her loss was formally reported at the end of 1855 in the *Immigration Report for Victoria*:

> The *Guiding Star* ... sailed from Liverpool on 8th January 1855, with 546 souls on board. She was last heard of on the 15th February, in lat 26° long. 34° west, since which period no tidings have been received of her. The cause of this deplorable catastrophe can only be conjectured; in all probability it has been owing to collision with ice. Many vessels reported that they had seen vast quantities of ice in unusually low latitudes and some of them had suffered more or less injury in passing among these floating masses.[4]

In nautical circles it was believed that the *Guiding Star* had become 'embayed' in an island of ice measuring sixty miles by fifty which had been sighted by another ship[5], but the truth was never determined.

Today it is difficult to imagine the long periods of uncertainty to which people were subjected as they waited for news of an arrival. It added to their anxiety that scarcely a week passed in Britain without

Wreck of the *Loch Ard*, thirty miles west of Cape Otway, on 30 June 1878. Of fifty-four persons on board, only two survived: Tom Pearce, an eighteen-year-old apprentice, who rescued Eva Carmichael, an eighteen-year-old emigrant. Seven members of the Carmichael family perished.

press reports of shipping disasters, reports often worded in the most dolorous terms. As if to ensure that the illiterate, too, could grasp the implications of the news, artists sketched their 'impressions' of the doomed ship, her spilled human cargo in the sea about her. Not surprisingly, anxiety 'for those in peril on the sea' was a commonplace of daily life; in fact, the hymn in which this line occurs was written when emigration was at its height; most of the people departing from Britain had sung it many a time in church or chapel.

It was a common practice among literate emigrants to keep a voyage diary. Usually it was addressed to family members left behind. Mainly the diarists wrote to strengthen their tenuous links with home and to alleviate their loneliness and apprehension, but some also realized that they had taken a step of great significance: they had left the land of their birth to found a branch of their family in a new and unknown country. As well as giving pictures of life at sea, the diaries convey the writers' reactions to strange, inimical surroundings.

The *Passat*, one of the last sailing ships to carry cargo on the Australian run, seen here encountering heavy weather in the North Atlantic. For the large emigrant ships, worse weather was to come as they reached the Roaring Forties and Howling Fifties.

Tis now ten o'clock and the wind is a frightful gale. I go out and with difficulty keep on the poop by holding to a chain. Mountains of water the waves assume, surrounding us on each side North South East and West, it is like as though every moment we should be engulfed at the bottom ... The wind increases and whistles through the rigging to a tune that none can remember but those who hear it ...

The writer is Nathaniel Levi, at twenty-three not long separated from his native Liverpool and his family; the year 1855. Earlier on the voyage he had experienced a dismasting — a spar had pierced the *Matilda Wattenbach*'s main cabin. Farther south there was no let-up:

Continuing bitter cold with showers and hailstones ... Lat. 51° 41 South ... crash after crash the sea breaks over us. All my thoughts I will not pen. Suffice to say I am resolved to persuade no one belonging to me who is not much more strengthened than myself to venture thus far on the wide ocean without telling them truly what they might perchance see.

He was to arrive safely, eventually to become the first Jewish member of the Victorian Legislative Assembly.[6]

Mary Anne Bedford, travelling out alone at twenty-one on the *Champion of the Seas* to marry a fiancé she had not seen since she was fifteen, addressed her diary to her widowed father:

... last night we had an awful thunderstorm which I shall ever remember. There was a report that the vessel was on fire and I shall never forget the sight — mothers clinging to their children — some running about almost frantic. We all thought we should go down any minute and, O dear Father, you cannot conceive the suspense we were in. No one can tell but those who go through it. The screaming and the noise was fearful until the captain came down to them to tell them that all was right.[7]

When real disaster occurred, the life of a government-assisted emigrant was of low priority. This becomes clear from the diary of Georgiana McCrae, travelling cabin class in 1840. Soon after her ship, the *Argyle*, had departed from London, it was struck by a gale which lasted four days. During this time the steerage emigrants were battened below for their own safety. Georgiana saw them when they were brought up into the fresh air:

... some of the women praying, others dumb with despair. After these returned to their quarters Captain Gatenby astonished me by saying: 'If ever we are compelled to take to the boats, only cuddy-passengers will be allowed to embark. *The emigrants must stay behind.*'[8]

The italics are the diarist's. Never during the era of sail were there lifeboats in sufficient numbers to accommodate all passengers on board.

With the one exception of the *Guiding Star*, there were survivors from all of the ships lost on the Australia run who were able to tell what had happened. On the *Strathmore*, wrecked in the mid-winter of 1875 when she struck one of the uninhabited Crozet Islands, only thirty-eight of the 400 passengers reached shore. Somehow they remained alive, but such was their isolation that six months passed before they were discovered by an American whaler.

Two other emigrant ships were lost only hours after the departing passengers had said their farewells. One of these, the *Tayleur*, left Liverpool in 1854 with 458 Melbourne-bound passengers and a crew of eighty-four. Less than 130 miles out of the Mersey she was driven by a southerly gale onto Lambay Island off the Irish coast. Her bowsprit actually overhung the rocky shore and most of those who survived were lowered from it; 290 drowned. Twenty years later the *Northfleet* was lost even nearer her point of departure. Carrying 350 emigrants for Tasmania, she left the Thames under tug and anchored off Dungeness to await favourable winds. There she was run down by a Spanish steamer that continued on its way. The emigrants panicked and 293 were drowned.[9]

In reading shipboard diaries one becomes acutely aware that many people, who were strangers to the sea, lived in a constant state of tension which could slip into panic. John Dill, a boy on his way to Sydney with his brother in 1857, never forgot a late night, far south in the Indian Ocean, when 300 emigrants heard the grating of ice on the vessel's copper bottom:

The deck soon presented an appearance not easily described

and impossible to forget with so many passengers, men and women and children all in dishabille who had rushed on deck thinking we were about to be wrecked. Among the passengers were about eighty Welsh people who could not speak a word of English, and the screaming of women and children and din of noises is still vivid in my memory. The passengers were all ordered to their cabins and some of them had to be forced down and the hatches closed over them ... The following morning we found we were pretty well surrounded with sheet ice and that there was a large iceberg about a mile from us ...[10]

Icebergs, fire and fever were the greatest terrors of a voyage. Because of the high risk of fire, especially in wooden ships, only a few lamps were left burning at night. In 1840, fire broke out on the brig *Australia*, when she was 500 miles west of the Cape of Good Hope. Fortunately she was carrying only 15 people and there was lifeboat room for them all. For eight days and nine nights the passengers drifted before they were sighted and picked up. Two lives were lost.[11] A slight enough experience compared to the loss of the *Cospatrick* which caught fire in much the same area when bound for New Zealand in 1874. Panic broke out and of the 473 on board only eighty-three were in lifeboats. Unlike the emigrants of the *Australia*, they were without either food or water and were in their night attire. As the days passed all but three of them died in the most harrowing circumstances.[12]

The landfall at Cape Otway, at the journey's end, was probably the greatest hazard of all. Until 1848 the cape was unlighted. Fifty miles south of it Cape Wickham, the northernmost tip of King Island, remained unlighted until 1861. Between these two points passed ships bound for Melbourne, Sydney, Brisbane and other east-coast ports, many of them doing so without sight of land since leaving Britain. Before threading this entrance to Bass Strait it was of the greatest importance that a master establish his position by the most certain means available to him: noon sextant sights of the sun. But as the area is subject to low cloud and gales, ships were repeatedly unable to see the sun for days on end, and consequently the approach was often made from uncertain positions. Most ships passed through without incident, though many a mariner was dismayed by too close a

Anchor of the freighter *Fiji* at Moonlight Head, seventeen miles west of Cape Otway. Wrecked on 5 September 1891, the *Fiji* lost eleven men from her crew of twenty-five, most of them washed off a lifeline between ship and shore. The French ship *Marie Gabrielle* was wrecked at the same spot twenty-two years earlier.

The western entrance to Bass Strait. For ships bound for Sydney, Brisbane and Melbourne this was the most hazardous section of the route. Eighteen ships nearing the end of long journeys were lost either on King Island or the Otway coast.

sighting of one coast or the other and some passed through in storms and darkness, never really knowing how close they had been to danger. Most of those that failed were lost on the low coast of King Island; a few others struck the Otway coast. By far the worst of those that failed was the *Cataraqui*, lost in 1845.

For 105 days the *Cataraqui* had laboured out from Liverpool, carrying 369 emigrants intended to build up Melbourne's supply of labour. At 7 p.m. on 3 August she hove to in heavy rain and gale-force winds somewhere west of the entrance to the strait. Darkness had fallen and, uncertain of their position, Captain C. W. Finlay decided to wait for daylight before going on. For four days he had been unable to obtain sights at noon.

There can be no doubting the wisdom of Finlay's decision to heave to until dawn, but, allegedly, it was ridiculed by the two surgeons in charge of the emigrants — possibly because of their eagerness to disembark and claim the bounty payable to them. At all events, Finlay reversed his decision at 3 a.m. and sailed on. He was much closer to King Island than he suspected.

About 4.30 a.m. the ship struck, taking the ground heavily and the sea breaking right over her. A scene of the utmost confusion ensued, as the passengers attempted to rush on deck. There was

Although Melbourne had been established only ten years when the *Cataraqui* was wrecked, colonists flocked to this benefit concert. As entertainment was limited, the drama inherent in shipwrecks made such concerts extremely popular.

(W. 5.   N 15)

QUEEN'S THEATRE

QUEEN-STREET, MELBOURNE.

Under the immediate Patronage of His Honor the Judge, and His Worship the Mayor.

Upon which occasion the proceeds of the Evenings Enter-tainments will be given in

AID OF THE SURVIVORS

From the late

Melancholy Wreck

Of the Emigrant Ship 'CATARAQUI,'

AND

To REWARD Mr. HOWIE'S PARTY for their meritorious assistance.

☞ The Manager does not think it necessary to solicit the support of the Public for this evening, feeling assured (from the well-known liberality of the Melbourne Inhabitants) the above—announcement will, in itself—without taking into con-sideration the attractive entertainments — fill the Theatre for the relief of the unfortunate.

THURSDAY EVENING,

18th September, 1845,

The Entertainments will commence with SHERIDAN KNOWLES' celebrated play, received last Thursday evening by a numerous audience with universal appro-bation, entitled the

HUNCHBACK;

OR, WOMAN'S LOVE.

Sir Thomas Clifford....Mr. NESBITT.	Master Walter..Mr. HAMBLETON.
Fathom................Mr. COPPIN.	
Lord Tinsel ...Mr. YOUNG.	Modus....Mr. THOMSON.
Master Wilford.......Mr. WATSON.	Thomas............Mr. OPIE.
Master Heartwell..Mr. ROGERS.	Stephen......Mr. WILKS.
Julia..........Mrs. COPPIN.	Helen.......Mrs. MERETON

Although not used to carry emigrants, the splendid *Cromdale*, complete with skysails, epitomized the beauty of sail. She was built in 1891 for the Australian wool trade.

The end of the *Cromdale*, wrecked on the Cornish coast in 1913, her steel hull smashed by the sea.

four to four and a half feet of water in the hold when the ship was sounded, and as the *Cataraqui* was grinding on the reef the ladders leading to the deck were soon knocked away, leaving many passengers still trapped below. The crew did what they could to get all on deck, but the sea, breaking over the ship on the port side, was sweeping the decks, and with every sea some passengers and crew members were swept overboard. About 5 a.m., when the ship tipped over on her port side, boats, bulwarks, spars and part of the cuddy were carried away. The masts were cut away in an attempt to right her, but by this time the ship was full of water and she did not respond. The passengers who had been unable to reach the deck were all drowned.[13]

The *Cataraqui* was scarcely a hundred yards from the King Island shore, but within that distance lay rows of serrated granite peaks with scarcely a break between them. Onto these, living and dead alike were pounded so that, in the end, 399 people perished. Nine men were swept through the reef and survived.

One might reasonably suppose from these disasters that the route to Australia was the most malign of sea routes. An emigrant must surely have had better prospects of crossing safely to North America — the Atlantic route, after all, was a quarter the length of the route to Australia and was familiar to generations of mariners. Furthermore, steamships as well as sailing ships plied it regularly and emigrants crossed it in hundreds of thousands.

Yet, paradoxically, the emigrant bound for North America had much *less* prospect of arriving safely at his destination. In the spring of 1834 alone, eighteen emigrant ships and 700 lives were lost on the North Atlantic.[14] The main reasons for this appalling rate of losses were the defective construction of the ships; their imperfect state of repair; the gross overloading of them by owners and, perhaps more than these, a system of marine insurance that allowed owners to recoup their losses.

Although these losses on the Atlantic by shipwreck were fearful enough they were greatly exceeded by deaths through illnesses at sea. These were at their worst in 1847, the year Ireland was ravaged by the Potato Famine. Large numbers of emigrants fleeing to America had contracted typhus before they embarked. Of nearly 107,000 who started out that year, over 6000 died on the voyage and a further 11,000 died soon after their arrival.[15]

The extraordinary contrast between emigration to North America and emigration on the longer, more hazardous route to Australia can be attributed to emigration to Australia being largely controlled by the British government. Emigration to North America on the other hand was left to private venturers. Emigrants bound for the United States received no assisted passages, nor did those bound for Canada — or not until after 1855. No government standard was observed in victualling and little attention was paid to the standards of accommodation laid down in the Passenger Acts.

The British government controlled Australian emigration because of the great distance involved. Prospective emigrants and shipowners alike were deterred by the economics of such a voyage. As far as the emigrants were concerned, they were not only deterred by the fare, but by the vast distance they would be removed from home — removed to a country only recently settled. By contrast North America had thriving towns and, being closer, fares were relatively low. Emigrants gave themselves some hope of return visits home. Furthermore, the hundreds of thousands wishing to go to North America could scrape together sufficient money to pay their own way, or at least the way of some members of their families.

Superficially it might seem that Britain showed concern for those going to Australia and indifference to those going to North America. In truth, she was looking to her own interests in both cases. Her greatest domestic problem was over-population. A landlord in Ireland might have been speaking for any of his class when he declared during the Potato Famine:

I consider the Failure of the Potato Crop to be the greatest possible Value in one respect — in enabling us to carry out the Emigration system ... every proprietor would be delighted if he had the Means to reduce his own Population.[16]

The overriding concern of the British government was to reduce the swarming surplus among the masses. If thousands of impoverished people were able to scrape together money enough to cross the Atlantic, why aid them? Why bother even to ensure that their ships

The *Hereward*, a steel ship built at Port Glasgow in 1877, was driven ashore at Maroubra beach on 6 May 1898.

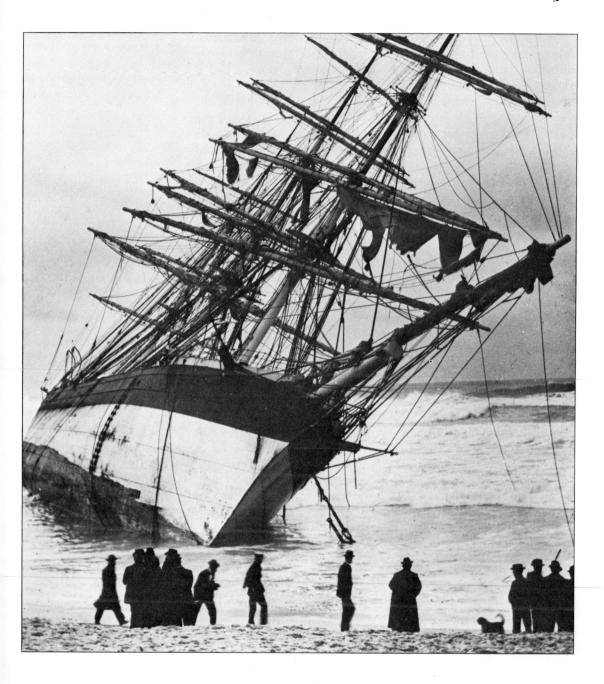

were safe? Whatever happened to them once they had left, their departure still effectively reduced the population. This attitude was much in accord with the prevailing policy of *laissez-faire*. Aid afforded emigrants going to Australia was contrary to *laissez-faire*; in Victorian England it was an anachronism. The contrast between the two forms of emigration sounds more palatable in euphemisms uttered by the British Agent-General for Emigration in 1838: emigration to Australia lacked 'an original impulse', whereas emigration to North America could be 'left to flow from natural springs' and thus needed 'no direct aid'.[17]

Once committed to backing emigration to Australia, Britain was able to produce the expertise for conducting it. For generations her ships had crossed the world's oceans carrying cargoes of soldiers, slaves and convicts. From this experience her government had long known how best to fit the maximum number of bodies into the available space aboard ship; how best to assess rationing; how to determine medical supervision. The run to Australia was well-known to her through trans-

Sails shredded in a sudden squall. This was likely to be the outcome if they were not furled quickly enough.

portation; indeed, from the beginning, Australia had been 'government country' and it is scarcely possible to over-estimate the role of government on the long voyage, or its moulding influence on those who would soon be Australians. When the colonial governments demanded a voice in the selection of their future citizens, to offset the home government's desire to be rid of her paupers, this too benefited the emigrants. As Geoffrey Blainey has put it: 'Once governments began to select migrants for Australia and to subsidize their fares, they tended to become responsible for their well-being during the voyage.'[18] North America, by contrast, was private-enterprise country, founded by merchant venturers, populated by people paying their own way. It is not surprising that the North American ethos contrasts with that of Australia.

As one reads emigrant diarists' accounts of their trials on the run to Australia, it is necessary to remember that, harsh though their experiences were, these people were infinitely better off than their relatives crossing the Atlantic. The fact that the route was so long brought them controls and benefits they could scarcely be expected to perceive, let alone appreciate. Their minds were too taken up in any event with the rigors of the voyage and the immensely long distance they were slowly putting between themselves and home.

2 The Route

Though you untie the winds and let them fight
Against the churches; though the yesty waves
Confound and swallow navigation up.
Shakespeare

When we think of a destination being 'far' or 'near' our assessment is based largely on the length of time one would take to reach it. It is difficult today to imagine being five months on the seas. Steamships reduced the five-month journey to five weeks; five weeks was reduced to five days by early air services and, by the late 1970s, subsonic aircraft had reduced the five days to considerably less than one day. Each reduction has had the effect of reducing our capacity to imagine creeping for five months toward the same destination. Yet this was the passage time for many of the early emigrant ships and convict transports alike on their voyage to Australia.

Nineteenth-century man's concept of distance was governed by factors quite the reverse of ours: since the voyage would take so long, it followed that Australia was unimaginably far from home. Reinforcing this impression was the knowledge that convicts were banished to a place so remote that there was small hope of their return.

The clipper *Lightning*, reputedly the fastest of all ships on the run to Australia. Designed by Donald McKay for the Black Ball Line, she was delivered to Liverpool from Boston in 1854 by Captain James Nicol ('Bully') Forbes. On this maiden voyage she covered 436 miles in twenty-four hours, a record never equalled by sail. Nor was Forbes' record of sixty-three days from Melbourne to Liverpool in the same year ever equalled. The *Lightning* burned at her moorings while loading wool in Geelong in 1869.

During the era of sail the route underwent considerable change. The actual distance to Sydney by the first route in general use was over 13,000 nautical miles. Fremantle was a couple of thousand miles less; New Zealand some 1200 miles more. This route had been laid down by the Admiralty and remained in use from the time of the foundation of New South Wales until the gold rush.

Most ships' masters had gained their experience on the Atlantic. The long easterly run across the southern Indian Ocean presented them with a problem few of them had previously been called upon to solve: determination of longitude. The coast of Western Australia in particular was apt to turn up either before it was expected or not until days after it had been expected. As late as 1871, by which time chronometers had long been in general use, the master of the *Ivy*, 109 days out from London, found himself in much the same difficulties as Dutch mariners had experienced on their way to Batavia for generations past.

Then came the morning when, by the captain's calculations they should sight Australia. There is no sign of it. They cannot even get a sounding. There is consternation and dismay. The captain is wrong. He 'dare hardly show himself on deck'. He is 'completely ridiculed'. But two days later, at evening, the carpenter and cook perched on the masthead, shout that land is in sight. That night the lights of Fremantle appear . . .[1]

And yet determination of longitude was a simple matter. Sextant sights taken as the sun approached its zenith determined noon on the ship. By comparing 'ship time' with Greenwich time, as kept by the chronometer, the master had a difference of so many hours and minutes. This difference in time he had only to convert to degrees. Each hour equalled fifteen degrees; it had to, because every twenty-four hours saw one rotation of the earth's 360 degrees. But there was often trouble when chronometers ran fast or slow and for years

Officer 'shooting the sun' at noon to establish the ship's latitude and longitude.

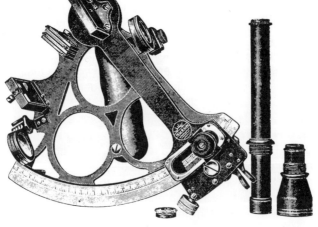

The marine sextant, developed in the mid-eighteenth century, was used primarily to measure the elevation of the sun above the horizon at noon. From this angle, the ship's latitude was derived.

there was distrust of them anyway by conservative masters. A battery of three of them was really also needed, for if there were only two, who could tell which one was correct? Most masters had to provide their own chronometers and few could afford two, let alone three. So the master of the *Ivy* was by no means alone in his embarrassment. The barque *Eglinton*, approaching Fremantle in 1852, had an undetected chronometer error which led the master to believe he had 140 miles yet to run. That night he crashed into the coast twenty miles north of his destination. Fortunately only two of his twenty-five passengers and one of his crew were lost. The 65,000 sovereigns he was carrying were saved.[2]

Latitude was also determined by the same noon sun sight — this by a fairly simple reference to tables. Consequently noon was a very important time in the ship's day: the ship's position was determined as well as ship's time. An artist who made the voyage for the *Illustrated London News* observed the rather solemn daily ritual:

> The sun is now fast approaching the meridian, and some little bustle is observed on the quarter deck. The captain, two of the mates, and a tiny midshipman, have all adjusted their several sextants and quadrants,* and are making a steady examination of the horizon immediately to the south ... After some minutes the instruments are lowered within a few seconds of each other; and the captain solemnly addressing his first mate, says, 'Mr. Jones, *make* it noon'. 'Ay, ay, sir. Forrard there; strike eight bells'.[3]

Mr Jones was, in fact, starting the ship's day — at midday instead of midnight. Passage of time was then measured by a sandglass that took half an hour to run through; the ship's bell was rung each time it emptied.

Another sandglass was used in conjunction with the log to determine the ship's speed. The log — named from the time when it was just that — was dropped overboard to float where it fell while a line attached to it ran out over the stern as the ship sailed on. At intervals along the line were knots indicating distances. The number of knots passing over the stern, as timed by the glass, gave the ship's speed.

Before changes were forced by the demands of the gold rush, pass-

The chronometer. This accurate clock, insulated against the ship's motion, was set on Greenwich Mean Time. It was used in conjunction with the sextant to establish the ship's longitude.

*The octant, a forerunner of the sextant, measured angles on a graduated curve which was the eighth part of a circle. The sextant is based on a sixth part of a circle.

age times to Australia were slow, both among emigrant ships and convict transports. Companies and masters and, for that matter, the government itself, did not press for speed. The route originally approved by the Admiralty for the First Fleet became the standard route. It led first to Teneriffe, the Cape Verde Islands, then down to Rio de Janeiro and across the South Atlantic to Cape Town. From there masters were advised to follow the thirty-ninth parallel of latitude to Australia. After about 1817 the Rio call fell from favour and Cape Town was left as the one certain port of call, though, if necessary, a call could still be made before this at Teneriffe or the Cape Verde Islands to replenish food and water. This was to remain the Admiralty's recommended route for well over seventy years.[4]

By the time the pre-gold-rush emigrants had reached Cape Town, their voyage was about half over. The mild climate and the beauty of the Cape led many to wish they were going no further, but their brief stay was like a half-time break in an arduous sporting contest when worse is to follow. Ahead lay 7000 miles of ocean with no land mass closer than India to the north and Antarctica to the south. It was an ocean crossing even more protracted than the one that lay behind, with a climate and ocean much less beneficent, and no rests in port. The convict transports had been the first British ships to sail it regularly; before their time, only Dutchmen had plied it on their way to their East Indian colonies.

Although the early emigrants found this long crossing of the southern Indian Ocean an ordeal, it was, in fact, relatively mild in comparison with the route to be developed later. On the Mercator projection, familiar to them from their school atlases, the thirty-ninth parallel *looked* the shortest way to Australia, furthermore, it offered mariners a single straight course to steer. But its apparent directness was an illusion.

Because the earth is a sphere, the shortest distance between any two points on it must be a curve. This can be seen if one stretches a cord between two places on a globe; the stretched cord will lie along the 'great circle' linking the two places. (A 'great circle' is one that encircles the globe, its diameter being the diameter of the globe.)

John Thomas Towson, who was scientific examiner of masters and mates at Liverpool, saw the advantages of a great circle route to Australia years before the gold rush. He knew full well, however, that it was impossible to keep to a great circle all the way from the South Atlantic to Australia, for such a route led into Antarctica; in any event,

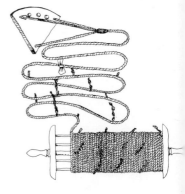

In its earliest form, the log was just that – a log of wood dropped over the stern. A line attached to it was allowed to run out as the ship moved on. With a sandglass, the passage of knots in the line was timed to give an estimate of the ship's speed.

The sandglass. There were four models, each used to measure different intervals of time: four hours, one hour, half an hour and half a minute. The half-minute glass was used in conjunction with the log to measure the ship's speed: the others to measure the length of the crew's watches. The ship's bell was rung each time a half-hour glass ran through.

Matthew Fontaine Maury, the American oceanographer, collected data on winds and sea currents from mariners all over the world and from these developed charts to guide shipping along routes that offered the best natural forces of propulsion. Use of Maury's charts greatly reduced passage times to Australia.

a curved route could not be followed by ships' compasses. His answer was a break-up of a curved route into a series of chords, or 'rhumbs', going as far south as ice would allow. Such a route cut out Cape Town completely, leaving it hundreds of miles to the north.

Towson presented his calculations in 1847 in a small but radical book: *Tables to Facilitate the Practice of Great Circle Sailing*.[5] Although the Admiralty published the book, it did not disavow its own ancient route to Australia. Three years were to pass before a master dared adopt Towson's recommendations, for the proposed route not only threatened to lead into hazardous waters, it also demanded high proficiency in the use of sextant and chronometer so that masters might know precisely when to alter course on to each new rhumb. Many of them lacked such a degree of proficiency. Nevertheless, in 1850, Captain Godfrey in the *Constance* ventured far south following Towson's theory. He reached Adelaide in a record time of seventy-seven days. Before the gold rush no one dared follow him. Thus, by the time the rush began, Towson had gained little recognition.

With thousands of would-be gold miners clamouring for quick passages, the shipping world was ripe for change. It was at this juncture, in 1852, that Captain James Nicol Forbes adopted Towson's recommendations and made an astonishing dash to Port Phillip in the *Marco Polo* in sixty-eight days and back again in seventy-six. Many ships were still taking as long to get to Australia as Forbes took to make a return journey! Although Towson's recommendations were now amply proved, remarkably few masters showed inclination to risk adopting them even now.

Fortunately support for him was at hand. In 1853 his theories were augmented by the work of the American oceanographer, Matthew Fontaine Maury. That year the already famous Maury visited England. He was a man known to most of the better navigators the world over, for he had persuaded them to correspond with him over a period of years in his efforts:

... to collect the experience of every navigator as to the winds and currents of the ocean, to discuss his observations upon them, and then to present the world with the results on charts for the improvement of commerce and navigation.[6]

Maury's Atlantic charts had long since proved themselves. On the Australia run he now sought not only the shortest possible route, as

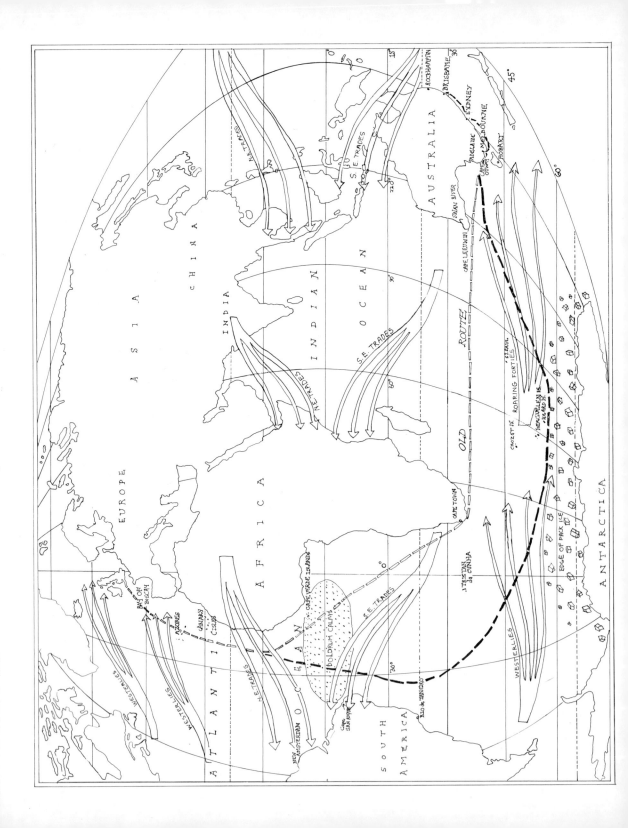

The original maritime route from Britain to Australia and the 'composite great circle route' recommended by John Towson, the scientific examiner of masters and mates at Liverpool. This route virtually halved passage times between Britain and Australia.

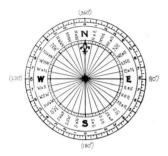

The mariner's compass. Mounted in the binnacle it was so positioned that the helmsman could read the course he had been ordered to steer.

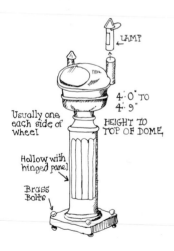

The binnacle. Its glass-fronted cover protected the compass and its light against the sea and weather.

Towson had done, but 'a route which, taking winds and distance both into account, would give the shortest attainable average'. Already, he observed, 'some ships that sailed out of Liverpool . . . under the advice of Mr. Towson . . . commenced to leave the Admiralty route, and to go further south in search of a shorter one . . .' [7] But the Admiralty still hedged:

> The Admiralty route to and from Australia is one of those tedious old routes, but very difficult to break up, because of the weight and authority which everything with the imprint of that ancient and renowned board upon it has with its navigators.[8]

The august lords still recommended a call at the Cape of Good Hope and 'the parallel of 39°S. as the best upon which to run down easting for Australia'.[9] Maury, like Towson, would have none of it.

> I have endeavoured to impress navigators with a sense of the mistake they commit in considering the Cape of Good Hope as on the way-side of their best route to Australia. It is not only a long way out of the best and most direct track for them, but the winds also, to the north of the fortieth parallel of south latitude are much less favourable for Australia than they are south of this parallel.[10]

Maury and Towson won the day, for the competing shipowners were hungering for quick passage times. In September 1854 Towson received whole-hearted recognition. The London *Times* referred to him as the 'inventor of the system of what is called great circle sailing, by the adoption of which the average length of voyage from this port [Liverpool] has been reduced from 120 days to 75 or 80 days.' He was awarded £1000.[11]

What do the recommendations of Towson and Maury add up to? From a position abeam Rio de Janeiro ships were to angle away south-east toward the middle of the South Atlantic and there begin looking for the assured westerly winds. Once they had picked them up they were to begin their bolt toward Australia — not on an easterly heading, as in the past, but swinging far south, so that the old haven of Cape Town was left 700 nautical miles to the north. Most of the skilled navigators then went on to exceed 50° south; some reached 55°. Maury's warning to the new breed of masters was clear:

The highest degree of south latitude, which it may be prudent to touch, depending mainly on the season of the year and the winds, the state of the ship, and the well-being of the passengers and crew.[12]

Once they reached their greatest southern latitude, Maury recommended that they stay there for the next two and a half thousand miles — 'if ice etc. will allow . . .' They were not to sail to the north of their 'greatest southern latitude before reaching 90° east'. There, in that emptiest and wildest of oceans, they were to begin 'hauling more and more to the north'. Unless a ship were bound for Fremantle, Cape Leeuwin was to be left about a thousand nautical miles to the north. In this context the eventual approach to the fifty-mile opening into Bass Strait will be seen as the hazard it truly was.

In terms of life on board ship, the new route meant that emigrants experienced a range of climatic conditions few of them could have imagined. At first they were fortunate: for while they were finding their sea legs they moved south from England into balmy weather. Flying fish and bonito were seen and, by night, the enchantment of phosphorescent seas. In these 'horse latitudes' the ship idled along pleasantly, but soon the sails filled and the north-east trades bowled them toward Brazil. As they neared the equator the winds inevitably fell off, for they were entering the doldrums. The area was inescapable. Maury himself described it as 'one of the most oppressive and disagreeable places at sea'.

The emigrant ships from Europe to Australia have to cross it. They are often baffled in it for two or three weeks; then the children, and the passengers who are in delicate health suffer most. It is a frightful graveyard on the wayside to that golden land.[13]

'There we remained firmly fixed for 21 days', wrote an emigrant of 1852.[14]

Scores of ships at a time were imprisoned in the deathlike silence, masters seeking every catspaw of wind, their crews making dozens of unavailing sail changes. Sooner or later the imprisoned ships crept out, passengers and crews breathing freely again as they headed for the tropic of Capricorn. But then came the plunge south. As it pro-

Cape Otway, on the coast of Victoria. Often this was the first land emigrants sighted after leaving Britain months earlier. Its lighthouse marks the western entrance to Bass Strait. Fifty miles to the south lies King Island. As the entrance is subject to gales and low cloud, several sailing ships were wrecked on the Otway coast and many more on King Island.

gressed many people found themselves inadequately clad; nearly all found themselves afraid — some desperately so. William John Adams, emigrating to Sydney in 1855, might have been writing for many of his fellows:

... the wind Blew and the Sails tore and Chains and Ropes Rattled and the Seaman and Captain Run and hollwed about and the Women Cried and Prayed and men Run about onley with there Shirts on and the warter Came in two hatchways By Streams and Sometimes the lamp was out and it Seems Verrey miserable and the Ship Roald heaved and Groand From one Side to the Oather and now and then a Rat Squik and Run Oaver Some Boday and then they would Sing out and then the Tables and all the Temprey Fixtures would Rattle and the tins Fall From the Shelves and Tables Sometimes on Your head as you lie in your Bed and the Jars and Books i had to hold in my Bed and Jar of Red Cabbag Fell over and Wetted the Bed ... when the Waves comes against the Ship it Makes it Tremble and when it Falls on Deck it goes off like a Cannon.[15]

William Scoresby, a lifelong authority on the sea, had seen nothing like the waves on the composite great circle route.

[They reached] a height frequently of forty feet — regular waves rolling in the direction of the wind, and incomparably higher peaks and crests produced by crossing waves ... The vehement storm not only blew off the lighter summits of the foaming crests, but actually seized upon great masses of the roaring peaks of crossing seas, cut them off ... and drifted them away. Thus the quantity of drift ... constituted a stratum of haze so thick and dense that ... vision from the poop of the *Royal Charter* ... was limited in all directions, and for hours of continuance, to about the third part of a mile.[16]

The cold became more and more intense, for here there was no warming Gulf Stream Drift, as there was in similar latitudes around Britain, only the chilling West Wind Drift. Moses Melchior, a Dane emigrating in 1853, wrote in latitude 51° south:

This morning snow lay about 5″ high on the deck, and the sails and the rigging were stiff from the frost ... Last night I kept some of my clothes on, had three blankets, my dressing gown and two winter coats on my bed, and even then I could not keep warm.[17]

One wonders how the underclad and impoverished among the steerage passengers fared. But the waves and the cold were as nothing compared with that other fear — icebergs. Charles Scott, a Kidderminster weaver, wrote in 1859:

About half past 12 o'clock at night a mighty Icebearge was close to the Bows of the ship, the lives of Hundreds depending on a few moments, orders was promptly given to turn the ship [so] that instead of striking it full she skimmed it sidewise with a terable bump, but fortunate with no injury to the ship, nearly all the sailes to be taken in so passed the night.[18]

Few emigrants had the power to write of icebergs as Richard Dana did in *Two Years Before the Mast*:

The 1335-ton composite ship *Torrens* after collision with an iceberg late in 1898. Saved from the full shock of the impact by her bowsprit, she was able to limp on to Adelaide.

... no description can give any idea of the strangeness, splendour, and, really, the sublimity of the sight. Its great size, — for it must have been from two to three miles in circumference, and several hundred feet in height — its slow motion, as its base rose and sank in the water, and its high points nodded against the cloud; the dashing of the waves upon it, which, breaking high with foam, lined its base with a white crust, and the thundering sound of the cracking of the mass, and of the breaking and tumbling down of huge pieces ... The main body of the mass was ... of an indigo colour ... as it grew thin and transparent towards the edges and top, its colour shaded off from a deep blue to the whiteness of snow.[19]

On the new route there were no voluntary stops. Antoine Fauchery, a Frenchman bound for 'the diggings' in 1852, wrote wryly of the new English obsession with speed:

One knows that it is useless to think about stopping places: for the English, however long the journey may be, it is always non-stop. The storm, taking you for a ride on a piece of wreckage, might occasionally allow you to touch or see the land, — the captain, never ...[20]

The new route proved itself abundantly, but it left an ineradicable memory on the minds of the emigrants and turned many against their previous idea of returning home after they had made their fortune. When at last he reached the end of a gruelling passage, Nathaniel Levi wrote:

It must be remembered that we went Composite Circle Sailing to get strong breezes ... But no more Circle Sailing for the writer. A steamer will always be my choice should I take such a journey again if it is possible to get one.

Many years were to pass before steamers could replace sail on the long run. Until they did so, Australia was served by the finest sailing ships the world ever knew.

3 *The Ships*

They mark our passage as a race of men
Earth will not see such ships as those again.
Masefield

As the route to Australia underwent change, so did the ships that sailed it. In the early decades of emigration there was no real difference, apart from fittings, between emigrant ships and convict ships; indeed, Charles Bateson tells us that a ship 'might carry prisoners one year and the next turn up in Australian waters with cargo and passengers or immigrants or simply as a freighter'. He goes on to describe these ships as 'ordinary British merchantmen', nearly all of them ship- or barque-rigged, 'mostly vessels of 200 to 400 register tons and later they were generally under 600 tons . . . They sailed badly and incredibly slowly, but speed was not considered essential, their masters were not great sail carriers . . .'[1] According to Basil Lubbock, 'the ordinary steerage passenger had to content himself as a rule with a ship that was little better than a hermetically sealed box . . .'[2]

In the thirty-two years from the First Fleet until 1820, ninety-two convict transports reached Sydney. Not one completed the passage in less than 112 days. From then until transportation to Sydney ceased in 1840, only five ships completed the voyage in less than 100 days. Throughout the same period a dozen transports exceeded 200 days — nearly seven months![3]

Both the transports and the early emigrant ships were dumpy-looking vessels:

Their hulls were full and round. They could sit almost bolt upright on the

A lithograph by T. G. Dutton of the clipper ship *Lady Melville* passing through icebergs. Watch for icebergs had to be kept day and night for weeks at a time.

Countess of Bective at Swansea, UK, c. 1843. She typifies the early ships that sailed to Australia. Rounded, slow and relatively safe, they were used for emigrants and convicts alike.

mud of a tidal harbour, their bows were blunt and they pushed a lot of sea in front of them as they went through it. They had a square stern and stern windows . . . They were safe in skilled hands . . . and tended to ride like a cork . . . They leaked continually and needed constant pumping. If they were not well maintained they were highly dangerous — leaky, flimsy masts, fire-prone.[4]

On the Atlantic things were different. Despite the voracious appetites of the first steamships, the short Atlantic passage was not beyond them. As early as 1838 a regular service was established; the ships *Sirius* and Isambard Kingdom Brunel's *Great Western* had begun running between New York and Liverpool. True, there was also the very dark side to the Atlantic emigrant trade: evicted Highland Scottish tenantry were fleeing to North America in almost anything that floated — and in many ships that failed to float — and the plague-stricken Irish were soon to follow them.

Competition from steam on the Atlantic spurred designers of sailing ships to their greatest efforts and this was eventually to improve ships in the Australian trade. Designers in America had already developed the Baltimore packet, which entered service in 1816 and became notorious as a fast slave ship. The Baltimore packets, in turn, were forerunners of the clipper ship. Both consistently outstripped early steamships.[5]

Sally, a 1400-ton wooden ship in dry dock at Sharpness, UK, in 1875. Wooden ships were subject to riddling by teredo worms, which could lead to waterlogging. As protection against the worms, 'yellow metal' sheathing was fitted below the waterline.

In the minds of later admiring generations, the term 'clipper' conjures an enduring image. We still envisage a ship with a sharp-raked stem and an inclined, overhanging stern — a design that reduced the area of hull in contact with the water; a ship carrying tall, tapering masts raked slightly aft (the rake was to be more pronounced on the American clippers), masts carrying masses of sail that caught every possible wind to drive the yacht-like hull through the water. Seen from abeam the hull was to have a lovely sheer curve from bow to stern, which touched its minimum point amidships.

As a type the clipper lasted only about thirty years — from the mid-1840s until the mid-1870s — then it lost the battle with improved steamships. It lasted longest on the run to Australia and New Zealand because it could race before the prevailing westerlies for much of the journey out and home; there were also no coaling stations for the competing steamships on the long easterly haul. Although the clipper eventually lost the race to steam, it remains in men's minds the most beautiful ship ever created. In nautical circles the term 'clipper' was applied very loosely to ships. Any shipowner wanting to attract emigrants to a mediocre vessel was likely to advertise her as a clipper and many emigrant diaries tell of weary months spent on so-called clippers.

Perhaps because Britain had borne the burden of the Napoleonic Wars, but more probably because she was less enterprising than her young rival, she lagged behind America in the design of swift ships. There was one notable exception: the building of the *Great Britain* (discussed at the end of this chapter). Another reason for American supremacy was the ready availability of softwoods. The *Sea Witch*, built in New York in 1844, is generally accepted as the first of the new breed. The *Houqua* and the *Rainbow* built there in 1844 and 1845 began the era of tea races out to China and home. At this very time, thousands of miles south of these clipper races, an inferior breed of vessel laboured out to Australian ports.[6]

The shipbuilding genius, who was eventually to have greatest impact on the Australian trade, was a Nova Scotian of Scottish parentage whose yards were in East Boston: Donald McKay. McKay's first clippers were built for the Atlantic trade — beautiful vessels, but very much smaller than those for which he gained his legendary name. He was spurred to design larger ships by the discovery of gold in California in 1848. When the rush began, the overland trek from the

Donald McKay, the brilliant Nova Scotian born shipbuilder who gained a reputation second to none through the ships he designed and built at his Boston yards. Several like the *Lightning*, *Sovereign of the Seas* and *James Baines* were built specifically for the run to Australia.

James Baines, founder of the Liverpool-based Black Ball Line. His ships moved the passage to Australia onto a new time scale, not only because of their design, but because of the shorter route their masters adopted.

The *Marco Polo*. Built by Smith and Co., of St John, New Brunswick, the *Marco Polo* halved the passage time to Australia in 1852. Under Captain James Nicol Forbes she carried 930 emigrants from Liverpool to Melbourne in sixty-eight days. Forbes, more than any other master, pioneered the composite great circle route.

populated eastern states took six months and lay through all manner of terrain and climates, much of it through territory of hostile Indians. Before long the 'Forty-niners' began offering high passage money to be taken by sea from east-coast ports to San Francisco, via Cape Horn. The pioneer *Sea Witch* completed the voyage in ninety-seven days; others followed and the passage time was quickly reduced. But McKay saw that large ships were needed to withstand the tremendous seas encountered around 55° south latitude. In 1851 he entered the run with a ship that cut the New York-San Francisco record to eighty-nine days — a passage never excelled by sail. This was the superb *Flying Cloud*, a giant of 1793 American tons which was destined to put up splendid performances on the Australia run, particularly in carrying emigrants to Queensland.

In the year that McKay built the *Flying Cloud*, gold was discovered in Australia. The immediate demand by thousands in Britain to get quickly to the ugly-duckling colony changed the emigration pattern overnight. In Liverpool a self-made shipowner, James Baines of the Black Ball Line, purchased a large ship for the Australia run which was to make history: the *Marco Polo*. She was not a McKay ship; she had been built by Smith & Co. of St John, New Brunswick and, although it has been claimed that she was built specifically for Baines and even that he had a hand in her design, it seems more likely that in his impatience to grasp a large share of the emigrant trade, he bought a ship already built. From a description of her in the *Illustrated London News* she had every claim to being termed a clipper:

> Her lines fore and aft are beautifully fine ... she has an entrance as sharp as a steamboat [and a] bottom like a yacht; she has above water all the appearance of a frigate.[7]

Baines had her refitted to such a degree that he was able to offer unheard of luxury accommodation to first and intermediate passengers. The 1625-ton clipper sailed from the Mersey in July 1852.

The design of the *Marco Polo*, the skill and daring of her master — the famous 'Bully' Forbes — and use of the composite great circle route, resulted in the ship taking 701 emigrants to Melbourne in an astonishing sixty-eight days. Forbes had moved Australia-bound ships onto a new time scale. It seemed to matter little that there had been fifty-three deaths en route. Well aware of the furore he had started, Baines capitalized on it. In 1853 he saw in the Mersey a superb American clipper. She was McKay's *Sovereign of the Seas* and aboard her was the designer himself — he had made the Atlantic crossing in the company of her master, who was his brother — to study her performance. Baines not only chartered her immediately, but in a daring business venture ordered four ships from McKay's yards. Each was destined for fame on the run to Australia: *Lightning, Champion of the Seas, James Baines, Donald McKay*.[8]

As a shipowner, Baines soon had speedy competitors: the Blackwall Line, the Golden Line, the Fox Line, but, most challenging of all, the White Star Line. The name ship of this last line, the Nova Scotian built *White Star*, and their American-built *Red Jacket*, ran Baines' ships closest, but never wrested from him the laurels of fastest passage. All of the ships so far mentioned were North American built and very large. The *Marco Polo* was the only one of the eight which was less than 200 feet in length and less than 2000 British registered tons.

George Campbell, a modern authority on sailing ships, regards Donald McKay's ships as 'probably the finest and fastest sailing vessels ever built'.

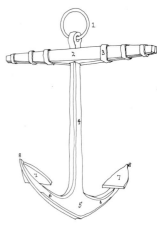

Common anchor

1 Anchor ring
2 Stock
3 Hoops of the anchor stock
4 Shank
5 Crown
6 Arm
7 Fluke
8 Pea or bill

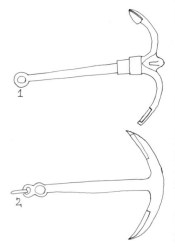

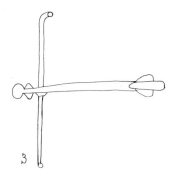

Types of anchors

1 Grapnel
2 Iron-stocked anchor
3 Trotman's anchor

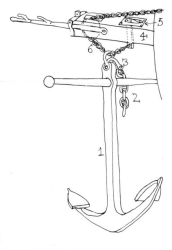

Cathead with anchor gear

1 Anchor
2 Cable
3 Shackle
4 Cathead
5 Releasing gear
6 Cathead stopper

The whole value of the clipper ships, however, lay not only in their ability to attain high speeds under ideal conditions for short periods, but in being able to move at all when most other vessels were becalmed, and in maintaining good average speeds for all conditions.[9]

In a definitive history of the Black Ball Line Michael K. Stammers, Keeper of Maritime History at Merseyside Museum, states that two of McKay's ships, *Champion of the Seas* and *Sovereign of the Seas*, were reputed to have sustained speeds of 22 knots; additionally, the *James Baines* sustained 20 knots and the *Lightning* 19 knots.[10] There are those who have doubted that the ships could have withstood the structural strains of such speeds and some contemporaries even dismissed the claims as 'Yankee boasts'. The fact remains that most were claimed by British masters of the ships. They made even more impressive claims for longest twenty-four-hour runs: no less than five of McKay's ships exceeded 400 nautical miles, the *James Baines* doing so on three occasions. In part, an explanation of such performances lies in the perfection of their design and in their enormous spread of sail — 12,000 square yards in the case of the *Champion of the Seas* — but much must be attributed to the great skill and audacity of Baines' carefully selected masters. Two of his McKay-built ships broke 70 days from Liverpool to Melbourne: the *James Baines*, 63 days, the *Lightning*, 69 days, and the same two broke 70 days for the return via Cape Horn: the *Lightning* 63 days, the *James Baines* 69 days.

Management of the true clipper ships was exceedingly demanding, for every change of wind meant a change of sail, not only to keep up speed, but, often, to avoid disaster. The leading masters knew to the minute how long they dared run with a rapidly rising wind before conceding risk and slackening sail. To many of the emigrants, sailing under such men, days and weeks at a time seemed to involve intolerable, inescapable risks; some began to think the masters mad. But most of the masters had developed skills to match the capability of their ships and well knew what they were about. Baines and the owners who competed with him, were responsible for the selection and nurturing of the greatest of these men: Enright, McKirdy, MacDonnell and, most daring and colourful of all, Forbes.

It caused a great deal of heartburning in Britain that, at the height

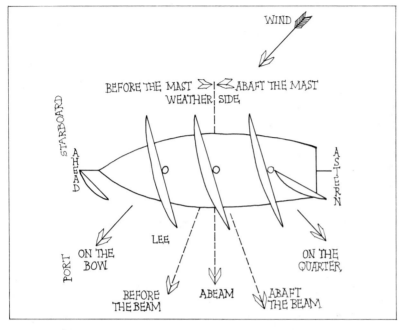

References used at sea. Starboard (right), port (left), hence expressions such as 'starboard bow', 'port quarter', etc. The side from which the wind is blowing is called the 'weather side'; the protected side, the 'lee side'. On large sailing ships the reference point on board was the main mast. Everything on board was either 'before' (in front of), or 'abaft' (behind) the mast.

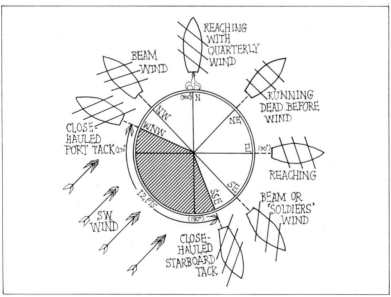

Until auxiliary engines were introduced, a sailing ship could make no headway in windless conditions. Given a wind, she could move in approximately 225 of the full 360 degrees, or, in nautical terms, in twenty of the full thirty-two points of the compass. When she sailed as close as possible into wind, her sails were said to be 'close hauled'. She was easiest to handle with a beam, or 'soldier's' wind. A wind from dead astern resulted in the after (rear) sails stopping the wind from reaching the forward sails. This diagram shows the directions in which a ship could sail in a south-westerly wind; the cross lines show the direction of her sails. If the wind were blowing a ship toward a nearby coastline, she was said to be 'on a lee shore' – a situation that demanded skill in handling and, even then, sometimes ended in disaster.

of her mercantile power, she was not able to produce ships to match McKay's. There was national rejoicing when Baines himself took up the challenge by ordering from Halls of Aberdeen, the giant *Schomberg*. She was 288 feet long and 2600 British registered tons; her mainmast soared to 210 feet and she spread 16,000 square yards (3.3 acres) of sail. To make doubly sure she would set a record, Baines appointed James Nicol Forbes as her commander. There was confident talk that she would reach Melbourne in sixty days, for 'Bully' Forbes was at the peak of his career. Whether the *Schomberg* was a good sailer will never be known. Forbes was unlucky in encountering adverse winds in her and this seems to have driven him to a state of frustration bordering on pique; added to this, there is little doubt that he was infatuated with a young female emigrant. At all events, he gave the *Schomberg* scant attention on the demanding approach to Bass Strait. On Boxing Day 1855, on a clear, relatively calm night, she drifted onto a sandspit near Curdie's River. Although no lives were lost, she was soon pounded to pieces by the sea. Thus ended Britain's hope of matching America's wooden ships with one of her own. As for 'Bully' Forbes, he was never given another first-class command.[11]

The stories of driving masters and record passages are stirring stuff, but a corrective is necessary: really fast passage times by sailing ships unassisted by auxiliary engines, belong approximately to the years 1852-8 — in other words, to the height of the gold rush. There was an extension beyond this in the settling of Queensland, as the government there entered into an agreement with the Black Ball Line in 1861.

For every fast ship there were ten or twelve very much slower ones. During the years 1858-63 the Director of the Flagstaff Observatory in Melbourne recorded 300 passages between Europe and Melbourne. Only one of the 300 bettered 70 days; seven completed the voyage in 70 days; fifty in 71 to 80 days; eighty in 81 to 90 days; sixty-eight in 91 to 100 days, and ninety-four, the largest group by far, exceeded 100 days.[12]

During the period of the Flagstaff Observatory records, iron ships were beginning to take over from their wooden forerunners. There were various reasons for this. As they became older, the softwood ships tended to become waterlogged and were subject to rot. They were also prey to teredo worm, commonly called 'ship worm'. Although teredo worm was a tropical mollusc, wooden ships had gradually brought it to the temperate latitudes. The teredo worm was of great size, sometimes three feet in length, and bored a hole up to an inch in diameter. Not surprisingly it could cause ships to founder. Shipwrights countered teredo worms first with lead and zinc sheathing, then with copper. But as this proved highly expensive, 'yellow metal' came into general use around 1846—sixty parts copper to forty zinc. Emigrant diarists sometimes mention the flash of sun on the metal bottom of a passing ship as a roll partially exposed it.

Yet teredo worms, waterlogging and rot were by no means the main reasons for the displacing of softwood ships by iron ships. 'The main advantage of the iron hull,' says George Campbell, 'was the increase in internal volume, structural members being so very much smaller' — smaller because of the much greater strength of iron over wood. Two main types of iron ship developed in parallel: those built wholly of iron and those built with iron frames planked on the outside with teak. The latter were known as 'composite' ships. Because the teak bottom could be sheathed with yellow metal, the composite ships had a great advantage over ships built wholly of iron — iron hulls became badly barnacled below the waterline and often dragged six or eight inches of marine growth along their full length. For many years the two types existed side by side. Probably the most famous of the composite ships on the run to Australia was the *Thermopylae*, which earlier had made her name as a China tea clipper. Not much more than a third of the *Schomberg* in size, she achieved in 1868 'Bully' Forbes' ambition of reaching Melbourne in sixty days — the unbeaten record for pure sail. Forbes by then had retired from the sea.

Basil Lubbock, who knew many of the iron ships, said that they had 'never been able to equal their wooden sisters in light winds' because of fouling by barnacles, but he gave three advantages the full iron ship had over wood: 'her hull would stand unlimited driving, especially into a head sea; secondly, she had more room for cargo than a wooden ship of the same size; and thirdly she was safer from that dreaded scourge at sea — fire.'[13]

Although America had limitless supplies of softwood, she was not self-sufficient in iron, also economic depression fell on her, then the Civil War. She could no longer compete with Britain whose iron foundries led the world. Nevertheless, she had provided the ships that gave Australia its most colourful days of immigration.

For some years iron hulls presented one alarming problem: they deflected the magnetic compass and this undoubtedly led to loss of

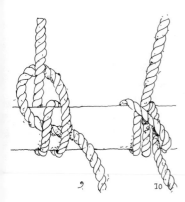

1   Overhand knot
2   Figure of eight knot, Flemish knot
3   Square knot, reef knot
4   Sheet bend
5   Double sheet bend, variation
6   Bowline
7   Clove hitch
8   Two half-hitches
9   Fisherman's bend
10 Rolling hitch

ships. John Towson turned to solving the problem, but the foremost authority was the remarkably versatile William Scoresby, who in 1854 spoke in Liverpool on remedies for the problem. According to the London *Times* the reception given him was chilly:

> **Something approaching to indignation has been manifested at this enunciation in Liverpool, above all places in the world, of a theory which, it is said, will tend to bring iron ships into disrepute and which has already produced a fluttering among the merchants on 'Change.**[14]

Scoresby fought back in an effort to have human life placed above shipowners' profits. He sought to have a second compass positioned by the crow's nest, remote from the hull. It has already been told how in 1856, at the age of sixty-seven, he went so far as to leave the comfortable parish of Torquay, of which he was incumbent, to test his hypotheses. He proved the case for a remote compass, but his constant venturing aloft in all weathers undermined his health: he died at home soon after his findings were published.[15]

Scoresby travelled out on the *Royal Charter*. She was not a pure sailing ship but one of a new breed — an auxiliary ship. This category needs defining, but definition is by no means easy, since many adopt the view that once an engine and screw were fitted into a ship, then it was no longer a sailing ship. But the fact remains that for days and even weeks at a time, the engines were not used; propulsion during these periods was wholly by sail. Engines were auxiliary to sail, not sail to engines.

By today's standards the engines were puny, but they gave the auxiliary ships enormous advantages. Even the greatest masters in the finest pure sailing ships were at the mercy of the wind in at least four different sets of circumstances: in departing during adverse winds; in passing through the doldrums; in coming into port; and when caught on a lee shore. Auxiliary power could save weeks of passage time. A hundred ships at a time often waited for favourable winds before they beat out of the English Channel or the Irish Sea. They might wait a week or more, often moving backwards, before they made some small progress. Auxiliary power finished this exasperating delay. In the doldrums the engine carried these ships past their immobilized pure-sail sisters. Approaching port, the auxiliary ship did not have to tack back and forth while waiting to pick up the pilot.

The fourth advantage was a very reassuring one: an auxiliary ship had some hope of standing off a dreaded lee shore when it might otherwise have been pinned there by the wind. 'Some' hope only, for there were times when wind and sea overpowered the horsepower of the engine, as in the case of the great *Royal Charter* herself. *

Apart from these periods when the engine was of great advantage, propulsion of the auxiliaries was by sail — it had to be, for the good reason that insufficient coal could be carried for masters to use their engines freely; also, their speed under steam alone was about half their best speed under sail. Even the most notable 'steamship' of all,

The *Great Britain*. Designed in 1838 by Isambard Kingdom Brunel, this 3500-ton iron ship carried more passengers to Australia, with greater reliability, than any other emigrant ship — an estimated 20,000 people on thirty-four passages. In her design and construction she was decades before her time.

*In October 1859 the *Royal Charter*, on a return voyage from Melbourne to Liverpool, was trapped on a lee shore off Point Lynas, Anglesey. Her 200 h.p. engine was unable to hold her off. Of 498 passengers, only thirty-nine survived. Also lost were 68,397 oz. of gold and 48,000 sovereigns. News of the disaster, which involved many successful diggers, did not reach Australia for nearly three months.

Isambard Kingdom Brunel's *Great Britain*, wound her screw out of the water for days at a time as she ran before the prevailing westerlies of the southern Indian Ocean. Ships were not able to depend on steam alone until the coming of the steam turbine and twin screws and the parallel development of steel — a combination belonging to the beginning of the twentieth century.

In the intervening years the auxiliaries greatly reduced passage time to Australia. The *Royal Charter* was an outstanding example. She reached Melbourne in the record time of fifty-nine days. Until they arrived, her passengers and crew did not know that the proud *Schomberg* had been lost three weeks before they had left home.

Although the *Royal Charter* set a record on her first voyage, the *Great Britain* had made the voyage three times before her and was to continue to make it for many years to come. The remarkable *Great Britain* was not built to carry emigrants to Australia, but to compete on the Atlantic. Nevertheless, she was destined to carry more emigrants to Australia in shorter passage times, over a longer period and with greater reliability than any other ship of the century. She was decades before her time.[16]

As early as 1838 Brunel had her on the drawing boards, thus her classic clipper-ship lines even pre-dated the American tea clippers. To realize how far ahead of his times Brunel was, we must remind ourselves that this was the era of poor, slow tubs inching their way to Australia with emigrants and convicts. The *Great Britain* was, in fact, so in advance of other builders' conception of what was possible that no one could be found to run the risk of building her. Her prospective owners, the Great Western Steam Ship Company, eventually decided to build her themselves — not willingly, but under pressure from the forceful Brunel. One can understand their reluctance: the proposal was to build a ship of iron three times as large as any ship built before! In the event, the project was to break the company financially, but the calamity was attributable not to Brunel, but to hazards of the sea.

When the *Great Britain* was launched in 1843 her specifications were: 3500 tons; 320 feet long; six masts; a six-bladed screw weighing four tons driven by an engine claimed to develop 1000 h.p.; accommodation for 730 passengers and a crew of 130. Her interior was plain but functional. Her first voyage to New York, made in 1845, was a triumph, but trouble with her screw led to it being changed to one of four blades instead of six. On her fifth voyage, in 1846, the blow on the Company fell: she ran aground on the east coast of Ireland, either through misreading of a light or because of compass trouble. Given Scoresby's later investigations, one would suspect the latter. Although the wreck broke the company, it did not break the hull of the *Great Britain*. Admittedly she was given some protection by a specially constructed breakwater, but nevertheless she must be the only ship to have convinced her detractors of her worth by her durability as a wreck. In 1850 she was refloated and sold to Gibbs Bright & Company, for a quarter of her original cost. For two years her new owners refitted her. They reduced her masts to four — she was still to carry 10,000 square yards of sail — and installed a two-cylinder oscillating engine. They then tried her on the Atlantic before switching her to move some of the thousands waiting to join the rush to Australia.

In 1852 she left on her first voyage to Melbourne with 630 emigrants. As she called at Cape Town to refuel, her voyage was not a fast one by her later standards, but her arrival led to great public enthusiasm: in Melbourne 4000 people paid a shilling each to see over her. She returned westward around the Cape of Good Hope, battling into the westerlies, as it was doubted whether she would stand up to Cape Horn seas. On her arrival in Liverpool her masts were reduced to three and she was fitted with full clipper rig; her screw was reduced to three blades. On her next voyage she followed the traditional easterly route all the way. Although she encountered an icefield for ninety-five miles and sighted twenty to thirty icebergs daily at the southern extremity of her homeward voyage, she weathered everything successfully.

Between 1855 and 1858 she was lost to the Australia run, being commandeered to carry troops to the Crimea and then to the Indian Mutiny. For the time, her trooping capacity was enormous: 1,650 infantrymen and thirty horses. Between 1858 and her withdrawal from service in 1877, she remained on the run to Australia. By 1866 it was estimated that she had brought out 10,000 immigrants — a figure probably doubled before her day was done. Her passage times were remarkably dependable: ten prior to 1870 averaged sixty-two days. Her best passage was 55 days 17 hours — a voyage on which she carried 670 passengers. On some passages she refuelled; on others she came out with no sighting of land before reaching Cape Otway. All told, she made thirty-four voyages to Australia.

Ship: A. Rigging B. Sails (square-rigged)

A. Masts, spars, and rigging:
1. Foremast 2. Fore shrouds 3. Fore-lower yard 4. Stunsail boom 5. Fore brace 6. Fore-stay 7. Fore topmast 8. Fore-topgallant mast 9. Fore-royal mast 10. Fore-royal backstay 11. Jib-stays 12. Bowsprit 13. Jib-boom 14. Bobstay 15. Mainmast 16. Mainbrace 17. Mizzen-mast 18. Gaff 19. Boom.
Decks and hull: 20. Poop 21. Companionway 22. Binnacle (holding compass) 23. Wheel or helm 24. Taffrail 25. Counter 26. Rudder 27. Keel 28. Bulwarks 29. Bilge 30. Waist or amidships 31. Deck-house (with galley) 32. Forecastle 33. Cat-head 34. Stem.

B. Sails: 35. Flying jib 36. Outer jib 37. Inner jib 38. Fore-topmast staysail 39. Foresail or fore-course 40. Fore-lower topsail 41. Fore-upper topsail 42. Fore-lower topgallant sail 43. Fore-upper topgallant sail 44. Fore-royal 45. Mainsail 46. Spanker 47. Fore-tack 48. Fore-sheet 49. Fore-lower stunsail.
The names of the upper masts, sails, yards, stays, and braces attached to the main- and mizzen-masts follow those given for the foremast.

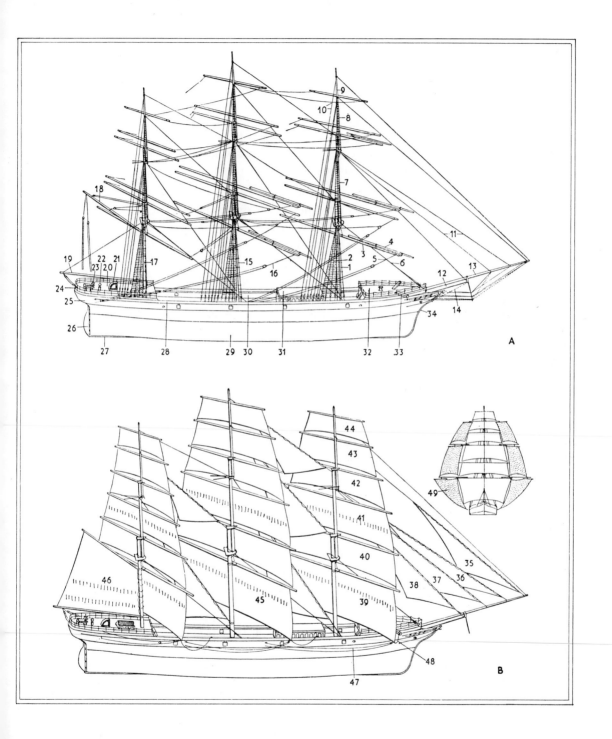

Her company described her as an 'auxiliary steam clipper'. A one-time midshipman of her crew, writing to the Melbourne *Age* in 1934, stated that her screw was of no use to her above eight knots and was used mainly at the beginning and end of her passages and in the tropical calms.[17] Rachel Henning, who returned to Australia on her in 1861, wrote of one of the greatest blessings the ship brought her passengers:

... we were fortunate enough to steer through [the doldrums] while the unhappy sailing-ships we passed were flapping their sails helplessly ... their inhabitants must have been nearly roasted alive.[18]

Her coal capacity was 1200 tons, 700 in bunkers and the rest 'in other parts of the vessel'. What this meant is apparent from the diary of Robert Saddington who came out on her in 1853. She refuelled on that voyage at St Vincent, in the Cape Verde Islands:

Our decks are now in a very uncomfortable state all the Fore-part is covered with Coal nearly as high as the Bulwarks and we are told that it must remain so for 2 days until the Engines have consumed a quantity.[19]

When one considers the extent of the *Great Britain*'s decks, some idea is gained of the reserves of coal piled there and the voracious appetite of the engine. Once the ship began running its easting down, Saddington recorded day after day when there was no use of steam and times when the screw was raised onto the deck. (He was distracted in keeping his record by 'the most disgusting Fleas and Bugs etc. with which the Ship swarms'. In a parcel he left on his bunk he counted twenty-five!)

All through her days on the Australia run the *Great Britain* enjoyed tremendous popularity and was accorded send-offs that usually exceeded those given other ships. The grand old lady richly deserved the honour bestowed on her in 1970 when she was brought back to England from the Falkland Islands where she had lain derelict for thirty-four years, her hull still defying the elements. Exactly 127 years after her launching, she was positioned in the Bristol dry dock in which she had been built and restoration on her was begun.

True steamships were yet far off. In Australia it was realized that only they would bring to immigration the capacity and reliability that was needed. Late in 1869 George Verdon, Agent-General for Victoria, put the matter plainly:

> Until there is steam communication between England and Australia, of which passengers of all classes can take advantage, we shall not have done all that is possible to shorten the distance, which is now one of the chief drawbacks to Australian immigration . . . It is the certainty of the time of starting, the knowledge that the passage is being made as quickly as possible, and that it will end in so many weeks, that gives a steamer so great an advantage over a sailing ship in the conveyance of large numbers of passengers.[20]

In the year that Verdon spoke, the Suez Canal was opened. For sailing ships the writing was on the wall, nevertheless, the 1870s and even the 1880s saw use for them in the emigrant trade.

The figurehead of the *København*, a Danish sailing ship built early in the twentieth century. The use of figureheads stems from the ancient superstition that a ship should be given eyes to see her way through awesome wastes of sea. Masters were known to have the figurehead removed in port so that they could personally safeguard it.

This brief account of the emigrant ships would be incomplete without reference to Lloyd's Register of Shipping.* In the early years of emigration, particularly on the Atlantic, many over-loaded, unseaworthy ships, well-covered at home by insurance, were lost at sea. As early as 1835 Lloyd's Register proposed a freeboard of three inches per foot depth of hold, but as this reduced loadings, many owners resisted it. Five years later ships on the register were still being lost at the rate of 1.5 a day. In 1854 the government intervened with an attempt to make draught marks compulsory, but its efforts came to nothing. Then in 1867 James Hall, a Tyneside shipowner, wrote to the *Shipping World* and to the *The Times* protesting that so many of the ships lost soon after leaving port were overloaded and unseaworthy. His condemnation applied less to Australia-bound emigrant ships than it did to cargo ships, but the result of his agitation eventually brought safeguards to shipping of all kinds.

When it was suggested that restricting the depth to which a ship could be loaded would put British shipowners into unfair competition with foreigners, Hall replied: 'If our success has to be purchased by sacrificing the lives of our sailors, then the foreigner, for my part, is welcome to the trade.' [22]

His words deeply impressed Samuel Plimsoll.

Plimsoll called on him congratulating him on his work on behalf of the seamen and telling him that he was anxious to help in the cause, and, as a Member of Parliament, was in a position to give considerable assistance. Hall handed over to him copies of the papers and addresses he had used in London and related many stories of the devilish work of some shipowners in sending their coffin ships to sea to get the insurance . . . When Plimsoll entered Parliament in 1868 his election address mentioned nothing about the inhuman behaviour of some owners to seamen, or the load-line, and for his first two years in the House of Commons he did not speak on the matter. Not till 1870 did he submit his views on the loss of life and property at sea by moving a resolution calling in general terms for legislation. [23]

Even then, the fight proved a long one. The marking of load-lines

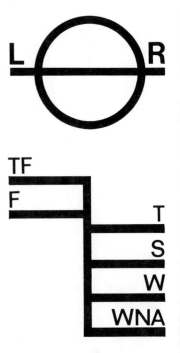

The Plimsoll Line. The line through the circle is the general line below which a ship may not be loaded. LR signifies 'Lloyd's Register'. Horizontal lines show variations permitted in different densities of water: TF, tropical freshwater; F, freshwater; T, tropics; S, summer; W, winter; WNA, winter North Atlantic.

*Lloyd's Register of Shipping should not be confused with the Corporation of Lloyd's Underwriters. It is the underwriters who are familiarly referred to as 'Lloyd's of London' and the register of shipping which gives point to the expression 'A1 at Lloyd's'. Though the two organizations have a common origin, they have long been separate entities. [21]

was not made compulsory until 1876 — and then it was left in the hands of the owners to make the marking. It became known as the Plimsoll Line, but in their hunger to overload their ships the owners cheated in the positioning of it. In 1890 the responsibility for the marking was taken over by the Board of Trade. By this time emigration to Australia by sail was over.

4　　　*Life at Home*

England is the Paradise of the first class;
it is essentially aristocratic, and the humbler
classes have made up their minds to this, and
do contently enter into the system.

Emerson

While it is true that of all emigrants under sail, those bound for Australia endured least, there is evidence enough from their diaries that they endured much, especially so couples travelling with children. Adventurous young men were troubled least; indeed, in their boredom they often proved troublesome to everyone else.

Close-packed steerage travel, which was the lot of most, could not be other than miserable. To read diaries telling of its trials is to wonder how emigrants endured what they did. But here again, it is necessary to see the travellers in the context of their times, to appreciate that a large proportion of them were conditioned to hardship.

One of the numerous guides printed for intending emigrants gave a categoric piece of advice:

[Men] of large capital ought not to emigrate at all ... England is the paradise of the rich — a man with moderate capital can command many sufficiently profitable ways of applying it without subjecting himself to the barbarisms of the bush.[1]

For most who went out steerage, the 'barbarisms of the bush' at least offered prospects of better living conditions; home offered none. As for the temporary barbarisms of the voyage, Basil Greenhill and Ann Giffard put these in perspective when they wrote of English rural workers emigrating from Somerset:

Communal water supply, Liverpool slums. Built during the Industrial Revolution to accommodate factory workers, these tenements became grossly over-crowded. They were not demolished until the 1930s.

49

The conditions [on the ship] were clearly not intolerable . . . if you lived on 7s 6d a week in a cottage built of mud and straw with an earth floor and a thatched roof, relieving yourself at the bottom of the garden into a pit with a rough seat bench over it, drawing your water from a well which might be several hundred yards away, and cooking your food on an open fire.[2]

The lot of the English farm labourer was lowly indeed. Even though the gulf between him and the landholder is familiar social history, it is nevertheless disconcerting to read such domestic exchanges as the *Dinton-Dalwood Letters*.[3] 'Dinton' was the English home of George Wyndham who left it in 1827 to establish 'Dalwood' on the Hunter River in New South Wales. As he toiled, perhaps he looked back nostalgically, but with new awareness, when he read of his male relatives' preoccupation with hunting while their tenant farmers attended the round of sowing, harvesting, ditch-digging and the like. His mother wrote:

William is with us at present, with his family of hounds, and the whole of his hunting establishment. He seems on the whole pleased with his occupation. I cannot but regret his having taken it upon himself, as it engrosses by far too much of his time and thought; but people must be employed, and he had better hunt than do many things I hear of.

In 1831 there were riots among the farm labourers and wholesale smashing of farm machinery. William had to give up his hounds for a time to help round up the rioters. George Wyndham heard of the outcome through his sister Charlotte:

The Special Assizes took place at Salisbury last week, before three Judges and a great many prisoners are sentenced to transportation. Two are to be hanged, I hear, one of them for having very nearly killed Mr. Oliver Codrington ... I think these convicts will be most valuable servants to you and other settlers in New South Wales, I fancy they will not be inclined to quarrel with the machines they will find there ...

It is evident that George Wyndham's father was a compassionate

Highlander's cottage on Isle of Skye, 1851. The woman has been collecting peat – the only available fuel.

Interior of a cottage on the Isle of Skye, 1851. The cottagers had little more than shell fish to live on, yet children such as these became sturdy pioneers in Australia.

man, but there was one culprit he and his family were glad to see go: Jem Larkam. George's mother wrote of Jem sharply:

... Your father ... having lost a considerable quantity of wheat, it was necessary to make enquiries about it, and there being a hole in the sack in which it was carried away, they were enabled to trace it step by step from the lower barn to Jem's lodging at Teffont, where it was found under his bed. He was taken into custody while at work in front of the dining room windows and the evidence was so clear he was transported for seven or fourteen years, I forget which.

Fourteen years later, George's sister Ella was still complaining bitterly about the fecundity of the local peasantry:

The whole place swarms with children that are being brought up to anything but obtaining an honest livelihood. It would be doing quite a service to them, and to the country at large, to transport them where they must exert themselves. But if any of the upper classes proposes their going to America or Australia, they are up in arms directly, and think it is to save yourself you make the proposition ...

This was ironically a time of great economic prosperity which reached its peak in 1851, the year of the great exhibition, in Joseph Paxton's Crystal Palace. The depressed lives of those in the mines and factories that produced Britain's array of exhibits is familiar social history. Such individuals counted for little. They could starve, fall ill, be maimed by factory machinery, or engulfed in mine shafts without concern extending much beyond their own families.

Harsh though the life of working people was, the lot of vast hordes of unemployed was worse. One may see them through the eyes of Nathaniel Hawthorne[4] who was U.S. Consul at Liverpool when it was the greatest port of emigration in Britain:

Almost every day, I take walks about Liverpool; preferring the darker and dingier streets inhabited by the poorer classes. The scenes are very picturesque in their way; at every two or three steps, a gin-shop; also filthy in clothes and person, ragged, pale, often afflicted with humors, women, nursing their babies at dirty bosoms; men haggard, drunken, care-worn, hopeless, but with a kind of patience, as if all this were the rule of their life; groups stand or sit talking together, around the door-steps, or in the descent of a cellar; often a quarrel is going on in one group, for which the next group cares little or nothing. Sometimes, a decent woman may be seen sewing or knitting at the entrance of her poor dwelling, a glance into which shows dismal poverty ... Doubtless, this noon-day and open life of theirs is entirely the best aspect of their existence; and if I were to see them within doors, at their meals, or in bed, it would be unspeakably worse.

Five days later he wrote after a further walk:

The people are as numerous as maggots in cheese; you behold them, disgusting, and all moving about, as when you raise a plank or log that has long lain on the ground, and find many vivacious bugs and insects beneath it.

Lord Shaftesbury visiting coal miners of the Black Country, 1840-2. 'Chained, belted, harnessed like dogs in a go-cart,' wrote the commissioner of a mining inquiry, 'black, saturated with sweat, and more than half naked . . .' But Lord Londonderry was disgusted that such woodcuts 'should have found their way into the boudoirs of refined and delicate ladies . . . weak-minded enough to sympathise with these "victims of industry" '.

Children of the 1930s in the Liverpool slums before the buildings were demolished. The over-crowding prevalent a hundred years earlier had been greatly reduced.

To Hawthorne the most depressing aspect of the poor was their acceptance of their lot.

... they really seem to take their distress as their own misfortune and God's will, and impute it to nobody as a fault ... the really hungry work-people . . . submit to starvation meekly and patiently, as if it were an every day matter with them . . .

Melancholy though these pictures are, they do not plumb the depths of bondage revealed by the inquiry of the 1840s into mining in Britain. In 1841, 1,189 women and 1,152 girls under eighteen were working in the East of Scotland pits alone.

A memorial in Silkstone churchyard, near Barnsley, Yorkshire, summarizes the attitudes and standards of the era in the chillest terms. One side reads:

This Monument

was erected to commemorate the re-
membrance of an awful visitation
of the Almighty which took place
in this Parish on the 4th day of July 1838.
On that eventful day the Lord sent forth his Thunder,
Lightning, Hail and Rain carrying devastation before
them and by a sudden irruption of water into the
Coalpits of the R.C. Clarke Esqr twenty six human
beings whose names are recorded here were suddenly
Summoned to appear before their Maker.

Reader Remember

Every neglected call of God, will appear against Thee
at the Day of Judgement.
Let this solemn warning sink deep into thy heart &
so prepare thee that the Lord when He cometh may find
Thee

Watching

The names of thirteen dead male miners are listed on another face of the memorial:

George Birkinshaw Aged 10 Years) Brothers
Joseph Birkinshaw Aged 8 Years
Isaac Wright Aged 12 Years) Brothers
Abraham Wright Aged 8 Years

So they go on, only one of them over the age of thirteen. On the opposite side of the memorial appear the names of eleven female miners with the addendum that their remains are 'deposited at the feet of the Males'. Their ages run from eight to seventeen; the average is twelve. Elizabeth Clarkson, aged eleven years 'lies at the feet of her Brother James Clarkson'.

Liverpool slum scene in 1934 before demolition. The railed area led to the basement rooms, which, in the late nineteenth century, were often affected by damp.

In Silkstone church itself a handsome marble plaque on the north wall marks the death in 1843 of 'Robert Couldwell Clarke Esquire', owner of the mine. It tells that 'He lived respected and died lamented'.

In these years, and for many years afterwards, people were accustomed to seeing those about them sent to the hulks, or transported to Botany Bay, or executed for a wide variety of crimes. Indeed, executions were one of the few forms of free public entertainment.

Samuel Warren [5], a lawyer and novelist, described in 1837 a crowd streaming to the execution of Pegsworth, a London murderer:

> Judging from the indifferent manner, the jocular volubility of these people, you would have thought them going to see a dog-fight rather than the execution of a murderer. As we approached Snowhill, which leads directly up to Newgate, all the avenues were seen crowded with the same description of people as had accompanied me down Holborn.

Twenty years later, in the relatively small cathedral city of Lichfield, 30,000 people attended the hanging of Palmer the Poisoner. Special trains ran; the pubs remained open all the preceding night; there was great jollity among the crowd.[6]

Brutish though much mid-Victorian life was, it would be a mistake to suppose that no improvements in living standards had come from the Industrial Revolution. Cotton underwear became available; glass for windows; kitchen ranges were manufactured, so were greater varieties of food. Soap, which had been made after a fashion in country cottages, was turned out in factories. But most of these innovations were beyond the purse of a tenement dweller, let alone the unemployed. As for soap, a tax placed on it in 1852 effectively discouraged any tendency a working man's family might have toward personal cleanliness. Indeed, with so low a standard of hygiene, the apparent fecundity of the country might well be wondered at. In reality it arose more through a fall in the deathrate, than a rise in the birthrate. When Jenner led the way to conquering smallpox and, a generation later, Snow to discovering the link between cholera and foul water, they were among those who lifted the country's average life expectancy from forty to fifty years in the course of a century. Compounding this was a long era of peace which meant that men were neither killed in battle, nor separated from their wives. With vast reserves of manpower available, and so many technical developments, England found herself with gluts in production on the one hand and in pauperism on the other. Not surprisingly, men of substance were alarmed by the restless masses and listened with foreboding to news of revolutions on the Continent. But no revolution came. The armed forces were at the call of the establishment, furthermore religious leaders did much to induce people to accept their lot peaceably. A farm worker born at the end of the century declared in his old age:

People believed in religion then, which I think was a good thing because if they hadn't got religion there would have been a revolution. Nobody would have stuck it. Religion disciplined us and gave us strength to put up with things.[7]

The greatest threat hanging over the lives of the compliant poor was the workhouse. In 1834, after 270 years, Elizabeth I's Poor Law was revised. Care was taken in the revision to ensure that the lot of the pauper would be below that of the lowliest labourer in case people chose to make the workhouse their home. Once committed, wives of child-bearing age were separated from their husbands, and often there was separation of parents and children. The workhouse was only a little less tolerable than transportation — and it held no hope of eventual betterment.

Such were the extremes of life in England. Conditions in Scotland and Ireland were worse. A reporter from the *Illustrated London News* wrote from Bridgetown in Ireland in February 1847 describing the fearful breakdown of normal life during the Potato Famine:

I saw the dying, the living, and the dead, lying indiscriminately on the same floor, without anything between them and the cold earth, save a few miserable rags upon them. To point to any particular house as a proof of this would be a waste of time, as all were in the same state; and not a single house out of 500 could boast of being free from death and fever, though several could be pointed out with the dead lying close to the living for the space of three or four, even six days, without any effort being made to remove the bodies to a last resting place.

Deeply attached though the Irish were to their country, all who could do so fled to North America — and as we have seen, many did not survive the Atlantic crossing. Only a few hundred left for Australia — it was not only remote, it was British.

There were many similarities between the depopulating of Ireland and the Highland Clearances of Scotland: eviction of cottagers by landlords; destruction of their dwellings; backing of landlords by police and soldiery; depiction by certain journalists of the dispossessed people as indolent beggars.

The depopulation of both countries was in the economic interests

Interior of a Liverpool slum in the 1930s. In the nineteenth century such a room was shared by more than one family.

of those selling and those buying the lands. In Scotland this encroachment had begun as early as 1792 when clan chieftains began selling their estates to Lowland and Northumbrian sheep breeders. Since the estates were encumbered by cottagers clustered in small villages, they had to be cleared before sheep were brought in. This was done by persuasion, threats and force. With a few admirable exceptions, persuasion and threats came from chieftains and church alike, the law supporting them.

The dispossessed families, bearing their aged, their infants and their sick, trudged away with what they could carry, not knowing where food and shelter were to be found. This process was to be continued for decades, exacerbated in its worst years by famine. In the famine years Scotland's homegrown crops were shipped out of the country.

At this the starving people rebelled, the women in particular fighting the constables with anything to hand. At Invergordon the landowners were immensely relieved when a hundred soldiers of an Irish regiment arrived to support them: 'Irish soldiers, in whose own homeland at this moment skeleton women were shrieking for food and maddened animals were gnawing at human corpses.'[8] They drove the people back with fixed bayonets — perhaps remembering England's use of Scottish troops in Ireland.

In 1851 the Highland and Islands Emigration Society was established. It told people that their country could no longer support them, that emigration to Canada or Australia was the only course open to them. The proprietors of the new sheep runs supported this policy wholeheartedly. Within two years the Society had sent 3000 assisted emigrants to Australia.

Having looked at the impoverished masses of Britain — 'as numerous as maggots in cheese', submitting to starvation 'meekly and

Inheritors of the Liverpool slums in 1934.

A staircase used by generations of Liverpool slum dwellers.

patiently', broken in Ireland and Scotland by landlords and famine — one would scarcely consider this a field of recruitment for labour in a new land. But the situation was not without a degree of natural selection. If in every thousand there were three or four or five who questioned their existence and sought means to escape it, then they were the ones likely to inquire about emigration. And always the literate had better chances than the illiterate, since they could read of opportunities overseas and of how to avail themselves of an assisted passage. Then there were the thousands of others who were coerced into departing. Vast numbers of 'the deserving poor' simply sank back into the quagmire of deep poverty. On the edges of the quagmire were further thousands who, because they were employed, managed to exist but not to save. From among them came larger numbers of emigrants. Further removed again were those who could save, but could see few prospects for their children; others again who saw small prospect at home of exercising professional qualifications. The upsurge of emigration to Australia in the 1850s saw thousands of these latter groups departing. Nevertheless, among steerage passengers most were people acutely aware of the quagmire: the prospect of unemployment, hunger, dependence on charity, denial of protest, the possibility of separation in the workhouse. Among the diaries that have survived, few have come from this group. Many among them were illiterate; others were thwarted in their intentions by steerage conditions. 'We intended keeping a Journal', wrote one of two Scottish sisters after she had arrived in Australia, 'but our part of the Ship being so dark many a day we could not see'.[9] Harsh though steerage conditions were, they were not as harsh as the lives of many of these people had been — and there was an end to the long voyage.

5 *Decision and Preparation*

Oh! emigration! Thou'rt the curse
Of our once happy nation's race!
W.[1]

To emigrate, or to remain at home? For many it was the most far-reaching decision of a lifetime; indeed, it is doubtful whether later generations have had to make up their minds on an issue so final in its implications. By firesides and over tables in homes all over Britain, emigration was the subject of long and painful deliberation. The optimistic tried to persuade themselves and those they were leaving behind, that they would soon make a fortune and return to bring comfort to the entire family.

... should their enterprise succeed, how blest,
The prospect 'homeward' to return and rest.[2]

In the event, only a small proportion made money enough to return so far with a family; others could not bring themselves to face the voyage again; perhaps more were to find that the desire to return had gradually left them, though for most there remained longings for the attractive aspects of 'home'.

The Emigrants' Farewell. Apart from the signpost this scene might have been anywhere in the British Isles. Many villagers were reluctant 'to cross the brook to the next parish', yet economic circumstances and government pressure forced them to leave the British Isles for ever.

Members of families knew that once parted, their only link with each other would be an annual exchange of letters; two exchanges within a year if they struck fast ships with each post. They were conscious, too, of the risks of the voyage itself. Then there was the remoteness of Australia, its prison atmosphere, its lonely bush, and its reputedly hostile natives. Would they be able to adapt themselves to such conditions, or would they have committed themselves to a lifetime of loneliness and longing?

In most cases the alternatives to leaving were equally depressing. Thomas Coggan, when he decided to emigrate, was twenty-five:

... like many others [I] had worked constantly from the age of eleven at wages ranging from two shillings to twenty shillings per week, which seemed to be as much as I had a chance of getting by remaining at home; and, although my parents did rear a family on such wages, I did not mean to try to, so I thought I would devote ten years to money-making in Australia and go back a bloated capitalist ...[3]

Both before the gold rush and after it, many people reached their decision after considering the advice of friends or relatives who had preceded them. In 1834 Anne and John Loomes, an industrious couple forced by circumstances onto poor relief in Cambridgeshire, went out to Australia. Anne wrote home:

... bless God, we are in a land of plenty, and it is a very fine country, and I think I should like it, if I had but one friend to speak to, but I dare say my dear friends when you read my letter, some of you will shed a tear for me, for I have shed a great many since I left my home, I think of you all when I am asleep and awake, but I hope my dear friends if we meet no more in this world, we shall all meet together in the next ...

Tell all inquiren friends we are in the land of plenty, we sit down every day to a good joint of beef ... oure stint of beef is 40 pounds a week, you may buy good beef at one penny per lb. if you take a quantity at once, sugger 2d. per lb., and good tea 1s. per lb., and tobacco 1s. per lb., good beer is 1s 6d. per bottle, rum 10s. per gallon in Sydney ... we are about 40 miles from Sydney; our wooden hutt stands on a hill and is very pleasant, we have about 20 acres of Indian Corn before oure door and it grows from 6 to 7 feet high and has cobbs as long as your arm. You may buye land at 5 shillings a acre, up the country; you may buy all sorts of clothing in Sydney almost as

These advertisements describe the contrasting types of accommodation: differing classes and all one class. The former was more common.

cheap as at home; shoes is cheap hear, it is a good place for trade; such as blacksmiths and wheelwrights, and carpenters and shoemakers, do very well in Sydney and in the country. Now my dear friends I must conclude ...[4]

The eyes of people who had lived harsh lives at home opened wide with incredulity when they found food to be so plentiful. It seemed at first, a country formed for the less fortunate. Ellen W. wrote from Sydney in 1846:

We pay eight shillings a week rent, but it is well we get on. Oh what a difference there is between this country and Home for poor folks. I know I would not go back again — I know what England is. Old England is a fine place for the rich, but the Lord help the poor.[5]

Another Ellen, Ellen Clacy, came from a higher stratum of society. She emigrated with her brother in 1853, married in Australia and was one of those who did sufficiently well there to return to England. There she urged those of her own sex who were considering emigration to take the plunge:

... if you can go under suitable protection, possess good health, are not fastidious or 'fine-ladylike', can milk cows, churn butter, cook a good damper, and mix a pudding. The worst risk you run is that of getting married, and finding yourself treated with twenty times the respect and consideration you may meet with

A contrast in living conditions depicted in a way likely to appeal to literate and illiterate alike. Though the attractions of 'there' were overstated, many readily recognized 'here'.

in England. Here (as far as number goes) women beat the 'lords of creation'; in Australia it is the reverse, and there we may be pretty sure of having our own way.

But to those ladies who cannot wait upon themselves, and whose fair fingers are unused to the exertion of doing anything useful, my advice is, for your own sakes remain at home. Rich or poor, it is all the same; for those who can afford to give £40 a year to a female servant will scarcely know whether to be pleased or not at the acquisition, so idle and impertinent are they; scold them, and they will tell you that 'next week Tom, or Bill, or Harry will be back from the diggings, and then they'll be married, and wear silk dresses, and be as fine a lady as yourself'; and with some such words will coolly dismiss themselves from your service, leaving their poor unfortunate mistress uncertain whether to be glad of their departure or ready to cry because there's nothing prepared for dinner, and she knows not what to set about first.[6]

J. A. Rochlitz wrote of the same overturning of the social system. Servants and ex-convicts threw up their jobs and went to the diggings. 'And gold they found, while all around the whole social system fell into ruins.' Rochlitz added that 'even if a man could afford a palace, he would have to scrub its floors . . . In short every lowly work became the share of everyone. Because a servant one could not find for any price at all.'[7]

Sophy Taylor, who went out to Adelaide to marry in 1851, wrote home to her sister:

... It wants persons to be active, enterprising and industrious to get on here. Some do very well indeed while others don't succeed at all ...

As far as the voyage is concerned, it does not seem to me as formidable a thing as it used to be ... You say 'would it suit you' — well, I do not think it would be exactly to your taste though after you had been one month on the water and got used to the kind of life and had plenty of your own little comforts and made up your mind to be comfortable, not caring for the little annoyances, I think you would stand it pretty well.

... it is much more comfortable for a family than for an individual. On the voyage, for instance, you can form a mess among yourselves, using the things you bring with you in the way of comforts, and thus being of so much more use to each other. I said when I came I would never go to sea again without a gentleman. It is only fit for men to go to the galley and cook etc., and many of our annoyances on board were because we had to do such things ourselves or go without. Many of the single gentlemen on board too, would have been much more comfortable had they had a wife to do things for them in other departments. You can help each other if two or three are together.[8]

None of Sophy Taylor's family joined her for she died in 1853 following the birth and death of her baby.

The high wages paid during the gold rush to those who remained in their jobs, left many of the newcomers with feelings of delight when they compared their lot with what it had been at home. John Smith, a young Scot, wrote to his mother from Templestowe, Victoria, in March 1856:

About a week ago I earned seven and 6d before breakfast, for killing a bullock for a neighbour. That is more than your Lochaber farmers would give me for working hard for a week. I will never forget working for three years and a month for Sandy Grant for my grub and clothes and a £5 note. I can get the same here in less than three weeks. I have never thought of going to the diggings as I have never been out of work ... I am glad you got the money I sent you, as I suppose it will be very useful to you.[9]

Two years later the rest of the Smith family followed the writer to the same district where they all eventually prospered.

At least one of those who had gone ahead and settled successfully, sent home an encouraging jingle:

... here in my adopted land no parent feels the pain
Of hearing loved ones cry for bread and know they cry in vain,
But labour meets a sure reward and want and hunger flee.
I love thee well old England but Australia for me.[10]

In 1834 the British Government was endeavouring to rectify the great shortage of single women in the Australian colonies. When such ships as this one arrived in Australian ports, some of the women received proposals of marriage before they had even stepped ashore.

Female Emigration
TO
AUSTRALIA.

COMMITTEE:

EDWARD FORSTER, Esq. *Chairman*
SAMUEL HOARE, Esq.
JOHN TAYLOR, Esq.
THOMAS LEWIN, Esq.
S. H. STERRY, Esq.

CHARLES HOLTE BRACEBRIDGE, Esq.
JOHN S. REYNOLDS, Esq.
JOHN PIRIE, Esq.
CAPEL CURE, Esq.
WILLIAM CRAWFORD, Esq.

CHARLES LUSHINGTON, Esq.
JOHN ABEL SMITH, Esq. M P
GEORGE LONG, Esq.
COLONEL PHIPPS,
NADIR BAXTER, Esq.
CAPTAIN DANIEL PRING, R N

The Committee for promoting the Emigration
OF
Single Women

To AUSTRALIA, acting under the Sanction of His Majesty's Secretary of State for the Colonies, HEREBY GIVE NOTICE, That

THE SPLENDID TEAK-BUILT SHIP

"*David Scott*," of 773 Tons Register,

Carrying an experienced Surgeon, and a respectable Person and his Wife as Superintendents to secure the Comfort and Protection of the Emigrants during the Voyage will sail from

GRAVESEND
On Thursday 10th of July next,

(Beyond which day she will on no account be detained) direct for

SYDNEY.

Single Women and Widows of good Character, from 15 to 30 Years of Age, desirous of bettering their Condition by Emigrating to that healthy and highly prosperous Colony, where the number of Females compared with the entire Population is greatly deficient, and where consequently from the great demand for Servants, and other Female Employments, the Wages are comparatively high, may obtain a Passage

On payment of FIVE POUNDS only.

Those who are unable to raise even that Sum here, may, when approved by the Committee, go *without any Money Payment whatever*, as their Notes of Hand will be taken, payable in the Colony within a reasonable time after their arrival, when they have acquired the means to do so: in both cases the Parties will have the advantage of the **Government Grant** in aid of their Passage.

The Females who proceed by this Conveyance will be taken care of on their first Landing at Sydney. They will find there a List of the various Situations to be obtained, and of the Wages offered, and will be perfectly free to make their own Election; they will not be bound to any person, or subjected to any restraint, but will be, to all intents and purposes, perfectly free to act and decide for themselves.

Females in the Country who may desire to avail themselves of the important advantages thus offered them, should apply by Letter to "The Emigration Committee, London," under Cover addressed to "The UNDER SECRETARY OF STATE, COLONIAL DEPARTMENT, LONDON." It will be necessary that the Applicant be accompanied by a Certificate of Character from the Resident Minister of the Parish, or from some other respectable persons to whom the Applicant may be known; but the Certificate of the Resident Minister is in all cases most desirable. Such Females as may find it expedient may, when approved by the Committee as fit persons to go by this Conveyance, be boarded temporarily in London, prior to Embarkation, on Payment of 7s. per Week.

☞ All Applications made under cover in the foregoing manner, or personally, will receive early Answers, and all necessary Information, by applying to

JOHN MARSHALL, Agent to the Committee, 26, Birchin Lane, Cornhill, London

EDWARD FORSTER, Chairman

NOTE.—The Committee have the satisfaction to state that of 217 Females who went out by the "Bussorah Merchant," 180 obtained good Situations within three Days of their Landing, and the remainder were all well placed within a few Days, under the advice of a Ladies' Committee, formed in the Colony expressly to aid the Females on their arrival.

LONDON, 1st May, 1834.

* By Authority :
PRINTED BY JOSEPH HARTNELL, FLEET STREET, FOR HIS MAJESTY'S STATIONERY OFFICE

Large-scale emigration to Queensland came later in the era of sail, but reasons for leaving for the colonies had changed very little. Mrs Thomas Hinshelwood wrote home from Rockhampton in 1883:

> I would advise people who are fond of comfort not to leave their good homes, but those who, like ourselves, are struggling on with a small income and a growing family, would do well to come here, but they must make up their minds to endure hardships of many kinds as we have done.[11]

Those in Britain who made up their minds to emigrate had next to find how they should prepare for the voyage. Here, again, the advice of a friend or family member who had gone out ahead was of tremendous help. Mr J. B. Hack wrote from Launceston in 1837:

> Bring plenty of jam and things to mix with the water when it gets stale, or you won't be able to drink it comfortably. Plenty of hooks and large nails to hang things on ... raspberry-vinegar and ginger beer powder, and indeed anything to take off the horrible taste of the water are indispensable.
>
> And now I am going to give you the most important advice of the whole, and that is, however agreeable and friendly the captain may be on the shore, have a written agreement with him as to the quantity of every allowance ... When you are on board keep up ceremony with all passengers; it is the only way to agree: if you don't follow this from the beginning, you will find the value of it before you are three months on board: I cannot too much stress on this.[12]

As the stream of emigrants to Australia increased, books and periodicals appeared, giving advice to those contemplating the break; indeed, once the gold rush began, the number of books multiplied correspondingly. *The Gold Colonies of Australia* declared:

> In England a man may rise up early, and eat the bread of carefulness, but from our complicated commercial system, or from other causes, with all his industry and all his care, he may find that he has all his life been only laying up poverty for his

old age. This is not so in the colonies; there the industry of man founds families; here it but too often breaks them up.

The editor went on to reassure those who were reluctant to accept an assisted passage:

... let the emigrant remember, he is under no obligation for this fund. It is not alms, but money sent by the colonists, to provide what is to them the first necessity of life, viz., additional labour ... It has been said, that an emigrant going out by means of this fund is looked down on in the colony: we can assure him, from personal knowledge of the colony, that this is not the case. No man there cares how he comes out, or asks a question about it; the only persons looked down upon are the idle, the dissipated ... Rank and title have no charms in the antipodes ... Great family connections and ancestry would only provoke, to any who should parade them, the remark that 'he was like a potato: all that was good belonging to him was underground'.[13]

Those who were perturbed by alarming stories of the Aborigines had Arthur Hodgson to reassure them:

It is not to be supposed that such savages as these will quietly submit to see their country wrested out of their hands without making some attempt to dispossess such formidable occupants; but fortunately for us, we have to deal with the greatest cowards on the face of the globe.

He added unctuously:

I have no hesitation in adding that New South Wales is one of the proudest monuments to the Christian civilization of our country ...[14]

Sidney's Emigrant's Journal appeared monthly and offered advice to those planning to go to any one of Britain's colonies.[15] An early editor was a man named John Capper who, in 1852, compiled a new and more specialized publication: Philips' *Emigrant's Guide to Australia*. This sold at a shilling and with the gold rush proved so popular that Capper greatly enlarged its scope and content:

FEMALES
to
SIDNEY.
under
SANCTION
of
GOVERNMENT

London Pub by J Kendrick 54 Leicester Sqᵉ
Augᵗ 10, 1833.

EMIGRATION in SEARCH
of a
HUSBAND.

What are you going to Sidney for, pray ma'am.
Vy they says as how theres lots of good husbands to be had cheap there
whereas the brutes in England can't see no charms in a woman unless she's got plenty
of money to keep 'em in idleness.

The man who will go out to the southern colonies, having no capital but his labour, with stout arms and a stout heart, with no old-world prejudices hanging about him, determined to work with a will and to adapt himself to the new country and its way — such a man will be sure to find what he seeks and what he cannot get here — certain and constant employment at more than ample wages ... Such as have not the means of providing a pass-

Although advertisements in the 1830s stipulated that single women travelling as government emigrants were to be between fifteen and thirty years of age, many of them were older – and numbers of prostitutes among them caused the authorities concern.

age and look to doing so by aid of government funds for emigration, must first ascertain whether they come within the rules laid down by the Commissioners for the Selection of Emigrants.

[For those selected] the Commissioners supply, free of charge, provisions, medical attendance and cooking utensils, at their depot and on board ship. Also new mattresses, bolsters, blankets and counterpanes, canvas bags for linen, knives and forks, spoons, metal plates and drinking mugs, which articles will be given after arrival in the colony to the migrants who have behaved well on the voyage.[16]

For people who had seldom been given anything free in their lives, this was extraordinary news.

Capper quoted a passage from another writer:

Gentlefolks with little money and much pride, are the least likely to succeed as emigrants, because while they have not the working powers which are always in demand in a colony, they seldom have courage enough to accept the advantages a colony offers in economy of externals. Although poverty drives them from Europe they cling to European prejudices, and continually sacrifice their independence to a short struggle to maintain appearances.[17]

What sort of clothing ought a family take? What else was needed? Capper had the answers down to the last kerchief:

For the wife: Three cotton dresses, one pair stays, four petticoats, sixteen chemises, two flannel petticoats, twelve pairs cotton stockings, four pairs black worsted ditto, six night dresses and caps, six pocket-handkerchiefs, four handkerchiefs for the neck, six caps, two bonnets, cloak and shawl, one pair boots, two pairs shoes, eight towels.

For the husband: Two fustian jackets, waistcoats and trousers, three pairs canvas trousers, one overcoat, two felt hats, one Scotch cap, sixteen striped shirts, two Guernsey shirts, twelve pairs cotton half-hose, four pairs worsted hose, six handkerchiefs, eight towels, two pairs boots and one pair shoes, strong but not heavy.

Children in like proportion. The family will also require a flock mattress and bolster, one pair blankets, one coverlet, six pairs cotton sheets, two or three tablecloths, six pounds yellow soap, three pounds marine soap, metal wash-handbasin, knives and forks, one quart hookpot, comb and brush, besides a supply of string, sewing materials, tape, buttons, etc.

A superior class of emigrants, men of a few hundred, may take the following as a sufficient list for the voyage: Three dozen regatta shirts, common, to be used first; one dozen best regatta shirts; six best white shirts, for town; twelve pairs drawers, cotton thread; three dozen pairs socks, cotton or angola; six pairs worsted socks; six pairs shoes or boots strong but not heavy; one cloth cap; one straw hat and one felt hat, as you generally lose one or two overboard; a south-wester; one pilot-cloth coat; two boady coats, alpaca; six blouses; two pairs cloth trousers; three pairs alpaca ditto; ten pairs white ducks; large canvas clothesbag; a horse-hair or cocoa-nut fibre mattress; a pair of 40s blankets; eight pairs of sheets; a coverlet; a cabin wash-basin and table; a pair of ship chest of drawers; a looking-glass, combs, brushes, etc; a ship cabin candle-lamp, with 10 lbs. composite candles; 6 lbs. soap; some marine soap, all packed in chest or in the drawers; with tapes, buttons, sewing-thread, needles, etc.[18]

Having read Capper's list for the 'superior' male, one can visualize his dandified figure on deck. But if he were a bachelor, he would find himself among the heaviest drinkers and gamblers — before the voyage was half over, many a regatta shirt had changed hands.

Some families took with them seeds of flowers and vegetables, even cuttings which they contrived to keep alive, all for planting in the new land. A young nurseryman, William Adams, listed in the front of his voyage diary seven pages of seeds. Sometimes, on a ship carrying few emigrants, one finds a cabin or intermediate passenger taking a dog, even two dogs.

It was all very well for John Capper and the other publicists to produce their informative booklets, but many of those in desperate need of guidance were illiterate. Unless a friend read to them, they might not so much as hear of opportunities in Australia, let alone that they could travel out free.

Caroline Chisholm, realizing the handicap illiteracy imposed upon many potential emigrants, visited numerous centres and addressed crowds of people with power and persuasion. She encouraged emigration by families, or in groups of friends, and formed the Family Colonization Loan Society which made small loans to members once they had paid sufficient instalments toward the passage money themselves. Her agreement with her groups was that they repay the loans on establishing themselves in Australia. Sadly, many of those she helped were to fail her.

Capper gave wide publicity to Mrs Chisholm's scheme:

When the emigrants have been accepted, and the necessary funds provided, a vessel is selected suitable to their number. So soon as the day of her sailing is fixed, the emigrants are all divided into family groups, containing twelve adults, who can

Caroline Chisholm (1808-77). In Australia her name is associated mainly with her work among newly arrived immigrants – single girls, the unemployed and the people of the gold fields – but her most significant contribution to emigration under sail was her establishment of the Family Colonization and Loan Society in 1849 and her exposure of conditions on the emigrant ships. The latter was one of the many forces leading to the passing of the British Passenger Act of 1852.

take their meals together during the passage. The object of this arrangement is that friends and relatives may unite and aid each other in their common emigration...

Families and individuals who cannot meet with persons wishing to emigrate from their own locality have thus an opportunity of meeting desirable associates and mutually forming a group advantageous both to their present and future views. Friendless females and orphan girls are introduced to families and placed under their special guardianship. In like manner, youths and young men are associated with family groups ...[19]

Capper turned from the Family Colonization Loan Society to the costs of shipboard accommodation: first class ranged from £40 to £70 per person, depending on the size of the cabin; there were reductions for children sharing cabins. Steerage ranged from £20 to £25.

... To young settlers, especially married people, who are desirous of making their small capital go as far as possible we would say, avoid the cost of cabin or even intermediate passage; engage a space between decks at the steerage price, £20 to £25 each, and employ the ship's carpenter to run up a little cabin ...

... a supply of provisions will be found acceptable, as the ship's dietary may not be such as the emigrant and his wife have been accustomed to — say 1 cwt of flour, 1 cwt of potatoes, a few pounds of tea, coffee and cocoa, some candles, a hundred eggs greased and packed in salt, some suet, butter, cheese and biscuits; a dozen or two tins of preserved provisions, a side of bacon and a couple of hams, with a little wine and some bottled beer. The whole of the above might be had for about £20, which added to the cost of the steerage passage for a couple, say £45, will not amount to more than the cost of a single cabin passage.[20]

Sidney's Emigrant's Journal also listed supplementary foodstuffs:

I need but take for my text the words — 'oatmeal and treacle'. Provide as much of these as will last the whole voyage ... Eggs may be preserved all the way by being slightly rubbed over with butter or lard, and then covered over in your salt or some sawdust, taking care to place them resting on their ends, so as not to touch each other, or otherwise by being thrown against each other in the jolting of the vessel the shells will be broken...[21]

The *Journal* went on to give advice on selection of a ship:

Let the emigrant use his own eyes in the matter, and he will not be deceived ... 1st, beware of runners. — 2nd, beware of dishonest passenger-agents. — 3rd, Choose a ship with a good height between decks. 4th, Choose a ship with high bulwarks. — 5th, A ship with proper water-closets. — 6th, a ship with proper conveniences for cooking. 7th, See that the ship is properly loaded. 8th, See that the Captain and mates have a good character.[22]

Some captains had gained such splendid reputations that their names were household words; it was wise, if one had opportunity, to seek out their ships. But for a barely literate person living far from the sea, there was scant hope of doing so. And how was he to check the loading of the ship, even supposing he knew anything about it? Many emigrants first saw a ship the day they boarded one. But the warning against 'runners' was timely. These extortionists infested Liverpool in particular, where their main prey were the thousands of Irish emigrants making for North America. In *Passage to America* Terry Coleman tells of the link between runners and other rogues — 'brokers':

Before the emigrants even got on board ship they had to have dealings with ship brokers, otherwise known as emigration agents or recruiters; with runners, otherwise called crimps, touts and man-catchers . . . The broker was a speculator. He did not own ships. He sold space . . . and received from the shipping company a commission on each berth sold . . . If a broker chartered a ship he had to fill it by a certain time, or make a loss . . .[23]

Runners got hold of passengers for him — literally got hold of them: 'they pull them by the collar, take their arms and, generally speaking, the runners who were successful enough to lay hold of the boxes are pretty sure of carrying the passenger with them.'[24]

Runners were also 'in league with the provision merchants, who allowed them 15% on anything bought by an emigrant they dragged in'. It is difficult now to determine to what degree these parasites fastened onto emigrants bound for Australia. The fact that the government played so large a part in the Australian trade left fewer opportunities for them. Emigrants usually had their arrangements made before they presented themselves at the port of departure. The shorter Atlantic crossing, with its hundreds of thousands of desperate emigrants, remained a free-enterprise free-for-all, the individual pitted against desperadoes who set out to fleece him. They ranged from 'respectable' shipowners to the lowest of lodging-house keepers.

The Gold Colonies of Australia urged intending emigrants to seek out ships A1 at Lloyd's, to avoid what was known as the 'red diphthong' — 'which denotes an old ship, probably abounding in rats and mice'.[25]

The *Emigrant Voyager's Manual* attempted to introduce the reader to his ship:

> All seems confusion and disorder. Below there is what you would call a long, narrow, low room, with very little windows and small bed-places, and posts, and tables without number; and trap-doors overhead, and trapdoors beneath your feet. On deck, in the open air, as you look up, you see a confused collection of poles, and ropes, and sheets of canvass of which it puzzles you, or any other landsman, to conceive the use. Now, let me assure you, that in what seems to your eye a confusion of ropes, a seaman sees perfect order and regularity.[26]

The editor of *The Australian Colonies* set out to reassure those held back by fear of the sea:

> Some people are frightened by the thoughts of the length of the voyage, and at first suffer a good deal from fear; should the wind blow hard, and the sea run high, they are sure to overrate the danger, especially at night, when the crew are busy 'reducing sail'; the trampling of the sailors over their heads, the loud voice of the captain and mates giving orders, and the rolling of the ship from side to side, very naturally create alarm. This is also increased by hearing other passengers express their fears. Fear begets fear, and the between decks very often present a

The village priest blessing departing Irish emigrants. The majority of emigrants from Ireland chose to go to the United States, but by the time of the Australian gold rushes, many thousands turned to Australia, despite their detestation of British rule.

Interior of a shepherd's hut in Australia, typical of those occupied by many early settlers. While it is difficult to believe that this abode of Joe, a shepherd, would have appeared attractive to people in Britain, the *Illustrated London News* artist added this inducement in the text: 'a plentiful repast of mutton chops and sassafras tea prepared us for our journey.'

scene of great confusion, without any just cause for it. Passengers should always bear in mind this simple rule, 'never be alarmed until the captain is'.[27]

One might well ask how passengers were to assess the captain's feelings when they were shut away from him. Usually they could only hear him bawling orders to his officers and their repeating them, whereupon there would be a rush of feet on deck, all of which *sounded* calamitous.

Nevertheless, thousands who read these booklets, or had friends read them aloud, or had informative letters from Australia, made the decision to emigrate. As for choice of a departure time, James Henty's advice to his father in 1829, was sound:

I am of the opinion that *early* in the month of September is by far the best time for leaving England you get well away before the equinoctial Gales commence and by the time you arrive [in the] south you have spring and summer.[28]

Those who could afford to do so made their own choice of a ship rather than go on an 'emigrant ship' chartered by the government. The shipping lines advertised their vessels in resounding terms; one would have thought every one of them a McKay clipper with comfort even for the masses in steerage, and every master a record-breaker.

There was a wide variety of choice. For example in January 1855 one could go with the Temperance Line's *Sampson*, a 'very superior vessel' with 'ventilating apparatus recommended by Mrs. Chisholm'; she also carried a minister of religion and her prospective passengers were assured that baths and wash-houses would be 'erected on deck'.[29] Perhaps they were. Or there was Marshall and Eldridge's Line, 'noted for their fast-sailing qualities' and for their 'superior accommodations for passengers'. Or, if one wished to be entirely free of steerage passengers, there was the *Guiding Star*, a 'superb new clipper-ship' of some 2000 tons, A1 at Lloyds, due to leave on her maiden voyage: 'Will be loaded to the best possible trim . . . for the express purpose of making the quickest passage on record, an expectation her magnificent model fully justifies; her accommodation for cabin passengers cannot be surpassed.' She attracted, in fact, 486 passengers, people whose circumstances were considerably better than those travelling steerage on other ships. Her passage was indeed to establish a record — a tragic one as we have seen in Chapter 1.

Bookings made, the emigrants' packing had to be done. As to what they took, this depended very much on their social position. Some of the dispossessed Irish and Scottish could carry all that remained to them in their own hands, while some of the first-class passengers had in the hold furnishings enough to set up a home.

Packing done, the emigrants said their local farewells. Some members of their own family would accompany them to the port, if it were not too far off. There were many ports of departure, but Liverpool and London were by far the busiest. It was possible also to leave from Glasgow, Plymouth, or a dozen smaller ports.

It is difficult to realize today how little the common people of Britain had been able to venture beyond their own county; sometimes, even beyond their own parish. There they were born, they married, they died; so it had been for all recorded history.

I was a boy of 10 years old when, with my parents and four brothers and five sister, we went on board the ship in St. Catherine's Dock, London. Coming from a quiet village in Worcestershire, and never before having seen a ship or a railway train, I felt myself in a new world . . .[30]

Thus were the breaks made. For few could there be any last-minute change of mind.

6   *Departure*

Farewell, England! Blessings on thee,
Stern and niggard as thou art.
Harshly, mother, hast thou used me,
But 'tis agony to part.[1]

No matter for how long people had contemplated departure, or how assiduously they had studied the advice of their mentors, nothing could prepare them adequately for final farewells and sudden strange confinement on board ship in quarters that soon would be tossed wildly for weeks on end. They were no more prepared for reality than an unblooded soldier is prepared for action by tales of war. They knew that the journey would last three or four months, but, if they were of the general run of people they knew little of the sea and less of ships and their destination was *terra incognita*. A sympathetic surgeon-superintendent, Scot Skirving, wrote of his charges:

> ... what tragic goodbyes there must sometimes have been, whether the last words were said in the thick air of a city slum or in a quiet English village or in 'the lone shieling' of some western isle.[2]

Emigrants embarking at an unidentified British port in 1880. A wide range of people is represented, none of them looking happy now that departure is imminent. It is probable that the Black will be travelling as ship's cook.

Young single men were an exception to the generally sombre mood of departures. They set off as other generations of young men had set off for wars, buoyed by each other's company and expectations of adventure. One of them recalled later:

> ... with a light heart ... I joined a band of youths of gentle birth,

83

assembled on the deck of the good ship *Delta* as she lay moored in the river Mersey ... one sunny morning in July, 1852. We were bound for a distant and little-known land (except for its proximity to the notorious Botany Bay), from which had just come tales of untold wealth awaiting our arrival. We merrily turned the capstan around with the hardy crew, as they weighed the anchor, and joined in their farewell songs to our native land ...[3]

It was a different matter for married couples, especially the thousands travelling steerage. Steerage passengers usually had to spend a few nights in one of the large emigrant depots at the port of departure while they waited to board. John Bramley Moore, Mayor of Liverpool, thought 'a depot as necessary for emigrants as sheds were for bales of merchandise'.

He said that he could only look upon emigrants as live merchandise: vessels were being constructed with the sole object of carrying emigrants, and it had become the most profitable carrying trade.[4]

These depots woke steerage passengers to the lack of privacy that was to be their lot in the months ahead. Joseph Tarry reported to the Birkenhead depot in 1853:

... a cold comfortless place — but an abundance of good provisions ... We were struck with astonishment when we arrived at the top of the stairs — to see the Room — the People and the Beds — Two or Three hundred persons were to sleep in one room — on Beds almost as hard as Stones — arranged in the same manner as in passenger Ships — the scene altogether seemed very ludicrous — so unlike anything we had witnessed before — Some were laughing — others crying ...[5]

The same vast room had not changed much thirteen years later when Robert Beckett arrived there with his family:

Strange dormitory: it would accommodate 60 to 70 different families. On the right side, about 4 feet from the ground, a wide

Depot at Birkenhead where government emigrants to Australia were received and housed. The vessel at the wharf is finalizing preparations for the voyage. Steerage passengers, drawn from various parts of Britain, spent their last nights ashore in depots such as this — their first experience of lack of privacy in dormitory-type accommodation. In these depots many emigrants, especially the children, contracted contagious diseases that brought tragic consequences at sea.

shelf stretches the entire length of the room; on this shelf planks about 1 & a half or two feet high are placed at intervals of 4 feet, the vacant spaces are receptacles for the beds; the under part of this shelf is similarly divided & the left side of the room is arranged the same as the right. We are thus all sleeping in sight of each other, but the light is so dim, that we can see but little of our neighbours.[6]

Although the depots were strictly regulated, they often proved unhygienic and numerous cases occurred of people sleeping in beds vacated by emigrants who had been suffering from contagious diseases; the infections were thus unwittingly carried aboard ship, sometimes with frightful consequences.

Usually the stay in the depot lasted only a few days, but this was sometimes extended owing to delays in fitting out the ship. The rough steerage bunks had often been torn out in Australia for easier carriage of return cargo — mainly wool. The pungent, unfamiliar smell of greasy wool greeted thousands of boarding emigrants and remained with them until it was expunged by the odours of crowded, unclean, seasick humanity.

Boarding for cabin passengers was usually delayed until steerage boarding was over. One of the steerage passengers, Charles Scott,

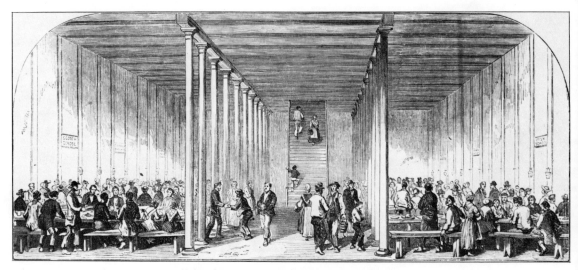

wrote with wry amusement of his boarding, though he had little enough to be amused about — he was an impoverished Kidderminster weaver who was probably already suffering from the tuberculosis that was to claim him six years after his arrival in New South Wales:

> The emigrants being 404 in number for the *Annie Wilson* all busy getting their Luggage on board, never saw such a droll act out in my life. Familys walking behind each other up the plank into the Ship loaded with thair Bags containing thair months Change of Linean and Cook-Utensils — like Noah and his Family going into the Ark and there was almost as great a veriety — there was English, Irish, Scotch, Welch, French and all sizes. Then to see something to amuse you still more, turn your eyes around the quay and you see Buckets, tubs, Barrels, and such like placed in ample order for the ships use, then before those stood a great Mountain of luggage belonging to the Passengers such as Boxes from the Hat Box up to the large packing Box, it stood before the rows of Buckets like a gander before the Geese — the procession moved on without interruption excepting now and then a Cannot you be asy behind there. Shure you are treding on my heels you Bogtrotter.

Robert Corkhill was a steerage passenger boarding the *British Trident*:

> ... what with the *singing* of sailors, the *swearing* of Officers, the *complaining* of passengers, the continual *croaking* of the German Brass Band and last though by no means least the *squealing* of pigs ... this ship [might be compared with] the Original Babel ...[7]

After steerage passengers boarded, their relatives and friends were permitted last farewells. *David Copperfield* contains a memorable description of a ship about to leave for Australia. David was farewelling the Peggotty family. He hired a boat, boarded the ship and went below deck:

> ... It was such a strange scene to me, and so confined and dark, that, at first, I could make out hardly anything; but by

SUMMARY.

	NUMBER OF SOULS.					EQUAL TO STATUTE ADULTS.
	ENGLISH.	SCOTCH.	IRISH.	OTHER COUNTRIES.	TOTAL.	
ADULTS....................	*157*	*15*	*68*		*240*	*240*
CHILDREN BETWEEN 12 AND 1..........	*52*	*4*	*3*		*39*	*19½*
INFANTS...................	*8*	*1*			*9*	
TOTAL,...............	*197*	*20*			*288*	*259½*

We hereby certify, That the above is a correct List of the Names and Descriptions of all the Passengers who embarked at the Port of Liverpool.

Signed *James Nicol Forbes* Master.

Emigration Officer.

Countersigned *Officer of Customs at Liverpool.*

Summary of passengers emigrating in 1855 on the new Black Ball Line clipper *Schomberg* under the line's leading master, James Nicol Forbes. Two and a half months later all were to survive stranding on the Victorian coast near Cape Otway and were taken by passing coastal steamers to Melbourne. Within a week of the stranding the Schomberg was smashed in storms.

degrees it cleared, as my eyes became accustomed to the gloom, and I seemed to stand in a picture by Ostade. Among great beams, bulks, and ringbolts of the ship, and the emigrant berths, and chests, and bundles, and barrels, and heaps of miscellaneous baggage, lighted up here and there by dangling lanterns, and elsewhere by yellow daylight straying down a wind-sail or hatch-way, were crowded groups of people, making new friendships, taking leave of one another, talking, laughing, crying, eating and drinking; some already settled down into possession of their few feet of space, with their little house-holds arranged, and tiny children established on stools, or in dwarf elbow chairs; others despairing of a resting place, and wandering disconsolately. From babies who had but a week or two of life behind them, to crooked old men and women who seemed to have but a week or two of life before them; and from ploughmen bodily carrying out soil of England on their boots, to smiths carrying samples of its soot and smoke on their skins.[8]

A picture surely drawn from life but invested with a Dickensian cosiness that conceals the emigrants' true feelings. How much more tellingly the mood of departing emigrants is conveyed by Ford Madox Brown's painting, *The Last of England.** This picture of a young couple looking back from the deck of a departing ship hung on the walls of numerous Australian homes and its details were familiar even

The Last of England. Ford Madox Brown based his famous painting on a departure he had witnessed in 1852 — that of his sculptor friend Thomas Woolner.

to the grandchildren of those who had emigrated: the man's broad-brimmed, black hat bent back by the wind; his young wife's veil blown out behind her; the protecting umbrella dripping with spray; the clasped hands — not only his hand and her hand, but, visible through the division in her shawl, a very small hand held in hers. Nothing more is to be seen of their infant. In his notes on the picture the artist said

[It] is in the strictest sense historical. It treats of the great emi-

*In his *Autobiographical Notes* published in 1892, William Scott Bell related that Ford Madox Brown painted this picture after he had seen the sculptor, Thomas Woolner, sail from Gravesend for Australia in 1852. The young couple at the rail are Brown himself and his wife, the hand shown is that of Oliver, their infant son. (The painting, now in the Birmingham Gallery, is dated 1855.)

gration movement ... I have, therefore, in order to present the parting scene in all its tragic development, singled out a couple from the middle classes, high enough, through education and refinement, to appreciate all they are now giving up, and yet dignified enough to put up with the discomforts and humiliations incident to a vessel all one class.

Emigrant diaries bear witness to the picture's truth. Hear John Sayers, about to depart on the *Osyth*:

When we got on board our feeling of sadness was not lessened by the appearance of our quarters. I felt at my wits' end for a while as both Harriett and Marianne were wishing to get home

The embarkation, Waterloo Docks, Liverpool. Liverpool was the main port of departure for all Europe. A constant stream of emigrants from the Continent would join the exodus of English, Irish and Scots. The great majority travelled to North America, suffering appalling loss of life on the way. Ironically, the longer voyage to Australia was safer because of strict government supervision.

again at any price. I felt much inclined to give up the whole business and return to Ireland for better, for worse ... After a weary walk to an outfitting establishment which did not repay our toil, we returned to our lodging for the night, full of struggling hopes and fears.[9]

Or William Rayment, leaving on the *Himalaya*:

I am sitting on the quarter deck. Everything is strange and I am surrounded by strangers, the majority with very elongated countenances. Children are running about apparently in search of a back yard, to give vent to their feelings in a game of marbles. Sailors are rushing about and passengers are rushing in their way. Everyone is out of his place. Be not surprised then when I say that my feelings were just a few degrees below happiness. When I was standing on the deck surrounded by my friends I thought things were not so bad after all, when they commenced wishing goodbye, I felt a twitching at the corners of my eyes, but when the boat pushed off and standing on the side of the vessel I waved my hand, I can safely say that I did not see the boat for tears.[10]

A reporter from the *Illustrated London News* watched 840 impoverished Scottish highlanders join the frigate *Hercules* in January 1853. They had been gathered up from North Uist, Harris and Skye, some of them by force, the single men not being permitted to marry their local women. Pressed into emigration they had been brought by steamer to Campbelltown where the *Hercules* lay waiting.

It was curious to observe them, as they stepped over the gangway of the great ship. The young women came first — some looking cheerfully round, some sad, and some in tears; but all took pains to adjust their shawls and handkerchiefs, their tresses, or their caps, as they made their appearance before strangers. The married women and their children followed, the latter skipping and dancing on the broad deck, overjoyed at their escape from the confinement on the steamboat; the former, so completely absorbed by the care of their children, and the fear of

Emigrant ship awaiting a steam tug. Once tugged from port she might have to wait several days for favourable winds to take her to sea.

losing them in the crowd, that they did not seem to be conscious of where they were, or what had brought them there. The men looked dark and stern, like men about to confront danger, and not likely to shrink from the encounter, but relaxed into a smile at the first kind word.[11]

To move briefly to the end of the *Hercules'* passage: when the ship arrived in Port Phillip, Edward Grimes, Immigration Agent, wrote feelingly to Lieutenant-Governor La Trobe:

... most of these people are in a most deplorable state of ignorance, and quite unacquainted with the English language; and of all those who were questioned by me through an interpreter, not one appeared to be in any degree aware that he had entered into no engagement to pay anything at all.

However desirable the system may be as a means of charitable relief, I scarcely look upon this class of Immigrants as one that should be brought out at the expense of the Colony: very few of them are acquainted with agricultural or pastoral employment, and from their indolent habits, I do not think they are likely to prove a very great acquisition to our labour market.[12]

Grimes probably knew nothing of the immigrants' own primitive system of agriculture, which had afforded them no opportunity of learning anything more advanced. As for the tag 'indolent', it had been affixed to them before they left. He underestimated a determined people.

Newspaper reporters were sent often to observe departures, but, secure in the knowledge that they would return to shore, they seldom succeeded in perceiving what lay below the surface excitement. A *Graphic* reporter on board the *Indus*, due to leave for Brisbane with over 500 emigrants, saw only the strange and the stimulating:

Forward between decks were the quarters of the bachelor emigrants. Here a tall thin sinewy Irishman was dancing a jig to the tune of a violin, the scraping of which, combined with the mewing of a litter of black kittens, and the laughter of the audience, to make up a very Babel of discordant sounds ... several passengers were busy letter writing ... Among [the married couples] were some Cornish miners bound for the copper mines of Queensland. Their strongly marked features, coupled with the sombre hoods of the women, and the broad-brimmed straw hats of the children, fluted at the edges, formed a most picturesque sight.[13]

An American reporter watching steerage passengers departing on the Atlantic crossing came much closer to the emigrants' mood;

Unlettered and inexperienced, everything seems dreamlike to their senses — the hauling of blocks and ropes, the cries of busy seamen as they heave round the capstan, the hoarse orders of the officers, the strange bustle below and aloft, the rise and expansion of the huge masses of canvas that wing their floating home, and will soon cover it with piled up clouds. Here are women with swollen eyes, who have just parted with near and dear ones; perhaps never to meet again; mothers seeking to hush their wailing babes. In one place an aged woman, who has nearly reached the extreme term of life, sits listless and sad, scarcely conscious of the bustle and confusion around her. She lives not in the present, but in the past ...[14]

The Emigrants – A Story without Words. From some ports emigrants were rowed out to their waiting ship. Although the moment of departure is sentimentalized here, there is no doubt that the eyes of the young usually looked forward to the adventure, while their parents looked back at their lost homeland.

Antoine Fauchery, the lively young Frenchman, later to make a reputation as a photographer of goldfields life, observed the departing emigrants around him on the *Emily* with a mingling of amusement and admiration:

As far as I can judge ... most of them belong to the English middle class. All ages and both sexes are represented. It is not without surprise that I see old white-headed men, smart ladies on the shady side of forty, and above all many children. About ten of them have already slipped between my legs, all between two and five; I can count an equal number of them who are at the breast; and the exaggerated stoutness of three or four of the ladies near me indicates an interesting condition which should soon cease to be so. That's the English all over. They alone can handle with bold indifference details that for us would constitute big obstacles. Once they have glimpsed their goal, nothing can stop them ...[15]

Cabin passengers remained ashore in private accommodation until the last possible moment, then they were brought out by boats to the ship, perhaps a day or two after the steerage passengers had been accommodated. Many of them boarded dressed for a grand entrance. But the last and most impressive entrance was made by the master himself. It was usual for him to delegate departure preparations on board to the first officer while he himself remained ashore for final discussions with the owners and the emigration authorities. As he boarded he was the cynosure of first and steerage classes alike: here was the god-like being who would now control their lives, in whose hands their safety lay. If his ship were a speedy clipper and he were aiming for a record, he made sure before departing that he had on board the day's newspaper, for on the highly competitive run to Australia the claims of ships' logs were sometimes suspect. The newspaper was a guarantee at the end of the voyage of his departure date — his starting gun for the long race.

As departure time drew near, bands on quays and following craft began playing popular airs: 'The Girl I left Behind Me'; 'Home Sweet Home' and, invariably, 'Rule Britannia'.

Robert Saddington departed on the *Great Britain*:

... different Bands of Music on various small Ferry Steamers playing 'Cheer Boys Cheer' and other Tunes ... I was startled by the heavy Boom of Cannon and for the next Hour Guns were fired Continually in answer to those from the Vessels Piers Docks et.

The hour had come for the boatswain to pipe 'all hands up anchor'. As Edward Snell put it:

... the sailors singing a barbarous sort of song about:

> Fare you well my lovely gal
> Heave y' I ho, I ho
> I'm aleaving of old England
> So I pray you let me go etc. etc.[16]

As the bands redouble their playing and passengers crowd to vantage points for last glimpses of relatives and friends, we return to David Copperfield who, having left the ship, watches her depart at sunset on a still evening:

She lay between us, and the red light; and every taper line and spar was visible against the glow. A sight at once so beautiful, so mournful, and so hopeful, as the glorious ship ... with all the life on board her crowded at the bulwarks ... I never saw.

Silent, only for a moment. As the sails rose to the wind, and the ship began to move, there broke from all the boats three resounding cheers, which those on board took up, and echoed back, and which were echoed and re-echoed. My heart burst out when I heard the sound, and beheld the waving of the hats and handkerchiefs ...

Fauchery's mood was lighter:

I walk from the wheel-house to the ratlines of the bowsprit, breathing in the last perfume of the shore ... Ships of all ranks and nations follow and cross us, pilot boats hail us; from the bottom of their nutshell fishermen greet us, and we move on steadily, softly, in a breeze that hardly makes us sway ...

The Englishmen shout frantic *hurrahs*, the English women wave their handkerchiefs ... Only the sailors remain unmoved by these demonstrations ... Their bearing is all but gloomy and they smile only after giving us all that look that is so searching and so peculiar to the navigator. A strange look, a singular smile.

To the crew the crowding emigrants were a trial, constantly getting in their way as the ship moved out. Crew procedure was precise. R. C. Leslie, an historian of ships and shipping, wrote that the tow by steam tug from East India Dock to Gravesend generally took half a day. 'Sailors with short iron hooks drag length after length of chain cable aft along the decks and lay it fair in fakes for running out'.[17] Many small craft continued following the ship, but gradually, as the Thames widened, they became fewer in number. At Gravesend the Thames pilot was dropped; the tug cast off and went its way with a farewell blast on its siren. Leslie again:

Roll call on the poop deck of an emigrant ship. The poop deck, offered the largest open space for assembly. Once at sea this deck was denied to steerage passengers and was reserved as the leisure area for the relatively small numbers travelling first class. The first-class cabins directly below the poop, were entered by the door at the centre of the picture.

All clear there for'ard? 'Ay, ay, sir all clear'. 'Let go!' The anchor falls from the cat-head, and the ship, trembling from end to end ... as the chains run out ... swings head to tide for the night.

So, if one were departing from London, the first night out was not a night at sea; the departure was drawn out by the length of the river. Some of the cabin passengers might even have decided not to board before next morning. Then a second tug and an estuary pilot took over. Approaching the Downs, Leslie relates, there was 'a quiet, "Ready about" from the pilot':

Very soon, 'All ready forward?' ... 'Ay, ay, sir!' from the mate. 'Put your helm down!' 'Helm's a-lee!' 'Raise tacks an' sheets'. The whole mass of canvas, ropes and blocks ... is banging, flapping and rattling among the spars and rigging as the ship comes upright and head to wind ... From the mate, 'Mainsail — haul!' The long yards swing round; gangs of sailors run along deck gathering in the slack braces etc. The ship turns from the wind and her after canvas slowly fills again, while her head-sails lie quietly, nearly aback against the foremast. Then comes another shout of, 'Let go and haul!' As the men run aft with the fore-braces the fore-yards swing round, and the ship's head is toward the Kentish shore. 'Steady your helm! Keep her full!'

There remained on departing ships, until the last boat left them, representatives of various Christian persuasions. F. W. Leighton, leaving Liverpool on the clipper ship *Bloomer** in 1853, wrote of the presence of 'a pale man with thin visage dressed in a shabby black surtout buttoned to the chin'.

He is standing by some parcels of books which we soon hear are tracts destined for the use of the passengers ... We learn that the habit of [his] useful Society is to put a number of tracts

---

*Named in honor of Mrs Amelia Bloomer, the American who devised the liberating female garment named after her. Additionally, a British railway engine was given her name.

in all vessels leaving the port of Liverpool thus they give food for the mind and instruction for eternity.[18]

The society was the Liverpool Seamen's and Emigrants' Friend Society and Bethel Union, an evangelical group which also conducted religious services aboard departing ships. The themes of their addresses were reported in their publication, *The Forget-Me-Not, or Last Hours on the Mersey* and from these today's reader may acquaint himself with the solace offered the emigrants before their long journey. James Buck, one of the Society's preachers, wrote in this journal:

[The Emigrants'] need of mercy as sinners condemned and unworthy and liable to perish, was clearly pointed out, and their peculiar circumstances as strangers in a strange land, and as intending voyagers over the mighty deep, where danger in a thousand trying forms might await them, rendering God's love, and God's wisdom, and God's power, their only felt dependence, and last resource, were all produced to give intensity to our appeal.[19]

Not surprisingly, the intensity proved too much for some who were already overwrought by farewells and strange surroundings: '. . . many [were] overcome by their feelings, even to tears'; others 'convulsively pressed my hand as they passed me weeping, and sobbed out their thanks for my labour among them'. When Mr Buck left the ship by the last boat, he was able to console himself also: 'if I never see them again, I feel I am clear from responsibility'.

It was not uncommon for people of the same religious persuasion to emigrate together. William Harbottle wrote of a chapel group gathering to sing as the *Scotia* moved down the Thames in 1849:

A brass-bound sea chest was possessed by most cabin-class passengers. It served a double purpose: trunk and chest-of-drawers. In the cabin it was lashed securely to prevent movement in rough weather.

. . . some of the more aged and graver are busy singing psalms — one group I think were spinning out the evening hymn in rather mournful strains, amid the almost indescribable confusion that necessarily prevails in their new habitations.

Next day, a Sunday, the *Scotia* had not progressed beyond the Thames: Two gentlemen from Exeter Hall — came down with us — they are from the 'Prayer Book and Homily Society' — to distribute tracts and religious books and to impart, as they term it, a word of exhortation. They have had Divine Service between decks, but it looked almost burlesque amid the tread of feet above and the rattling of blocks and chains — but they seemed to listen with great attention, expecially the married portion . . .

The day after this the *Scotia* put to sea.

. . . **The emigrants have been singing psalms between decks, but the tars have commenced some sea songs on deck in opposition.**[20]

There were sometimes amusing diversions during departures — amusing, anyway, for the observers. Thomas Small, a young Scottish bootmaker, wrote while still in the Mersey:

There is a laughable incident connected with one of the passengers which I cannot pass over. He is a Yorkshire man & having sold his small farm, he & a buxom young woman of about 23 summers thought they might do worse than try the Colony, so after they got themselves snugly berthed, & had slept two nights together as man & wife, what should appear in the distance but the tender coming along with the letters, & on board was a woman with a fine boy of about 8 years old who claimed to be the farmer's wife. Well, he was summoned to appear on the poop before the Captain, wife & child, & he had to make a clean breast of it, so the lawful wife was kept & the young one was taken back. When she was going away he gave her his handkerchief and told her he would soon have her out. Some of the passengers were going to put him overboard. His wife has given birth to a fine daughter since that.[21]

Ships departing from London dropped the estuary pilot at Deal. R. C. Leslie has written that the 'big breast pocket of his oilskins was regarded as the final letter box'. There was a last reminder often uttered in families being split by emigration: 'Now mind you write by the pilot.' Many, unable to write, lacked the outlet that pen and paper might have afforded them.

A young man whom we only know as E. Lloyd experienced a fairly ordinary departure from Liverpool, but he was more than ordinarily articulate:

The pilot was to leave us after we passed the light-ship and then we were to have taken a step from which there was no retreating.

My meditations were interrupted by a person informing me that the pilot was about to leave us, and that if I had any message to send, I would now have the opportunity. I hastily scribbled a few lines, and gave them to him; and once his form had disappeared over the side, and the sound of oars from his boat died away in the distance, I felt as if the last connecting link between me and the old country were severed. The night was setting in, and adding an external gloom to the already sombre colour of my thoughts. 'You are at sea now,' said a voice at my elbow, 'and will have to make the best of it.' That was exactly what I thought, and turned round to see the speaker, but he was gone.[22]

The ship was likely to be at sea before cabin passengers experienced their first night on board. 'A first night on board ship has in it something very strange', wrote Ellen Clacy, 'and the first awakening in the morning is still more so.'

To find oneself in a space of some six feet by eight, instead of a good-sized room, and lying in a cot, scarce wide enough to turn round in, as a substitute for a four-post bedstead, reminds you in no very agreeable manner that you have exchanged the comforts of Old England for the 'roughing it' of a sea life.[23]

Not 'roughing it' as steerage roughed it. By contrast, Henry McIntosh was among single men who did not even have bunks:

It is a very curious sensation one feels when taking off one's clothes on board ship, and looking into his hammock, naturally supposing that he is to be there for three months. A perfect hole, one not so large as you would give a dog to lie in, and there you are, and the vessel going to and fro as if you were drunk.[24]

The pangs of departure were almost inevitably overwhelmed by seasickness. Young Samuel Shaw wrote:

We all started full of mirth which was soon changed, for in

The Emigrants. For months family members have discussed emigration; the decision has been made for some to leave. Now the moment of departure has come. The coast of the motherland is slipping over the horizon, probably never to be seen again.

less than two hours after sailing there was scarcely a one but was sick and lying about the deck helpless.

And next day:

There is still no difference in the state of the sick, I believe they are worse than ever as they are lying in their beds heaving up and the smell is very bad.[25]

Mrs Thomas Hinshelwood was one of 400 emigrants packed into the *Nebo.* Two days out seasickness prostrated most of them:

... the well-dressed, respectable company that left Glasgow is to be seen reeling about in all stages of apparent intoxication.

But the day was not far advanced ere we were all in the same miserable condition, aggravated by the roughness of the sea and the consequent ceaseless rocking of the vessel. I think I shall never forget the sensation of loathing I felt every time our food was presented.

Two days later things were little better:

We may long remember our first Sabbath on the deep; our sickness at its height, with the waves breaking over the deck, the ship rolling from side to side by the force of the cross seas we had to encounter; each family clinging together in their berths, unaccustomed to such an experience; thinking it a terrible storm, while the sailors laughed at our fears . . .

As a surgeon-superintendent, Dr Scot Skirving felt for the 'shocking trials' of the departing emigrants under his care:

Unused to the sea, seasick, homesick, cold, wet, fearful and battened down, few aggregations of human wretchedness could be much greater than was to be found . . . in the close dark 'tween decks of an outward-bound emigrant ship.

While the passengers were enduring this misery, the coast of England was likely to be in sight still; in fact, dependent as a ship was on the wind, it might be becalmed or even steadily moving backwards. A week or more might be spent with the home shore tantalizingly close at hand — seen, but beyond treading upon. Only the coming of the auxiliary ships ended this period of delays.

When England at last fell from sight, people began to realize even more fully the extent of the step they had taken. Here is E. Lloyd:

The Sea was rolling the ship from side to side in impotent spite; the tall masts describing segments of circles in the clouds, and the giant sails flapping loudly against the masts. For the first time since my departure I experienced a depression of spirits. No doubt the prospect had its influence, but, singular enough, this was the first time I seemed fully to comprehend my position, and the undertaking in which I had embarked. It is curious, but nevertheless true, that occurrences take place

Good Bye. A typical scene of departure, as men preceded their womenfolk to Australia.

around us and concerning us, and we at the same time are fully cognizant of what is going on, yet a sort of incredulousness pervades the mind, and it is not till some period after that we awake to a perfect consciousness of their reality.[26]

Some days later he wrote:

Heavy and fitful are my slumbers; old and accustomed faces crowding round me, bidding goodbye and melting again, in a strange jumble of times and places and occasions.

Lloyd's mood is echoed by Joseph Beale, a Quaker who had been obliged to precede his wife and younger children. In a letter opening: 'To my best beloved wife, I write thee alone in our cabin with a dark blue sea before me', he continued:

Kiss each of my loved children for me, remember me aff [ectionately] to all interested about me — be assured that *all* that lies in *our power* will be done for you and if favoured to meet you in Australia it will be indeed the happiest day of my life and will recompense for all the trials hitherto administered to me ... Farewell my dearest, and believe me to be thy ever attached and loving husband.[27]

Soon, for all of the thousands of emigrants, nothing remained on the heaving sea to remind them of home. They now only shared the sun, the moon and the familiar stars with those they had left behind. But the constellation most familiar to them, that celestial signature of their hemisphere, eventually vanished too. Looking back to that final loss, Mrs Charles Meredith wrote:

I do not know one thing that I *felt* so much as the loss of the North Star. Night after night I watched it, sinking lower—lower; the well-known 'Great Bear' that I had so gazed at even from a child, that it seemed like the face of an old friend, was fast going too; it was like parting from my own loved home-faces again ...who might say that we should ever meet again? Those stars seemed a last link uniting us, but it was soon broken—they sunk beneath the horizon, and the new constellations of the southern hemisphere seemed to my partial eyes far less splendid.[28]

Plan of the Accommodations of the A1 British Built Ship
Sir Charles Forbes
To sail from Liverpool 1st Jan 1839 for
South Australia

Gun Deck.

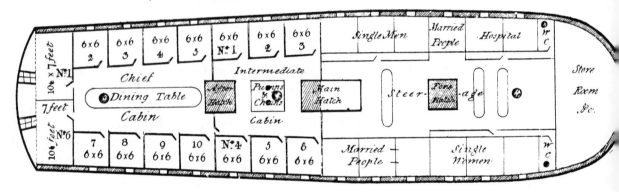

Poop Cabins.

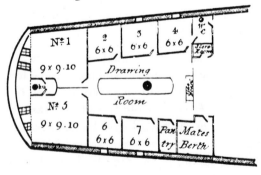

Apply to William Waddell
3 India Buildings
Liverpool.

7   *Accommodation*

When the stress of farewells was over the emigrants gradually became aware of their surroundings — of the billowing sails; the purposeful, agile crew, so unmoved by the departure; the cramped accommodation. The accommodation above all. Between bouts of seasickness it dawned on them that these few square feet of space were to be their home for months of travel, a home that would seldom be still.

Products of their time as they were, it probably did not surprise the emigrants that life on board ship mirrored the class structure of Britain. The masses below deck represented the masses at home. At the other extreme, the captain's table was the seaborne equivalent of a manor house, the captain its squire. And yet, this was a spurious image. On shore the captain might not have amounted to much socially at all and those who shared his table might not have been particularly elevated themselves — the aristocracy was rarely represented on the run to Australia; the upper classes infrequently. But a hierarchy had to be established; the passengers' habits of life demanded it. There must be some to look up to, others to look down upon. While steerage emigrants well knew the axiom, 'I have learned in whatsoever state I am, therewith to be content', there was among cabin class a sifting to be done: claims to degrees of respectability to be staked, a pecking order established. Sometimes there were annoying incongruities to be sorted out. A successful gold digger might have made a trip home and be travelling back to Australia in accommodation much above his former station. Was one to tolerate the fellow, or cut him?

Like several of the early emigrant ships the *Sir Charles Forbes* also saw service as a convict transport. Between 1825 and 1837 she made five voyages as a transport, on two occasions carrying female convicts. Her maximum load was 150 convicts plus guards. Here she has been refitted to carry over ninety emigrants — forty in her very limited steerage and more than fifty paying fares for cabins.

Rachel Henning, returning to Australia on the *Great Britain* in 1861, encountered 'several commercial gentlemen, or rather not gentlemen' at the captain's table. But the company was at least better than she had suffered on her first voyage. On the *Calcutta* in 1854, among fifty first-class passengers, she had found 'very few ladies . . . at all, and hardly any in the real sense of the word'.[1]

In the same year a pretentious young Scotsman was similarly troubled when travelling cabin class on the *Meteor*, but his language was less delicate than Rachel Henning's:

[Mrs Millett] is quite a lady and a very agreeable person. [Mrs Clark] although a vulgar woman She had some sence and Makes herself useful. As to the rest it makes one like to *spew* to come in contact with them. The one called Henderson is a very bad specimen of Vulgarity slipshod & dirty in the *extreme* . . .[2]

Cabin and intermediate passengers did not usually regard themselves as emigrants. Their definition of 'emigrant' qualified the dictionary definition. To them an emigrant was not one who left his own country to settle in another, but one who was financially assisted to do so. Snobbery apart, the distinction is understandable as ships carrying large numbers of assisted emigrants naturally became known as 'emigrant ships' — particularly so if they were chartered by the government. The tag was to remain after two world wars and until all emigration by sea ceased in 1977. Many who travelled on emigrant ships but paid their own way, wanted it known that they had reached the new land by their own efforts. Where the effort was considerable, their pride in their independence is understandable. It is chilling, on the other hand, to read some of the references made by cabin passengers concerning the lesser mortals below deck. William Johnstone, travelling on the *Arab* to Launceston in 1842, wrote:

Our greatest annoyance was in the Emigrants — a most awful set, about 20 respectable out of the whole number. Scenes are daily occurring, which tho' unnecessary to describe, are yet most revolting — and can scarcely be prevented. Fighting and swearing from morning till night — I would advise no-one to come out in an Emigrant Ship when another is in berth. They were chiefly agricultural labourers from Somersetshire, who had been earning upon an average of 7s. 6d. a week, on which they supported their wives and families.[3]

A decade later an inquiry into emigration revealed that few steerage passengers were familiar with use of the waterclosets provided for them:

The people who are put on board, the laboring classes, are not in the habit of using that form of convenience, and they use it very ill, and throw bones and all sorts of things down it. They are the greatest nuisance that can possibly be on board ship ... we are at our wits' end on the subject of waterclosets.[4]

Jessie Campbell, emigrating to New Zealand in 1840 with dispossessed Scottish Highlanders, was shocked by her poorer countrymen:

Captain Grey and the doctor complaining woefully of the filth of Highland emigrants, they say they could not have believed it possible for human beings to be so dirty in their habits, only fancy their using the dishes they have for their food for certain other purposes at night ... poor as I am no consideration on earth would tempt me to trust my little family in a ship with Highland emigrants if I still had the voyage before me ...[5]

The best accommodation — cabin, saloon, or first class — was located under the raised poop deck in the stern of the vessel. The most desirable cabins were the two with stern windows — except that, when the vessel was pitching, the occupants' vertical arc of travel was much the same as that of the crew in the fo'c'sle. These cabins — sometimes termed the 'great cabins' — were relatively large; those on the *St Vincent*[6], in the middle of the nineteenth century, measured nine feet six inches by nine feet. How many of a family the passenger fitted into them depended upon his children's ages and the length of his purse. If he could afford to do so, he would place his children in separate cabins.

The doors of the great cabins opened into a corridor that led forward twenty or thirty feet and was seven or eight feet wide. On either side of it were more first-class cabins, smaller in size than the two in the stern. They usually measured about seven feet by six and were sometimes separated by a shared WC. The total number of cabins under

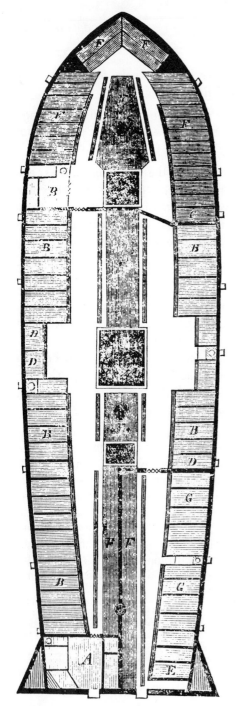

PLAN OF EMIGRANT SHIP BETWEEN DECKS.

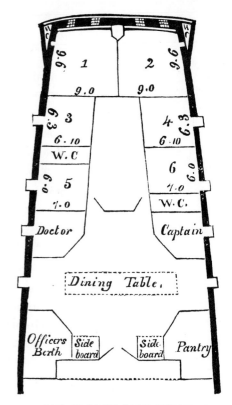

PLAN OF CABIN ACCOMMODATION.

A   Hospital for females (6 beds)
B   Hospital for males (4 beds)
Between A & B are 48 beds for married people
From B around to C - 46 beds for single men & youths
Between C & D are 24 beds for married people
From D to E, are single females
FF are tables the entire length of the ship

The plan of accommodation on the emigrant ship *St Vincent*, first, or cabin class (right), steerage (left). The best cabins measured nine feet six inches by nine feet; steerage provided dormitory accommodation below deck — six feet by eighteen inches for each adult. Children were required to share a bunk.

the poop varied with the size of the ship, but total cabin passengers seldom exceeded a tenth of the whole number the ship carried.

The central corridor between the cabins led into the dining saloon, the most capacious and pleasantly decorated of the ship's enclosed sections. The captain's cabin and the doctor's and usually the purser's opened directly into it on its opposite side. This saloon extended the full width of the ship — twenty-five or even thirty-five feet at this point. On many of the famous White Star and Black Ball ships and others of lesser fame, the surroundings here were on a most lavish scale: 'inlaid with rosewood, set off into Grecian arched panels, and ornamented with pilasters, papier mache cornices, gilding and flower work, the windows filled with transparencies.'[7] This description of the ill-fated *Schomberg* went on to tell of her velvet-pile carpets; her doors of bird's-eye maple; her chairs covered with damask. In the saloon was placed the long dining table, sometimes fore and aft, but more often athwartships. Here it was that the captain presided over first-class passengers at meal times.

The raised deck directly above these quarters — the high and relatively dry poop deck — was the promenading place of the cabin passengers, but most ships offered use of part of the area during specified hours to other fare-paying passengers. At the rear of the poop deck was the wheel and the binnacle and there the helmsman and the officer of the watch had their stations.

First-class accommodation was a world apart from the rest of the ship and one that offered the privacy of a cabin with the solace of a comfortable bed. Of course, when its occupants appeared on the poop deck, they could be seen by the throng of lesser beings on the main deck eight or nine feet below them.

Cabin accommodation was for 'emigrants of a superior station in life, who, as a matter of course, defray their own expenses'.[8] The service provided them was explained to those contemplating emigration to Australia by W. Shaw in his *Land of Promise*:

Cabin passengers, who rank first on board, keep to the poop, and live at the cabin table, where the captain presides. As they fare in good style, any private provisioning is unnecessary. The society of each other is their principal recreation.[9]

An 1855 copy of a newspaper produced on the *White Star*, spelt out the arrangement so that all the literate on board might understand it:

> A numerous staff of stewards and stewardesses ... attend
> saloon passengers and perform for them the various offices per-
> formed by their own servants at home.

For those who either could not afford cabin accommodation or preferred to conserve their limited capital until they reached Australia,
most ships offered 'house on deck', intermediate, or second-class
accommodation. (On some ships the term 'saloon' was applied to
these cabins and not to those below the poop.) Privacy was assured
here also, but in these deck cabins a couple were apt to be in a
constant state of collision if both were out of their bunks at the one
time. Deck cabins for four diminished privacy and increased collisions.
Although house-on-deck passengers were accommodated on the
same deck level as cabin passengers, they did not have unlimited
access to the high poop and consequently were more exposed to
the elements. Their dining saloon was of relatively limited dimensions.

First-class passengers parading
on the poop deck of the
Macquarie on the run to Australia.
A companion way beyond them
leads to the crowded deck space
allocated to the steerage
passengers.

On the large *White Star* they sat 'looking point blank against the bulk-head'.[10] Robert Poynter gave an amusing description of the small cabin he shared with his wife. This was on the Dutch *Cornelis Gips* and appears to have passed as first-class accommodation.

> You would laugh to see us turn out in the morning. My wife gets out first as there is only room for one to dress at a time. Whilst she is dressing I put on my stockings and drawers and shave as I lay, or rather sit up in my berth, I do so without the aid of a glass, and manage pretty well altho it is rather dangerous work sometimes . . .[11]

In all of the quarters so far described, passengers were required to provide their own furnishings — even to beds in the two great cabins. They were permitted to put up shelves, hooks, even partitions. Louisa Meredith travelled first class as a bride in 1839. Her husband had made the voyage before:

> [I] was greatly amused by Mr. Meredith's extreme caution in lashing every article with ropes to the sides of the cabin, as well as by having deep cleats of wood nailed to the floor to keep our chest of drawers, etc. in place. Even my dressing-case and work-box were tied fast, like a couple of terrible wild animals, lest they should make a sudden rush at us, and the candlestick was securely confined in their company. A convenient shelf, with a strong rail in front, formed an excellent bookcase; and by the time our various little arrangements were completed, our apartment, which was considered a most spacious one, being eight or nine feet square, began to look more snug and habitable than I had believed possible.[12]

All of the cabins so far mentioned accommodated between them no more than a seventh or eighth part of the total number of passengers carried*, but most accounts of life during the voyage have come from this literate minority. A few inches below the soles of their feet lived the hundreds who made up the great majority of people on board.

*Three typical examples may be cited: *James Baines*, 1854 — 620 steerage, 80 in other accommodation; *Schomberg*, 1855 — 350 steerage, 50 in other accommodation; *Lightning*, 1856 — 453 in steerage, 51 in other accommodation.

Indeed, on several of the larger ships there existed an orlop deck below the soles of even those passengers' feet. On these two steerage levels most of Australia's ancestors under sail made the long journey. They shared dormitory-type accommodation, based on government experience in transporting convicts. They were assessed not as so many bodies, but so many 'statute adults'. Children under the age of twelve counted as half adults in the numbers the law permitted a ship to carry.

To gain some idea of the dimensions of 'tween decks quarters we can do no better than read a description of the ship referred to earlier, the *St Vincent*:

The between decks ... are 124 feet in length, the breadth at the main hatchway twenty-five feet three inches, the height from the deck that is walked upon to the deck overhead six feet four inches. From the stern of the ship right away to the stem on the larboard side, and back again to the stern on the starboard side, the space is entirely occupied by a double tier (one above the other) of standing bed places etc ... [There] are forty-eight bed places, six feet by three each, for married people above, and for their children below, every one furnished with bedding, pegs on which to suspend their clothes being placed to every upright stauncheon, and each bed place divided from the next adjacent by stout planks from the deck below to the deck above ... a bulkhead goes across the ship to separate that part of the vessel forward which is appropriated to single men and youths, whose bed places range ... round the bows to the termination of the bulkhead on the starboard side. Of these the number is forty-six, and as every one sleeps alone they are six feet by two ... a bulkhead enclose[s]. the apartment of the single females [which contains] twenty-four bed places, each six feet by three, as two are required to sleep together ... Thus it will be manifest that the single women have an enclosed apartment to themselves, and so have the single men — one abaft and the other forward; the married couples filling up the intermediate space ... the sleeping boxes are all athwart ships, except [at] the main hatchway, where they are placed fore and aft, to afford more room

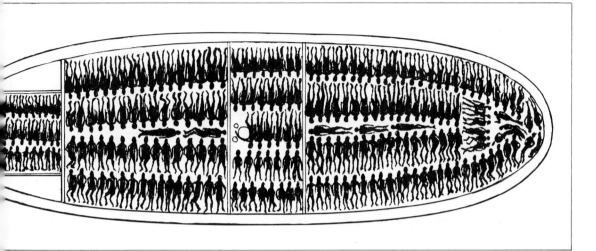

Before emigration to Australia began, Britain gained experience in transporting large numbers of human beings by sea through the carriage of slaves, soldiers and convicts. The lot of slaves was by far the worse. Packed into every available area aboard ship, they were allowed a space of only sixteen inches on which to lie. Although convicts and emigrants were allowed only two inches more of space, that is, eighteen inches, they were never carried in such numbers per ship.

This sketch is attributed to Captain Parrey, 1786, as part of a British government report on slavery. It purports to show conditions on the Liverpool ship, *Brooks*.

... Tables [run] the entire length of the ship, with fixed seats on each side of them, and beneath which are plate racks and battens to hold the breakers [small casks] containing the daily allowance of fresh water, and hanging shelves are secured between the beams. Seats are also fixed at the outer extremity of every bedplace ...[13]

Additionally there were two small hospitals 'tween decks, the one for women having six beds, the one for men, four. Scarcely adequate for 288 people, among them several pregnant women whose infants were to be delivered at sea.

One might well wonder if this was the accommodation people imagined when they decided to emigrate cheaply. Terry Coleman doubts it. In *Passage to America*[14] he expresses the belief that most emigrants imagined they would be allocated a berth. Instead, each was to occupy 'a quarter'. 'Each berth was six feet square, and into each berth four people were fitted', that is, eighteen inches of width for each person. The allowance for convicts had been precisely the same[15], for slaves, sixteen inches[16].

If we analyse the dimensions of the *St Vincent*'s steerage quarters, which may be taken as being typical of 'tween-decks accommodation, a clearer picture emerges of its packed nature. To begin with, head-room of only six feet four inches was claustrophobic, though on many

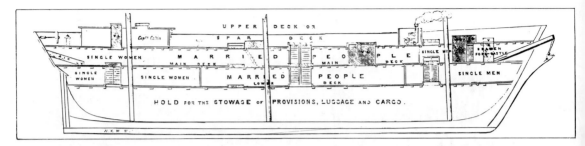

ships it was more than this by a foot, or even by two feet. Heavy beams cut into this headroom. Within this vertical space fitted the two levels of bunks, the lower one with a space of six inches beneath it for passengers' heavier belongings. (Their bulkier possessions were stowed in the hold.) On the *St Vincent* this left five feet ten inches for two bunks, or two feet eleven inches from lower bedboards to upper bedboards, reduced to perhaps eighteen inches when occupants and bedclothes were in place. The bunks themselves were three feet wide; it will be remembered that they were shared by a couple, or by two girls. It was stipulated in 1843 that 'as far as possible, not more than two children above the age of 10 years ought to be in the same berth'.[17] 'Ought' and 'as far as possible' were far from binding terms.

The table that ran the length of the *St Vincent* was five feet six inches wide. This considerable width must have proved a great convenience — at least, when seas were moderate. A raised edge prevented utensils from falling with the normal roll of the ship. As the fixed forms on either side of the table had to leave an allowance for legroom, they took up a further three feet, thus a passageway varying in width from three feet six inches to less than a foot was left between the forms and the foot of the athwartships bunks. (On some ships most bunks ran fore and aft, an arrangement that meant that the inside occupants would have to crawl over the outside bunk.)

Since children occupied lower bunks in the married couples' section of a ship, any couple without children had either another couple, or another couple's children sleeping below them. Although this allowed little real privacy, it was not the closest proximity in which couples found themselves. The *St Vincent* was generous in having dividing planks 'from the deck below to the deck above' between each couple, for the law demanded nothing more than a dividing plank

From this section view of the *Bourneuf* it is clear why her passage to Australia in 1852 was disastrous. The upper accommodation for government emigrants was in the normal ''tween decks', but below this the *Bourneuf* had an orlop deck (marked 'lower deck') so close to the waterline that portholes could seldom be opened. Of the 754 passengers packed into her, eighty-four died at sea from contagious diseases.

twenty-three inches high (earlier the requirement had been only ten inches). Thus, on most ships, a couple had not only another couple below or above them, but a second couple within arm's reach to one side. Within a six-foot square, four people slept; four more lay directly below them. Engravings show that on some ships curtains suspended from rings could be drawn across the open ends or sides of bunks, but they were not fitted on all ships, and were also too stifling to use in the tropics.

Close-packed though the steerage accommodation was, there is evidence that as early as 1839 some, at least, of the government emigration agents were doing the best they could for emigrants. One was Lieutenant Lean, Emigration Agent at the Port of London.

I draw out a plan of the between decks, with the berths properly numbered. With this plan before me, previous to the emigrants embarking, I take the list of the persons selected, and insert the names and ages of every individual in the berths they are to occupy, so that the moment they go on board they are directed without confusion to the numbers of their berths. I consider the retention of this plan by the surgeon superintendent a very convenient reference for him. All the single women and girls above fourteen are placed in the after berths on the side of the ship next the female hospital, which is usually on the starboard side, two in each berth; adjoining to them, and next to their daughters, I berth (as a kind of safeguard to the whole) the oldest and most respectable married couple.

The married people I place in the upper berths, taking great care to put relatives, friends and persons from the same neighbourhood alongside of and near each other, which is an advantage also in messing them. Their children are put in the berths immediately under them, observing to separate boys above seven years of age, and avoiding, if possible, putting more than three children in each berth ... The single men and boys above fourteen are berthed in the forepart of the ship, in the space partitioned off for the purpose of separating them from the rest of the people, two in each berth ...[18]

The plan of the *St Vincent* shows that water closets for women were

The standard water closet provided a chute to the sea and a protective flap for users. On many ships the women's toilet was in the 'tween decks area, while the men's was on the open deck — which presented problems during storms.

provided in steerage, but that those for men were on the upper deck. Many males made little attempt, at night, anyway, to use them. Filthy though the consequences were, one must recognize that it was expecting a great deal to have the men make the night journey onto an open deck when the ship was in heavy seas, or among icebergs. What was to be done, anyway, on those occasions, night or day — perhaps several nights and several days — when the decks were awash with seas and steerage passengers were battened below?

Jessie Campbell's Highlanders were not without extenuating circumstances when they 'used dishes . . . for certain other purposes'. As for places set aside to wash, there was usually no such thing. Passengers had to make do with shared handbasins. But then, this practice was familiar to most of them in their own cottages or tenements.

The *St Vincent* was by no means large when compared with the ships that came into being at the time of the gold rush. On some of the larger ships, on which an orlop deck was introduced, the waterline was so close that portholes could seldom be left open. The only sure method of bringing clean air to these quarters would have been by 'windsail', but it is doubtful that windsails came into use until after carriage of passengers on an orlop deck was outlawed. Windsails were probably first used in mining; their use in ships was first reported by the Victorian Health Officer in 1855:

The following important improvement in the ventilation of vessels has been introduced into ships carrying government immigrants. The contrivance consists of a large tube, divided into two compartments, and protected from the weather at the top, which passes from the main to the 'tween decks, the heated air ascends through one division of the tube while the cold air descends through the other, and a constant current of pure air is thus afforded to the passengers. I have only seen it employed in one vessel, but the result was most satisfactory.[19]

Having heard the essentials of steerage accommodation, we can visualize every peg with its smocks and coats and headgear hanging from it; every shelf laden with such home foodstuffs as the passengers were able to bring; the wide table strewn with metal mugs and plates and cutlery; each bunk occupied by men, women and children, some sitting, some lying. Then we can imagine the whole in motion, rolling from side to side, timbers creaking loudly as seas rise, children falling and crying and seeking comfort from parents who want only to lie down or to vomit — and where is there to vomit? As seas rise higher, scuttles must be screwed down by the ship's carpenter, plunging the whole steerage into semi-darkness while utensils are dashed into the long passageways.

Dr W. H. Leigh, surgeon on the *South Australia* in 1839, wrote compassionately of his charges:

I cannot but remark here on the great cruelty (to give it no harsher term) of cramming the unfortunate emigrants into unwholesome berths, like the unhappy Africans in a slave-ship, during a voyage of so many thousand miles, and of four months duration. If it be through ignorance that they are wedged together, the offence is scarcely more pardonable; for the *misery is the same*...[20]

Yet nearly fifty years later most ships offered nothing better. Dr R. Scot Skirving, coming out in charge of Sydney-bound emigrants on the *Ellora* in 1883, wrote feelingly of the steerage accommodation:

... it was horrid, and even indecent for decent married people to be herded together like beasts, with almost no privacy to dress or undress, and where, in the close and stuffy double bunks they slept in, only a thin board separated each couple from another alongside, another below, and another lot end to end. The ventilation was very poor, and in the tropics, with a temperature of 90°, the air was mephitic ... The married couples slept in bunches of 16 human beings in two tiers ... the very young children slept with their parents and the older children piled in together somehow in other double bunks.

Of course the mattresses were just 'donkey's breakfasts' ... I think sheets would have been out of place ... they could not have been washed. It would not be pretty ... to enter into all the adventures, embarrassments and awkward moments of a domestic day and night spent in such conditions of communal crowding, which, in happier conditions, are rightly separate, personal or familial.[21]

When the few allowable padlocked lamps were lighted, the scene must have resembled a Hogarthian bedlam. A newspaper correspondent, identified only as 'An Observer', was not far from the truth when he gave rein to his imagination in describing a departing steerage emigrant's lot:

Fancy the ship passing Holyhead with a quarter wind and yourself in one of those inside berths. What would you say or what would you do? There are no lights; spray comes in; the side holes are ordered to be closed. You pass the night, and you are not dead; but you hear that some have died and are to be put into the deep. If you have a wife and family what a situation you are in! All are sick. You cannot eat; perhaps if someone would wait on you you could sip a little tea. The side holes are again at daylight opened, but just as you draw near Land's End it blows again; side lights closed; sickness again commences and lasts two or three days. The very smell of the vessel in twenty-four hours is sufficient to produce cholera or to kill you all. Those outside are better off, but if a disease breaks out this is their abode. Now, in passing Holyhead, Land's End and Cape Clear, what is the use of the long dining table? You might eat on the floor or on the deck, if you could turn this place to better account . . .[21]

Given the prudishness of the time, it is easy to imagine the daily embarrassment in the simple business of dressing and undressing. A man could pull on a pair of trousers while lying down — provided his spouse afforded him something more than his eighteen inches of bunk space — but with a woman's voluminous clothing, there was no chance of concealment. All were probably thankful for the dimness of the light.

Steerage emigrants settling into their confined quarters. Top left, a mother settling her children in their shared bunk. The married couple in the bunk below show an interesting contrast of attitudes — the wife apparently contented, the husband dejected by his lot.

By night the teeming married quarters must have blessed the screen of background groans from the ship's timbers as they argued, wept, urinated, broke wind, copulated, snored, vomited, prayed, or cried out in dreams of the land they would never see. It was their only screen and even it was stripped away when the foetid doldrum days were on them.

In the tropics many of the male passengers slept on the open deck, willing to risk sudden downpours of rain for the sake of fresh and reasonably cool air. Very seldom does one read of a woman doing so. Those few who did were travelling in the segregated quarters of the unaccompanied women. George Tucker, an ebullient bachelor of twenty-six, wrote amusedly to his brother of the scene when the men returned to their bunks at daylight and tried in the overpowering heat to resume their sleep.

Their ship being ready to depart, these unaccompanied needlewomen are brought on deck for final admonishments by emigration officers and clergy.

They lay without a single stitch of bedclothing on them, and the majority of their shirts are either very short, or else get tucked up by their constant twisting and turning; in fact, it would do May good to see the number of bluebottles exposed to view.[23]

Strict segregation was enforced among unaccompanied men and women on the run to Australia. While this may seem typical of Victorian morality, in early impressed emigration of pauper girls open concubinage developed between some of them and the ships' officers with the result that deserted, pregnant girls became a very great problem in the receiver ports. Generally speaking, this had been stopped by the time of the influx of free emigrants. One can easily find what results the abolition of segregation would have had by glancing at the case of German ships running to Australia.

In using her own ships Germany was an exception among the nations of continental Europe. It was usual for other European emigrants to make their way to British ports of departure, but use of her own ships by Germany was warranted by the large numbers of emigrants leaving the country for Australia — leaving partly because of

The ladies' cabin. On larger ships ladies travelling first class had their own attractive reading and writing room.

religious persecution, partly because efforts were made by Australian vintners to attract workers experienced in German vineyards. Eventually the Germans were to become Australia's largest population group of non-British origin. Since the ships in which they came were not subject to British law, they were run according to German practices at sea — and segregation of the sexes was not one of them. There arose such a spate of complaints by newly arrived immigrants about this and other aspects of the voyage that an inquiry into German immigration took place in Sydney in 1858.[24]

Adolph Shadler, who had come out as second mate on a German ship, was asked at the 1858 inquiry if lack of separation between males and females had 'been very injurious to the moral condition of the emigrants'. He answered:

It was shocking in that respect. There were about forty young girls on board, some of them not more than from ten to twelve years old, and I am sure, and can lay an oath upon it, that I know for certain that every one left the ship as a prostitute.

Did they belong to families, or were they coming out as single girls?

They belonged to families.

Were their parents on board?

Some of them, some not, others had only relationship on board. They were all mingled together in the 'tween decks; there was no division whatever ... All the sailors, every one, had their girls in the forecastle ... It was a regular thing with the sailors, as they took watch and watch below to have their girls with them. The crew consisted of about twenty-four, and when the watch went below, twelve sailors, twelve girls went with them, and when they came up the other twelve took down their twelve girls. These girls used to dine with the sailors in the forecastle, and were constantly there, mending their clothes, and so on ...

The effect was to demoralize them?

Yes. I know that four of those girls were common prostitutes in Adelaide.

One cannot suppose that the results would have been any different on an unsegregated British ship. Incarcerate scores of men and women in a ship at sea for three or four months; subject them to fear of shipwreck; allow them no privacy and the outcome is easily predictable.

Because there was little government supervision on the Atlantic, 'proper division for the separation of the sexes' did not exist on British ships there. The prevailing state of affairs is clear enough from Terry Coleman's *Passage to America*. He cites evidence given before two British Select Committees into emigration — those of 1851 and 1854. Although the Passenger Act of 1848 had forbidden the berthing together of single men and women, companies flouted this regulation by allowing a third party to occupy a vacant space next to a married couple. No less an authority than the chairman of the emigration commissioners, giving evidence before the 1851 committee, when asked 'whether women were ever berthed together with men against their will', replied that 'this happened only very rarely, and that it did not matter so much on board Atlantic ships because the voyage was shorter than on the Australian run.'

Surely, he was asked, when persons of different sexes are berthed together it does not require forty days to produce a bad result?

No, he agreed.

The mate of a ship on the Atlantic run, 'asked how he managed with marriages at sea; how he managed to bed the couple on board', replied, 'There is no difficulty as to that; there is plenty of that work going on every night to keep them all in countenance.'

Not until the Passenger Act of 1852 were British companies required to provided separate sections in steerage for single men and women on the Atlantic; segregation on the Australia run on the other hand, was adopted at least as early as 1834 — witness the description of an unidentified ship of that year:

The men's berths are in the forepart of the vessel and strong bulk-heads, excluding both sight and sound, separate them from all communication with the females, and it is determined to preserve the strictest delicacy and separation of the sexes throughout the voyage.[25]

It is clear enough, for all that, that government regulations were often flouted, though not in the wholesale way of the Atlantic. Caroline Chisholm criticized the common practice of unaccompanied girls being passed off as daughters of married couples:

I have seen so much of this kind of protection that I loathe the thought of it. Some families there are who have indeed acted a parent's part — in every ship *there are some*, but I have known some of these married men tear up their marriage certificates, leave their wives in Sydney, and extend their protection far into the interior.[26]

Women seem always to have been the losers. One very rough night Mary Anne Bedford had her bunk collapse with the force of the ship's rocking. She groped into bed with two other young women, but her startling night was by no means over:

We were just going to sleep when we were wakened by a person who slept close to us that was confined. We were all very much surprised as we none of us knew anything about it. She had a baby boy. She was a married woman going out to her husband and he had been in Australia eight years.

The steerage families, with their numerous utensils and cherished additional foodstuffs brought from home, found themselves in a weirdly animated world as soon as the weather deteriorated. Robert and Eliza Beckett had four young children around them:

Awoke last night at the small hours and found ourselves sleeping head downwards, then heaved over and had a stand-up sleep; then kept turning up and down with a jerk at every motion. Then there was music for all the pots in the cabin began to jostle each other, then set to dancing a sort of country jig; this soon grew too tame for some of them, and after a preliminary fling or two, they leaped over the wooden borders to the tables and danced a fandango in the middle of the cabin. The glass bottles were also in high spirits (tho' we are strictly prohibited from putting spirits into them) and in spite of the temperance beverage (lime juice) which they had nearly all been filled with on the previous day, they gradually grew hilarious, then boisterous and unruly, finally cracking their sides revelling piece-meal on the deck. Had there been light enough to see it, it might have been a spectacle to see sundry water-kegs strolling about the cabin in company with amorous-looking teapots, who had evidently slipped out without leave ... fragments of dead pig seemed to be resucitated and diverted themselves upon the floor in company with puddings and cakes & other edibles. Of course the proprietors of all these articles were awake & we had some droll conversation on current events ...

Humour in such circumstances undoubtedly gave a great lift to morale. George Tucker experienced a similar night on the *Northumberland* in 1876:

... as the vessel would give an extra severe roll, away would go everything, tins, lamps, lanterns, boxes, bottles, everything, in fact, that was loose went flying. We were all in the dark. About 2 o'clock in the morning there came a roll even more severe than any we had had before, and away they all went again, making such a din that was really terrifying, but very laughable to those used to being on board ship. Amid the noise we could hear some of the men's voices, exclaiming, 'Where's a light? I shall be killed'. A hurried tramping of feet, a run, a rush, a stare, a moment's silence and then — such a ringing burst of laughter from all hands, which lasted about ten minutes, and thoroughly roused all the sleepers in steerage. The cause of this was, that two of the men sleeping in the top berths had fallen through, the woodwork having shrunk, and allowed them to drop through on the top of the men underneath, who had been sound asleep underneath, giving them a dreadful shock, and making them think the ship was sinking, and they were going to Davy Jones's locker. A bunk that held their provisions ... was likewise about half opened, and a shower of pickles, vinegar, limejuice, a thin, sloppy currant pudding in a baking dish, butter, mustard, and all kinds of provisions, in fact, went tumbling through, mixing in delightful harmony with our provisions, such as pickles with butter, vinegar with sugar, mustard with flour, etc. Of course the men could not go to bed again that night, as they would only have shared the same fate again ...

When true storms struck the situation passed beyond humour. Then every effort of the crew could not prevent seas cascading among passengers already prostrated by seasickness and fear. Mrs Thomas Hinshelwood, emigrating steerage to Rockhampton, experienced successive days of storms:

> ... about four o'clock yesterday morning ... we were roused from sleep by a huge wave coming down the main hatch, and completely flooding the inmates of the berths on the lee side of the vessel. The screams of the women and children were terrible.

Next afternoon:

> The storm increased all day, and many tons of water came down amongst us. The hatches were closed and our windows darkened in case the heavy seas should break the glass. One of the lifeboats was smashed to pieces, the hen house carried away. Though we had no canvas up we made 268 miles, fairly flying before the wind. The Captain never was in bed for two night and stood at the wheel himself.

Early in this chapter William Johnstone, a cabin passenger, was appalled by the steerage emigrants on the *Arab*. After a storm he sounded close to sympathy for them:

> The between decks where the Emigrants were all stowed away (sometimes a man and his wife and two children in the one bed) were in a most horrible condition. The seas washed down the hatchways and the floor was a complete pond, many of the beds drenched through and through. In addition to these delights, with some four or five exceptions, they were all violently seasick — some of the women fainting, and two going into convulsions — all calling out for Brandy, which they had been told by the Emigration Agent had been put on board for their use — but which they now found 'nonest inventus'. The squall had come on so suddenly that their boxes were all adrift, flying about from one side to the other, with nearly 50 whining sick squalling children to complete their misery.

These unfortunates Johnstone had first seen as the *Arab* departed:

If steerage emigrants sought to escape crowded quarters below deck by coming into the open air, they were sometimes sent sprawling by waves.

The quarters of the unaccompanied women on an emigrant ship. These were below deck in the stern, as far removed as possible from the crew's quarters in the forecastle and separated from those of the unaccompanied men by the married quarters. The bunks are to either side of the central table.

... about 200 in number, including men, women and children chiefly on deck and mostly engaged in reading their Bibles and Tracts — some of them had mounted on the Poop, from whence they were most unceremoniously expelled by the Captain, who commanded them never to have the impudence to shew their faces there again.

Improbable though it may now seem, most steerage passengers did adapt themselves to 'tween deck conditions, nor were most days unbearably rough. Although close confinement inevitably led to fighting, it led also to friendships and interdependence, an interdependence that led some groups to stick together in the new land.

Given the ships that were available and the masses of people that were to be carried, the passage under sail would have been a sore trial even if shipowners had done everything possible to alleviate discomfort. Of course few shipowners did anything of the kind; had it not been for the watchfulness of governments, they would have done little at all that would have reduced profits.

One man who evidently believed that steerage conditions could be improved was the redoubtable Dr John Dunmore Lang. In his sustained efforts to attract a sound type of emigrant to Australia, he not only carried out personal recruitment drives in Britain in 1831 and 1848, but also chartered four ships. Three of these — the *Larpent, Travancore* and *Clifton* — had their steerage quarters fitted with a temporary line of cabins on each side of the ship with a passage down the centre . . .'[27] The cabins were dismantled and their pine timbers sold on arrival in Melbourne, where the ships took on cargo for the return voyage. But the person who really demonstrated to governments how emigrants could be carried was Caroline Chisholm.

Mrs Chisholm had gained valuable experience in caring for immigrants during eight years in Australia; she well knew from them the trials to which the voyage had subjected them. As a person, her stature was extraordinary. In the overwhelmingly male-dominated world of Victorian England, she confronted men of the highest office. She shone with compassion, courage and energy. Backed by a devoted husband, she eventually won a vastly improved voyage for those who chose her scheme of emigration.

She refused to accept the prevailing lack of privacy; the quartering together of strangers; the rigid segregation of single males and females, which involved separation from members of their own families; the drunken fights; the contrasting conditions of the classes. She aimed to have the family as the basic unit of emigration. She envisaged families paying small amounts into a co-operative organization toward their own fares — a fare of £15 for an adult or for two children. Emigrants first embarked under her scheme on 28 June 1850. She had chartered the *Slains Castle* and had it fitted out to her specifications. There was no division into classes. Instead of long rows of open bunks between decks, she devised small cabins of varying sizes, much as Dr Lang had done.

Those intended for a man and his wife were of a certain size, while those for a party of females were larger. The bedsteads for a married couple consisted of broad stout laths one-half of the length of which were placed to fit into the other, so that when not needed to sleep upon they could be slid back, and the bedstead became one-half size. By this contrivance there was a couch formed for the day, and by a board sliding in a support for the back, while the room gained left a private cabin for the occupants. A washstand in a corner and other trifling articles, completed the fittings. In some there was a small bedplace a little above for a young child ... By a space being left at the bottom [of the paritions], and the frame-work not reaching the roof by several inches, a free and perfect circulation of air was allowed in each cabin besides there being a small window covered by a piece of coloured cotton; thus there were privacy, air and light ...[28]

On government-sponsored ships alcohol was forbidden, but the regulation was so poorly enforced that drunken fighting was common. On Caroline Chisholm's ships alcohol was entirely banned. If the ban seems drastic, one can only consider the evidence against its free consumption that crops up in numerous emigrant diaries. Furthermore, her pre-embarkation groups voluntarily drew up and passed a pledge:

We pledge ourselves as Christian fathers and heads of families to exercise parental control and guardianship over all orphans and friendless females proceeding with family groups. To protect them as our children and allow them to share the same claims as our daughters.

We further resolve to discourage gambling and not to take cards or dice with us or to enter into any pernicious amusements during the voyage. We likewise resolve, by parental advice and good example, to encourage and promote some well-advised system of self-improvement during the passage.

Many gregarious single men would probably have applied a later Australianism to Caroline Chisholm: wowser. But the task she set about doing must be remembered: transporting hundreds of poor, mostly ill-educated people to the other end of the earth with the lowest possible degree of misery and maximum preparation for the life await-

ing them. For these ends, four months of restraint was a small price.

Generally speaking the groups lived harmoniously on the long voyage, though the system was not without its critics. Mark Amos, a Caroline Chisholm emigrant of 1852, wrote later:

> There were no class distinctions as all the passengers were on an equal footing, but this system did not work well — the ignorant and uneducated associating with the refined and intellectual.[29]

Happenings on at least one of the Chisholm ships, the *Nepaul*, sound anything but 'refined and intellectual':

> The other day we detected a young man in the act of being sick in his mess dish! Well, of course that drew the rage of some few upon him, and the majority seemed inclined to make him throw it overboard, and while compelling him to do this (for he became obstropolis and refused to do it) they discovered

An accurate illustration of married couples' accommodation in steerage: bunks to the left and right (the occupants' feet to the centre of the ship); a wide central table; an open area gaining light from the uncovered hatch. Privacy scarcely existed and, in a storm, conditions were often dark and chaotic.

that the pie he had been eating did not belong to him!! Therefore
they lynched him. Binding him hand and foot amidst the jeers
and taunts of most on board they carried him on the poop ...
He was condemned to have his face well tarred and to be lashed
to the mast for an hour and a half & it was well executed too ...[33]

Given the attitudes of Victorian England, such harshness was probably inevitable among 370 cooped-up people, despite Caroline Chisholm's tireless efforts.

The Family Colonization Loan Society reached its peak with the
building of the *Caroline Chisholm* by W. R. Lindsay, London's foremost shipbuilder. Lindsay had for long been disturbed by shipowners'
betrayals of emigrants' trust and was glad to incorporate the founder's
innovations into the ship's design.

Caroline Chisholm's scheme was overwhelmed by the vast numbers
of the gold rush. In all, probably only 5000 emigrants came out under
it — an infinitesimal part of the whole. But it proved conclusively that
shipboard accommodation could be provided that would afford a
degree of privacy and comfort and minimize harm to human beings
bereft of homes.

8 *The Crew*

*Sir, a ship is worse than a jail. There is in a jail, better
air, better company, better convenience of every kind; and a ship
has the additional disadvantage of being in danger. When men come
to like a sea-life, they are not fit to live on land.*

Dr Samuel Johnson

Although Samuel Johnson did not so much as see the sea until he
was in his fifties and was never on a large vessel, one can believe
that many emigrants, observing the crew's life at close hand for
months on end, would have been inclined to agree with him. The lives
of two groups in such close proximity inevitably impinged upon one
another, but it was not until the emigrants began to gain their sea
legs that they took much notice of the strange group of men who
were conducting them across the world.

If illiteracy was common among steerage emigrants, it was much
more so among men before the mast. It is not surprising that accounts
of crew life by the men themselves are few in number until late in
the era of emigration by sail; even then most are recollections of those
who eventually became officers. The most outstanding exception is
Richard Dana's *Two Years Before the Mast* which was recognized
as a classic soon after it appeared in America in 1840. But Dana saw
with the eyes of a well-educated young man, one who was able to
return to his studies after his experience of the sea; nevertheless, he
shared every aspect of the crew's experiences.

Until the demand for fast passages to Australia led to demand for
high skills in seamanship and navigation, even officers were an ill-
educated uncouth lot. Examinations for them were not introduced

Crew of the *Loch Ryan*, c. 1890.
Even though they were wearing
best rig to go ashore, their
appearance is anything but
gentle. One wonders how the
apprentices, cross-legged in
front, fared at the hands of some
of them, yet the standard of the
Loch Line crews was higher than
most others.

133

until 1845 — and then they were voluntary. They did not become compulsory until 1851. Charles Bateson claimed that the East India Company alone ran well-disciplined ships in the earlier years.

> The personnel of the rest of the merchant marine . . . was drawn from the dregs of society. With hardly an exception, the officers had worked their way up from the fo'c'sle, and were men of little education or refinement. They were hard-drinking, hard-swearing and brutal, often so illiterate that they could barely scrawl their own signatures. They were wholly unskilled in the higher branches of navigation and seamanship. The men, recruited from the waterside taverns by unscrupulous crimps and living aboard ship under conditions of squalor and hardship, were tough and quarrelsome. Their indiscipline was notorious, and desertions were frequent.[1]

Although desertions were still a problem during the gold rush, standards among officers had risen, especially in those lines of ships that gained high reputations. These pages will look mainly at what the emigrants saw and heard and thought of the men with whom they shared their Johnsonian 'jail'; the men upon whom they were utterly dependent. The emigrants were only committed to the gaol for a matter of a few months, yet here they found a breed of men who incarcerated themselves for a large part of their lives, men truly dubbed 'prisoners of the wave'.

Of course, circumstances that emigrants looked on with foreboding were regarded by the sailor with unconcern. He was assured of a place to lay his head; of a wage, of sorts; of constantly tested male comradeship; of escape from family responsibilities and, sometimes, from the law. An illusion of freedom was conferred on him by the encompassing sea and sky and by days in port when he could drink and womanize without fear of responsibility. The Victorian Age did not offer many men of his class such freedoms as these.

The emigrant could more readily understand the lot of the officers, since these men held a degree of power and had prospects of captaincy; also their accommodation was a few removes better than the fo'c'sle. Captains themselves came in for particularly close scrutiny for they were not only masters of the crew, but uncrowned kings of shipboard society. The surprising thing about many of them was their youth: several accomplished masters were in their twenties. But young or mature, their power was absolute. The master was 'lord paramount', said Dana:

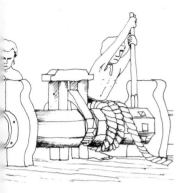

The windlass. A cylinder on an axle, turned by a crank or brace, used for hoisting and hauling. Usually it was positioned near the break of the forecastle. (See bottom picture on page 139.)

He stands no watch, comes and goes when he pleases, is accountable to no one, and must be obeyed in everything, without a question even by his chief officer. He has the power to turn his officers off duty, and even to break them and make them do duty in the forecastle as sailors.[2]

Emigrants witnessed numerous abuses of masters' power. William Greenhalgh, coming out on the *Marco Polo* in 1853 under 'Bully' Forbes, saw Forbes become enraged with a steward over a relatively minor matter and strike him 'several times with a large glass ship's lamp, cutting his face in several places, breaking his nose and giving him a pair of black eyes'.[3]

In the next month, when the *Marco Polo* was far south in very cold weather, a sailor, in a drunken outburst, insulted the first mate, whereupon Forbes put him on bread and water for several days. Greenhalgh wrote:

He would not be silent, so the captain, who was determined not to have his noise, ordered him to be gagged, which consisted of a piece of rusty iron [being] placed in his mouth and tied behind his head. A very painful operation, soon fetched blood; was in this state for an hour and then allowed to have it out.

Forbes, though a tougher master than most, was by no means unusual in handing out severe punishments. Mary Anne Bedford, a gentle, articulate girl coming out on the *Champion of the Seas*, saw a steward punished for drawing a knife during a drunken squabble.

They went to put him in irons but he went on so they tied his hands up over his head, his feet just touching the floor and he was there from 3 o'clock this morning tell 12 today on the poop where everyone could see him. I saw the captain cut the rope to let him loose. I never felt so sorry for any one before. He looked ready to drop. He was taken and put in irons for the rest of the day.

It must be remembered, of course, that crews consisted of very tough men indeed. When Arthur Manning was coming out on the *Earl Grey* in 1839-40, he heard the captain find fault with a sailor named Mills for negligence:

... the fellow began in a most shocking manner to abuse his Commander; finishing by saying 'I have been a pirate and caused the death of many a man. My life is forfeited to the laws of my country, and I do not value it a pin. I am ready to swing to the yardarm as any man, but, dam'mee, I'll have life for life.' ... When Mills was among his companions he became almost wild, and took out of his sea-chest a long sharp knife, which he flourished about saying, 'There — that is as good nine inches of steel as ever a man saw; and I would no more care about sticking it into a fellow than I would to run it into a pig!'[4]

Mills had to be watched carefully all the way to Cape Town where he was off-loaded.

Trouble was even more serious if master and first mate fell out, for some of the crew were likely to back the mate. Thomas Boykett, a London solicitor who emigrated with his family in 1853, wrote of a confrontation of this sort on *The Gypsy*:

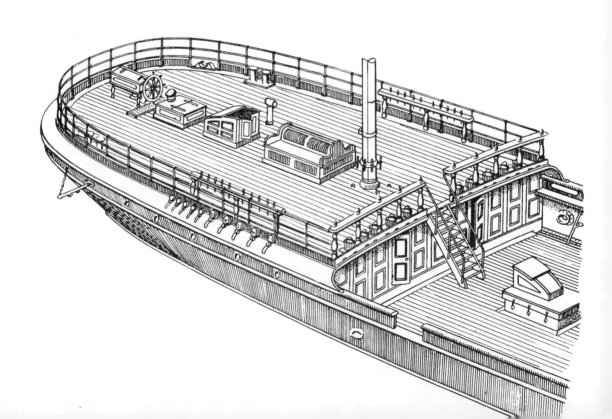

Full deck height poop. In the stern is the wheel and directly before it, the binnacle housing the compass. The poop was the promenading place of first-class passengers; their accommodation and that of the captain, the first officer and the surgeon-superintendent were below it. On most ships steerage emigrants promenaded on the limited space of the lower deck.

... one night, just as I got into my berth, I heard a great noise on the poop as of men struggling, and heavy weight falling. Several of us went on deck, where the Captain, and Chief Mate were found to be in mortal combat. It was very stormy and very dark night. Lanthornes were quickly produced and the mate was handcuffed and irons were put on his feet, but he was so powerfull that it took half a dozen persons to subdue him.

The crew refused to interfere in any way. They stood sullen by. My three sons and other passengers armed themselves and formed a patrole on deck for the night ... Next morning we saw that most of the sailors had prepared themselves for a fight. Whereupon eighteen passengers [armed] to the teeth, with the Captain at their head, commanded the men to surrender their weapons. This they did, but in a surly manner. They appeared to know that the slightest resistance would be followed by instant death. It was no joke to them to stand within six feet of the muzzles of nineteen brace of pistols. Happily the men gave us no further cause for anxiety, but on the vessel coming into port they all ran away.[5]

E. Lloyd was by no means exaggerating when he declared that the captain of a ship had to be prepared for anything 'from a shipwreck to a seizure, from a manifest to a mutiny, from a topsail to a tornado'.[6]

Celeste de Chabrillan, a passenger on the *Croesus* in 1854 wrote vividly of the ship's master, Captain Hall. But first a word on the extraordinary Celeste herself. Better known as Celeste Mogador, a former French courtesan, she married Count Lionel de Chabrillan, who was appointed French consul in Melbourne. Of Captain Hall she wrote:

He knows four languages, plays several instruments, draws marvellously, and is a charming companion; when he talks to one in private his voice is so soft that it makes one completely forget that he is ugly enough to frighten little children. But when it comes to his command, his whole personality changes in a flash and he becomes a raging porcupine, swearing, shouting, and threatening. His movements are brusque, his eyes squint with anger and his voice is strident. The sailors duck as he goes by, the children run away, calling him 'The Ogre'. I can understand his great responsibility, but he frightens me a little too when I see him in 'one of his states', as he calls it.[7]

'The Ogre' knew there were extremes in which men passed beyond control. As he watched a group of his sailors dancing round a barrel of spirits after crossing-the-line festivities, he remarked to Celeste: '. . . they're no better than savage beasts who have to be tamed with threats and blows.'

A short time before this, they had roughly handled an apprentice. The boy had hidden himself in his cabin, 'but was found and carried off by force'.

In spite of his tears. and cries, his merciless captors 'baptized' him even more brutally than the others. When they released him the wretched boy looked like an idiot — his face was dead-white, his teeth were chattering and his whole body trembled convulsively, but the more he suffered the louder they clapped. The instincts of those people are ferociously savage.

The boy had been in poor health and died before the ship reached Melbourne.[8]

At fifteen, or even younger, it was a harsh life for an apprentice. A boy was bound to the owners who agreed to have him taught navigation and seamanship, and to feed and accommodate him for four years. 'He received £4 for the first year; £12 for the final year and £24 over all.'[9] E. Lloyd saw one of these lads as his ship left the Thames in 1843.

[He] was leaning with his face upon his hands on one of the hatches. Captain J — said, 'Poor fellow! his troubles are just beginning; nobody knows but a sailor what these boys have to go through.' I can easily conceive what real grief they will suffer in such a complete transition, at a time of life when reflection and fortitude are of no avail, and when the mind is so susceptible of impression.[10]

For a boy from a good home whose parents wanted to see him trained to become an officer, the crew must have come as a great shock. Dana observed of sailors as a breed:

Forecastle arrangements. Here were the anchors and the capstan; below deck were the confined quarters of the crew. As the bows drove into heavy seas, the noise and vibration in the crew's quarters increased — so did the ever-present damp.

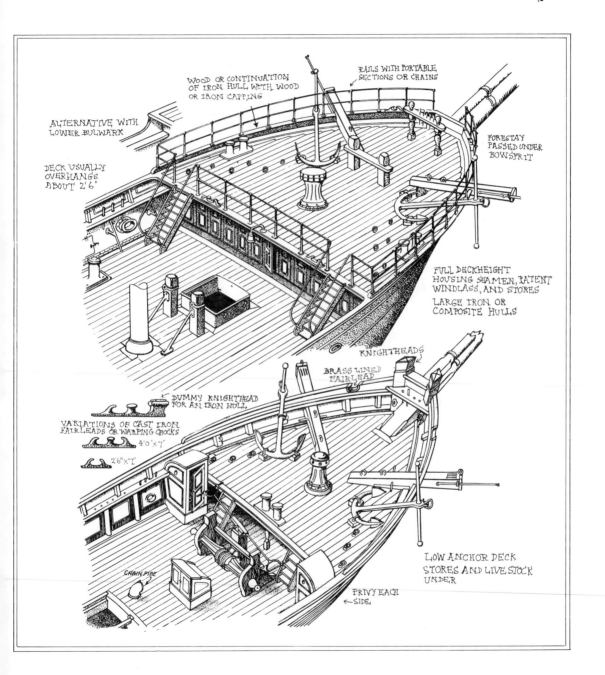

WOOD OR CONTINUATION
OF IRON HULL WITH WOOD
OR IRON CAPPING

RAILS WITH PORTABLE
SECTIONS OR CHAINS

ALTERNATIVE WITH
LOWER BULWARK

FORESTAY
PASSED UNDER
BOWSPRIT

DECK USUALLY
OVERHANGS
ABOUT 2'6"

FULL DECKHEIGHT
HOUSING SEAMEN, PATENT
WINDLASS, AND STORES

LARGE IRON OR
COMPOSITE HULLS

KNIGHTHEADS

DUMMY KNIGHTHEAD
FOR AN IRON HULL

BRASS LINED
FAIRLEAD

VARIATIONS OF CAST IRON
FAIRLEADS OR WARPING CHOCKS

4'0"×7"

2'6"×7"

LOW ANCHOR DECK
STORES AND LIVESTOCK
UNDER

CHAIN PIPE

PRIVY EACH
← SIDE.

An overstrained sense of manliness is the characteristic of sea-faring men ... no notice must be taken of a bruise or cut; and any expression of pity, or any show of attention, would look sisterly and unbecoming a man who has to face the rough and tumble of such a life. From this cause, too, the sick are neglected at sea ... A *thin-skinned* man could hardly live on shipboard. One would be torn raw unless he had the hide of an ox.[11]

To return to Lloyd: as the voyage progressed his sympathy for the sailors' lot increased:

People on shore have a very dim idea of a sailor's life when they talk in a complacent way about his hardships and discomforts. These benevolent landsmen should see him reefing topsails in a gale of wind; or holding onto the ropes he is pulling, when a heavy sea breaks over the side, and taking him abreast high in the lee scuppers, rushing along the decks like a swollen torrent, carrying hen-coops and spars along with it in a sheet of foam, striking him from his footing, and beating him against the side like a helpless log of wood — this amidst work that must be done; and drenched or soaking, there is no going below to dry himself till his four hours of watch is out, when he goes below, with orders to stand by for a call. This may be in an hour, or the moment he gets into the forecastle, and is beginning to make himself comfortable.[12]

Crow's-nest. The descriptive name of a high look-out on the fore mast. It was much used when making landfall and in regions of icebergs.

The sailor's lot was no better nearly thirty years later when John Ramsay came out on the *Loch Sunart*:

Everything has a damp feel. I don't know how the Sailors can stand it, as they get themselves wet to the skin nearly every watch for some days, but they all say that you will never catch a cold with being wet with *salt* water. It must be true or sailors lives would be short indeed, for no sooner will they turn out to work and be engaged all in a row pulling a rope than over comes a sea on them and they emerge from it like drowned rats. I have seen a squad of men get half a dozen such drenchings in half an hour.

Ramsay continued with an explanation of the arrangement for keeping watch:

> The sailors are divided into two squads which are named the Port Watch and the other the Starboard watch. They work four hours and sleep four hours turn about night and day. The First Mate has command of the one and the second mate the other.[13]

The mates did their own choosing of their men, turn and turn about, at the beginning of the voyage. The first mate's men grouped on the port side of the ship, the second mate's on the starboard side, hence the origin of their names. Their lives were regulated by the ship's bell and before long the emigrants knew the significance of each group of clangings.

Clanging bells, shouted orders and loud tramping were concomitants of sailing-ship life.

> Six bells are struck. 'Square the yards', says the captain. 'Square the yards' roars the second mate, while the ready, 'Aye, aye, sir', is responded in a deep voice from the forecastle, and all the ahoying consequent upon such an order goes on.[14]

Dr Francis Workman, surgeon-superintendent on the *Sobraon*, became utterly weary of crew noise:

> Sailors (on sailing ships) surely make tenfold more noise in their work than any other men I know of; they cannot haul at any rope without yelling at the top of their voices. I know there are some who find their chanties musical; but it is not nice, as one is just going off to sleep, to hear the mate shout out, 'Now then the main tack', and about ten fellows seize hold of it, and run tramping overhead on the deck, hauling at it, and bellowing like a herd of bulls; and this occurs, in light winds, every night two or three times, as the yards have to be trimmed to meet a shift in the wind.[15]

Of course, 'bellowing' together, assured a pull together and did much to lighten the men's miserable toil. During his voyage on the *Bolton* Edward Snell became fascinated with the singing of chanties, especially with their differing tempos:

The Captain grumbled at the sailors for singing 'Cheerly Men' at the topsail halliard instead of hoisting them up hand over hand, so they changed the tune to 'Hurrah my Boys' and the yards went up like smoke. 'Cheerly Men' is a slow-time and the pulls are long and far apart. It goes like this:

In London city — hi ho — cheerly men (pull)
The girls — are all — pretty — hi, ho, cheerly men (pull)
Haul y I oh, cheerly men (pull)
Haul y I oh, cheerly men (pull)

It sounds very cheerful, but is only used when there are very few hands at the halliards and it is necessary they all pull heavily

Imperator Alexander making the long easterly run across the southern Indian Ocean for Australia. Lifelines are rigged on deck. Although this photograph was taken after the era of emigration by sail, crew life was as hazardous as ever it had been.

and together. In this case about 40 of the passengers had hold of the fall and the song went:

> Hurràh — my boys, we're home — ward bound
> Hurràh, my boys, hurràh

sung in quick time with a pull at every other syllable shown by the black dots. Many sailors' songs sound very well especially when pumping the ship at night — one man will sing the song and all the rest will join in with a regular rattling chorus, which I should think might be heard for miles in a calm night. The words of the song are usually extempore and do not possess any great poetical merit; the tune is everything.

As the *Bolton* approached the tropics Snell recorded a chanty sung at the pumps on a warm evening:

> Tis time for us to leave cold weather
> Time for us to go — oh — oh

Crew of the *Illawarra* raising the anchor by capstan. The tempo of the work dictated the chanties sung by the men. The ship's bell, which sounded each half hour, regulated the crew's life. In the 1880s the *Illawarra* made several passages to Australia of less than ninety days.

Hurrah, hurrah my lively fellow
   Time for us to go ho
Hurrah, hurrah my lively fellow
   Time for us to go
The tickly seasons coming on boys
   Time for us to go ho
Hurrah for Adelaide town my bullies
   Time for us to go.

Only a handful of diarists bothered to record the words of chanties. Another was an Irishman Francis Maybury, emigrating in 1856:

How cheery the sailors sing in chorus, while they pump the ship so merrily:

Haul the Bowline
Kitty you're my darling,
Haul the bowline
The bowline haul.

One singular fellow is apart by himself, actively at work patching the sheets. He hails from Kentucky and in merry mood is singing, as I catch the words:

Did you ever see the Devil
With his wooden spade and shovel
A digging of potatoes
With his tail cocked up.

No I never saw the Devil
With his wooden spade and shovel
A digging of potatoes
With his tail cocked up.[16]

Of all the crew's activities, it was work aloft among the trapezes of rigging that overawed the emigrants, especially if the ship was rolling. Snell, an engineer by training, rigged up a pendulum in his cabin during a voyage home to England, and from this he was able to read degrees of roll. One day he was reading off 40° when a wave caught the ship and drove her to 60°! If one considers a ship swinging 40°

The daily task of holystoning the deck with blocks of soft sandstone. Since the crew did the work on their knees, they called the large blocks 'bibles' and the small ones 'prayerbooks'.

out of the vertical, a man 150 feet above the deck would swing, arcwise, over thirty yards toward the sea on one side, pause there, then swing back perhaps as far on the other side, all at a considerable pace. At 60° he would swing over fifty yards on one side alone. If he were on the mainyard he would not, of course, swing so far, but, at the outer end of the yard, he could be dipped into the sea with each roll of the ship — a sight often watched by emigrants with terror. One who saw it was Celeste de Chabrillan. She had been asked to take care of a girl named Celia, an eighteen-year-old servant who was much in love with James, a young officer on the *Croesus*. The ship had just left Cape Town when a gale struck it.

... three sails were torn as if they had been made of paper. Their shreds beat against the masts with dreadful violence; the wind alternately crowed like a cock or hissed like a nestful of serpents; that night seemed to last a hundred years ... we trembled for ourselves and for those poor men, high up in the yards, balancing precariously above the abyss. One slip of a foot, a broken rope, and their lives are lost! The danger seemed so dreadful that we spent all night on deck. I could see Celia standing there in the darkness, as still as a statue. Her eyes were staring above, and as I followed her glance I could see James up there in the rigging with the sailors, transmitting to them the orders he was receiving from the officers below, and actively helping the crew in their struggles ... A sudden blow from the sea, and the *Croesus* heeled over to port. Celia gave a cry of despair. James and his companions disappeared in a huge wave. It only lasted a second, but it seemed a century. When they reappeared Celia had fainted.

Work aloft remained arduous all through the long era of sail. It demanded endurance, strong nerves and close team work. Sometimes when decks were awash and the crew were hanging to lifelines, the emigrants in the half darkness below heard with foreboding the shout, 'Lay aloft and furl!'

Going aloft in these times [wrote Captain James Gaby] we climbed with the roll, and then hung like flies when we felt the whole fabric moving across our heads on the weather roll.

Furling sail in heavy weather on the *Garthsnaid*. This was the most exhausting and dangerous of a sailor's tasks. The cold was often intense, the air full of flying spray, the masts swinging in giant arcs.

'Lay aloft and furl!' To slip off the foot rope was to plunge to almost certain death on deck, or in the distant sea.

On the yards, especially the t'gallant yards, it was worse. It was just like a high see-saw; one moment we were up above the man on the other yard arm, and next, we were away below looking up at him.[17]

When the temperature was near freezing, going aloft became even worse. 'Shalimar' described an occasion that was probably the experience of every sailor going far south:

On deck we had been drenched by breaking seas and spray, now we were scourged by flying hailstones. Eventually we reached the yard and laid out on it ... the canvas was wet and heavy and ballooning out as stiff as a board ... the ship lurching heavily so that the ... yard swayed giddily in wide circles through the air. Our only foothold was the wire foot rope that stretched below the yard ... the only grip ... the iron jackstay that ran along the top of the yard.[18]

Occasionally, in fine weather, the nimbleness and speed of sailors aloft was turned into a sporting contest. An anonymous emigrant on the *Somersetshire* in 1879-80 told of 'a Sailors' Race'.

[It] was held from the lowest ratline to the top of the foremast. Ten seamen competed, and the winners were Jonessen, a Scandinavian, who accomplished the task in 2 min. 8 sec; Brown who occupied 2 min. 20 sec; and Anderssen, who was one second longer than the last-named.[19]

In stormy weather the ship and her complement were dependent to a great degree on the helmsman. In the years of sail the helmsman stood at the extremity of the stern. In some ships a canvas dodger was erected behind him — not to protect him, but to prevent him from seeing the advancing waves and becoming so alarmed as to run from his post. When there was no dodger, the helmsman was firmly warned not to look behind. Lubbock tells of an occasion when a helmsman on the *Ben Voirlich* did look and did flee: 'As the ship broached to, a huge wave broke over her quarter. The avalanche of water smashed in the break of the poop, gutted the cabin and took nine men overboard.'[20] Two of the men swept away had been aloft on a yardarm!

William Scoresby, coming out on the *Royal Charter* to study the

effect of her iron hull on the compass, spent much of his time in the crow's-nest while the ship tore before the Howling Fifties. As a master mariner himself, he repeatedly watched the drama at the helm:

Furling the lofty main royal on the grain barque *Pamir*. Although the *Pamir* was not built until 1905, work aloft had changed very little since the years of emigration by sail.

> There you saw four men — the best class of seamen . . . keeping the wheel in active play, as they endeavoured to counteract any sideway tendency of the ship's head . . . Then there was the captain, standing a few yards forward of the helm . . . giving impulse and guidance to the helmsman in usual emphatic words: 'Starboard! starboard! — steady so — port a little — meet her again — mind your starboard helm', and so on . . . externally, the assailing mountain-like wave, following close on the starboard quarter . . . threatening, as many waves do, to overwhelm the ship in mightiness of waters.[21]

In extreme seas it was not unusual for helmsmen to be lashed to the wheel. Nathaniel Levi saw this on the *Matilda Wattenbach* in 1854:

> Two men lashed to the Wheel and every now and then nearly up to their necks in water. A huge sea strikes her by the wheel

and then washes away the binnacle lamp and at first we were told the compass . . .

As it was dark, the master of the *Matilda Wattenbach* tore up a handkerchief which he tied to a pole close to the helmsman so that they could keep the head of the ship with the wind.

Occasionally the wheel itself was wrecked. Aleck Gibson, coming out on the *Stebonheath* in 1855, recorded a wave that towered fifteen feet above the stern. It smashed the wheel and washed the two helmsmen along the deck, still clutching spokes. Only three spokes remained and an auxiliary tackle had to be fitted swiftly.[22]

Inevitably, losses of men overboard in this sort of weather were frequent and rescue of them rare. A. G. Harvie was writing up his diary on the *Scottish Wizard* when alarmed cries reached him:

Just as I am writing, I am interrupted by the shocking noise of 'a man overboard' and too surely Fred Pratt when helping to take in the mainsail fell from the yard-arm. With a heavy sea rolling, a pitch dark night and a heavy squall on, nothing could possibly be done to save him as the ship is going over 11½ knots through the water. He was a nice gentlemanly lad the senior apprentice on board — just 19, who was taking his last voyage previous to going up for his exam for Second Mate . . . the sea was too high for anyone encumbered with thick clothes, sea boots and oil skins to swim in, or keep above water any length of time.[23]

After loss of one of the crew, it was usual for the master to auction the missing man's belongings. Dana described just such a scene:

. . . his chest was brought up upon the forecastle and the sale began. The jackets and trousers in which we had seen him dressed so lately were exposed and bid off while the life was hardly out of his body, and his chest was taken aft and used as a store-chest, so that there was nothing left that could be called *his*. Sailors have unwillingness to wear dead man's clothes during the same voyage, and they seldom do, unless they are in absolute want.[24]

After a death sailors were more than usually superstitious. On the

Helmsman on the iron barque *Barossa* (built 1873). Often in heavy seas two men were at the wheel, sometimes lashed there so that they would not be washed away. In such weather it was essential to keep the ship's head before the wind, as it could be overwhelmed if it 'broached to' — that is, slewed around to windward.

Scottish Wizard they had been catching albatrosses, but following Fred Pratt's death they desisted:

> [They] don't want any more birds caught — at least this week, as they think it unlucky as his spirit may be in one of the birds that fly round the ship.

Harvie himself was in no mood to smile at the superstitions, though earlier on the voyage he had written lightly enough of another: the ship's carpenter had informed him that he carried a caul in his sea chest with which his mother was born; he carried it as protection against drowning:

> I told him that in order to be quite efficacious he ought to wear it about his person, but he sees some difficulty in doing this, and fully believes its virtue even when kept in a little tin canister in his sea chest.

Harvie also recorded what he called an 'informative' superstition:

> The Steward killed the first of the pigs this afternoon, watched with interest by the crew as they have a superstition that a breeze which they call 'the Pig's Breeze' comes from whatever direction the animal's head pointed at when it died. This pig died with his head in the starboard scuppers pointing to the starboard quarter — a direction that will suit us nicely.

Superstitions were rife. Captain George Calcutt wrote of a common one: whistling was taboo, for the crew regarded it as an imitation of strong wind — a tempting of providence.[25] On the other hand, 'Bully' Forbes was seen by one of his passengers to be 'whistling for a wind' when he wanted to make a fast passage in the *Lightning*[26] and there were even masters who used a bosun's pipe for the same purpose.

On the *Africaine* in 1836, there was outcry among the crew when an emigrant's cat disappeared overboard:

> I heard one of the [sailors] say he would hang a man for a glass of grog but would not drown a cat for a sovereign, for they consider it as the certain forerunner of a storm.[27]

This concern for cats does not seem to have extended to dogs.

20 fathoms — piece of cord with 2 kn
17 fathoms — piece of red bunting
15 fathoms — piece of white linen c
13 fathoms — piece of blue serge
10 fathoms — leather washer
7 fathoms — red bunting
5 fathoms — white duck (linen ca
3 fathoms — 3 leather strip
2 fathoms — 2 leather strips

The lead line. A weighted line heaved by the leadsman into the sea to sound the depth of water. The markings on it, which could be identified at night by touch, continued to twenty fathoms.

Snell saw a dog thrown overboard by one of the crew without a voice being raised in protest:

> A dog which has been running about the decks ever since we left Plymouth was thrown overboard this morning by the ship's cook on suspicion of being mad — the poor thing swam very hard after the ship and looked very pitifully up at us but gradually dropped out of sight astern.

Contrary to the story of Coleridge's *Ancient Mariner*, sailors did not normally regard the albatross with superstition. They did, however, feel animosity toward it, as they believed it would take the eyes of a man struggling in the sea. They 'fished' for it unmercifully, using as a 'hook' a baited triangle about the size of a man's hand, two sides of metal and one of wood, so that it would float. Baited with waste meat, the triangle was streamed astern. In going for the bait, the hook of the bird's beak would catch in one of the angles of the triangle whereupon the sailors — usually it took two of them — would gradually draw it in.

Having used the bones of its long legs for pipe stems, its skull cavity as a snuff box, the webbing of its feet for tobacco pouches, and its breast feathers for ladies' muffs, they soaked the carcase for several hours in salt water, then, unpalatable though the dish must have been, they ate it — 'only so because we were so ravenous,' said Captain A. W. Pearse.

> We were always on the verge of starvation ... the beef and pork were half bone, so didn't amount to much after they were cooked. Biscuits were our main food, though certainly we had

For the benefit of the first-class passengers, fowls, sheep and pigs were carried on deck. The fowl pens were so often awash on the long easterly run that egg production was poor and the fowls became emaciated. Sheep and pigs fared better, but occasionally all pens were swept overboard.

pea soup on Monday, Wednesday and Friday, and boiled rice on Saturday, with plum pudding on Sunday.²⁸

The Loch Line allowed 1/6d. a day in 1876 for feeding a seaman.²⁹ If this was typical, it is not surprising that crews devised all manner of ploys to get hold of additional food: a harpoon for reaching bread through the galley skylight; grease on the deck to cause the steward to slip on his way to the dining saloon; an apprentice on watch at night for a hen putting its head out of its pen to drink, whereupon his task was to run a needle through its brain — and then in the morning beg from the steward the 'diseased' fowl that had died in the night.

One standby was boiled rice — dubbed 'strike-me-blind'. Failing even that the men made themselves 'dandyfunk': ship's biscuits placed in a canvas bag and pounded with a hammer, with scraps of salt meat or bully beef added to it, along with a dash of molasses. The dish was dampened and put into the oven.

Salt meat reached the sailors after the officers had cut off the least offensive pieces. They termed it 'old horse' and addressed long, traditional verses to it, the final words being:

> . . . killed by blows and sore abuse
> They salted me down for sailors' use.³⁰

Sometimes impossibly hard chunks were dried in the sun and afterwards sculpted.³¹

In the fo'c'sle there were seldom any of the refinements of eating ashore. Dana, in describing conditions on American ships, might just as well have been describing English ships:

> **There are neither tables, knives, forks, nor plates, in a forecastle; but the kid [a wooden tub with iron hoops] is placed on the floor, and the crew sit round it, and each man cuts for himself with the common jack-knife or sheath-knife, that he carries about him . . .³²**

Many masters took care to have these knives rounded up as soon as the ship was at sea, for fighting was rife. In the earlier years of emigration, when there were ports of call and easy access to grog, fighting was at its worst as men struggled back to the ship. When the *Indus* called at Port Praia in the Cape Verde Islands in 1839, Anne Drysdale saw the returning crew on the docks, drunk to a man:

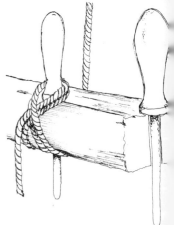

Belaying-pin. A strong pin around which a ship's ropes could be fastened or 'belayed'. During outbreaks of violence, sailors sometimes wielded them as a formidable weapon.

They all fought, sometimes with each other and sometimes with the mate, who they all hate ... It was fearful looking over to see the men fighting stripped naked to the waist and the blood streaming down their faces.[33]

At times a tot of rum was handed out officially, especially after men had been aloft in bad weather, but on emigrant ships crews were often plied with liquor by passengers and this could prove highly dangerous. William Howitt came on deck on the *Kent* and, on seeing 'the sun whirling around', discovered that the man at the wheel was lying on his back, drunk. Fortunately the sea was calm, nevertheless the wheel was spinning so rapidly that the carpenter, in a rash attempt to arrest it, broke his thigh.[34]

When officers became drunk — as they often did — the outcome could be drastic. On the night of 16 July 1853 the mate of the *United*[35] sighted the Cape Otway light and went below to report this to the captain. The captain was lying drunk on the chart. He was still drunk next day when the ship sailed into Port Phillip. Warned by a customs officer that he 'would be on the sands in five minutes', he replied, 'I know how to steer my ship.' Then onto the sands he went and stuck fast. He disappeared below after this, but on coming on deck at dusk demanded, 'What's all this about? Why are we not going on?' He ordered all sail to be set and a good breeze took the ship off. But when the ship ran onto another bank, the crew struck and the first mate took over. The ship was saved — but not the master: on the outside of the court brief is written: 'Guilty 2 & 3rd Counts 3 Years on Roads'.

Insobriety was the subject of many shipboard yarns, one of which was related by Sir Charles Gavan Duffy — he had it from the master of the *Ocean Chief* on which he travelled to Australia in 1855:

A skipper of his acquaintance entered a complaint in the logbook against one of his officers. 'I regret to state (so it ran) that during the greater part of this day the first mate has been intoxicated and disorderly.' Some days later the first mate made an entry in the log. 'I am rejoiced to be able to state that during this entire day the captain has been quite sober.'[36]

For each 100 tons an emigrant ship was required to carry five men

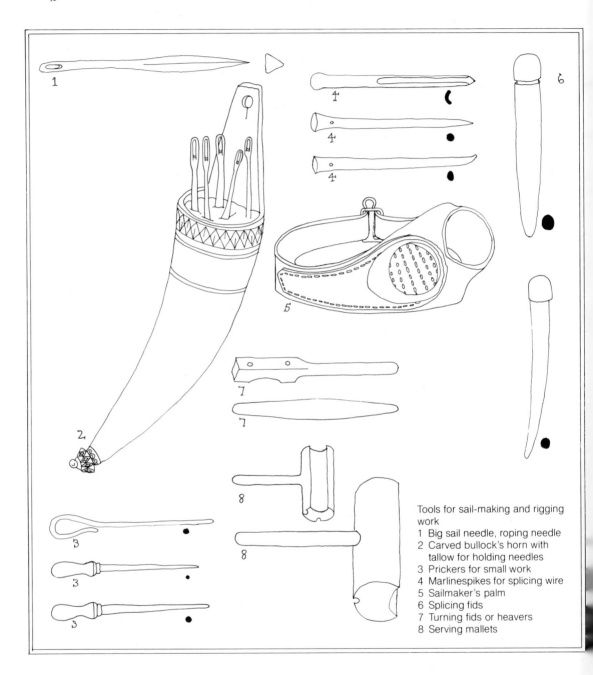

Tools for sail-making and rigging work
1 Big sail needle, roping needle
2 Carved bullock's horn with tallow for holding needles
3 Prickers for small work
4 Marlinespikes for splicing wire
5 Sailmaker's palm
6 Splicing fids
7 Turning fids or heavers
8 Serving mallets

and one boy. Taking the *Marco Polo* as typifying the larger emigrant carriers, we can read in her 1854 newspaper that she carried:

2 carpenters, bosun, bosun's mate, sailmaker, 14 stewards, 2 stewardesses, 6 cooks, 2 bakers, 12 musicians, 1 butcher, 34 seamen and 5 boys. Officers: master, 2 surgeons, 2 pursers and 4 mates.

Taking the Loch Line ships as typifying smaller vessels, their crews numbered thirty-five to forty.

Whether a ship was large or small, crew accommodation was incredibly confined. Shut in the converging bows, the men's constant companion was the booming sea — 'the old grey widow-maker'. On some ships they slept in bunks; in others in hammocks still. There could be no privacy.

Havelock Wilson, who in 1887 founded the National Amalgamated Sailors' and Firemen's Union in Britain, wrote of fo'c'sle lighting:

... we had oil-lamps with the wick down to the funnel — when they were lit we could not see each other for smoke. This particular lamp was known as the 'luxury' lamp, only to be lit when we were in channels or dangerous waters. When we got into fine weather, our substitute of this lamp was a tin plate filled with fat ... floating on this was a piece of cork with a hole in it, and a piece of rag pushed through the hole for a wick.[37]

Such hobbies as model-making, scrimshaw work and knitting could only be carried on by day; even then, the light was wan — worsened by sailors' love of their short pipes. They were a rough lot — intemperate, superstitious, illiterate, often violent, yet, in their way, innocent and not without wonder at the vast world surrounding them. They brought most of the hundreds of thousands of their charges safely through and received little in return. When they failed to reach their destination, they and the emigrants shared the same deep and common grave.

9 *Surgeons and Health*

Cur'd yesterday of my disease,
I died last night of my physician.
Matthew Prior

Prior's lines, written early in the eighteenth century, are perhaps an unfair introduction when one allows that the application of medical science had not developed dramatically between his time and the era of emigration by sail. But what those at sea most needed were straightforward preventive measures rather than skilled medicine: cleanliness, good diet, dry quarters, exercise, fresh air. These lessons had been learnt by the time of James Cook. Experience gained in the early transportation of convicts to Australia had driven the lesson home, but when the flood of emigration began, there were unaccountable areas of neglect. One of these was the standing of the surgeon in relation to the ship's captain — a problem already faced and solved in transportation.

During the period of early transportation few worthwhile surgeons had been willing to accept a subordinate position that exposed them for months on end to confrontations with dictatorial masters. Dr Murray Verso has pointed out the consequences: the early surgeons accompanying convicts tended either to be young and inexperienced or old and failures. In 1792 Royal Navy surgeons were appointed to the transports, but even then, their rank only equated with that of a petty officer, so the situation was not greatly improved. Dr Verso has explained the next steps taken:

It was not until 1814 that surgeon-superintendents were appointed to the convict vessels and given responsibility for the

Burial at sea — a frequent occurrence on emigrant ships. The sailmaker stitched the body into canvas with lead weights at the feet; the captain or an emigrating clergyman read the service as the ship raced on.

157

care and discipline of convicts as well as for their welfare, their behaviour, their proper rationing, their treatment and for seeing that they got regular exercise. However, their powers and responsibilities were not clearly defined until the early 'twenties when explicit instructions were issued to masters, captains of the guard and the surgeon-superintendents themselves. From then on this arrangement worked well.[1]

It also worked well because after 1832 the surgeon-superintendent on a transport could lodge complaint with the senior British naval officer at the ship's next port of call if his reasonable requests to the master, so far on the voyage, had been refused.[2] The quality of surgeons now began to improve distinctly.

As early as May 1838 detailed instructions were promulgated for surgeons on emigrant ships[3], but the relative standing of surgeon and master remained imprecise. Orders given the surgeon of the *Georgiana* in 1840 typify the situation:

> The master of the Vessel will give you every assistance in his power in enforcing order and regularity and to him you will address yourself if necessary.[4]

By this time emigrant surgeons were drawn from among civilians — generally speaking, better educated, more humane men than ships' masters. Most had trained in hospitals, others in the Society of Apothecaries. But lack of precise instructions in the standing of surgeons *vis-à-vis* masters still bedevilled the system. It led Caroline Chisholm to address a booklet to 'the clergy of Australia' in 1842. As usual, she was forthright and clear:

> The duties of captain and surgeon ought to be fully explained *before* a ship sails. And I would beg leave to suggest, that the issue of rations should not be under the control of the captain ... Captains of ships are the last persons in the world we can expect to give attention to the weighing of oatmeal, or to be judges of the quantum of food required for a sick child: the duties of captains and surgeon ought to be as *distinct* as possible ... a surgeon-superintendent ought to be ... able to compel cleanliness, and pursue proper discipline among [the emigrants]

— to regulate the supply and distribution of extra rations according to climate or particular circumstances — to see and be aware that the rations distributed are of proper and sufficient quantity and quality . . .[5]

As all of these matters had been solved over a thirty-year period by the transportation authorities, one is left wondering whether one department kept the other properly informed of its conclusions. The instructions to surgeons of emigrant ships were gradually expanded and their standing in relation to masters was clarified: strictly these requirements applied only to government-chartered vessels, but when emigration was at its height, the instructions set a general standard which became expected of all major emigrant ships.

The lesser ships were not required to carry a surgeon at all. The British Passenger Act of 1848 had a release clause: if a vessel carried more than 100 passengers it could either carry a surgeon, or the passengers' space allowance could be increased from twelve square feet to fourteen square feet. Presumably the small increase was reckoned to reduce risk of disease. The 1849 act was tighter: a vessel carrying more than fifty passengers was required to carry a surgeon or, once again, allow each passenger fourteen feet of space. The act of 1852 required vessels carrying more than 500 passengers to carry a surgeon, but 500 was a total seldom reached.

Terry Coleman, in *Passage to America*, contrasts surgeons on British ships bound for Australia with their counterparts on ships bound for North America. On the Atlantic some surgeons were not even qualified.

The surgeons on the Australia run were better. They had to be qualified, and they were paid by the government and supervised by the commissioners in London. Evenso, many of them were pretty doubtful doctors. Of the seventy-eight surgeons sent out on Australian ships in 1849, twenty-two were found to be either inefficient or wanting in energy. Here are short reports on five of them:

'Surgeon died on voyage from a disease brought on by intemperance.'

'Surgeon efficient, but guilty of gross misconduct after landing, with respect to a female emigrant.'

'The surgeon extremely inefficient, apparently from intemperance. He was mulcted £48.'

'Great neglect of his duties on the part of the surgeon, owing, apparently, to his having become insane.'

'Surgeon inflicted improper punishments on some single females.'[6]

Numerous diarists made adverse comments of their own. Charles Scott, coming out on the *Annie Wilson* in 1859, struck a martinet:

... as regards the Doctor and his attendance on the sick [it] is everything but satisfactory. If a man or woman feels indisposed and goes to him they are treated anything but civilly — viz. 'What's the matter with you.' 'I feel inwardly ill and I want something from you.' 'What do you mean by that, I am not the almighty how can I tell whats the matter with you' — and such like expressions such being the case the invalided are afraid to apply to him — he has the air of a Commanding Officer more than a comforter in the dire calamitys that befall the human family.

One can sympathize with a surgeon constantly demanded by seasick people who scarcely knew what was wrong with them and who were, into the bargain, disoriented by the unfamiliar life. And many surgeons were seasick themselves. William Merifield, in the depths of seasickness himself, wrote:

Bay of Biscay ... enough to pitch my insides out. Evening — it's all up with me. I am not able to stir. [Four days later] ... very ill — weak. The Doctor can give me no relief — but at that I am not surprised he is very young, never been to sea and is just as ill as the other people.[7]

A tragedy occurred on the *Northumberland* largely owing to the surgeon being seasick. An elderly man had been temporarily bedded down in quarters set aside for invalids. In this small cabin, jars of carbolic acid were stored. George Tucker, a twenty-six-year-old printer, related what happened:

... The night being stormy, the jars clashed together and of course smashed. When the old man rose in the morning he commenced baling this stuff out of his berth, and wiping it up. Several people tried to dissuade him from doing so, but he would persist. It was not long before he was observed to be lying in

Box of instruments required by a surgeon at sea. Only in the last years of sail was chloroform available, consequently most operations had to be performed quickly — usually with the help of morphine or spirits.

Amputating saw

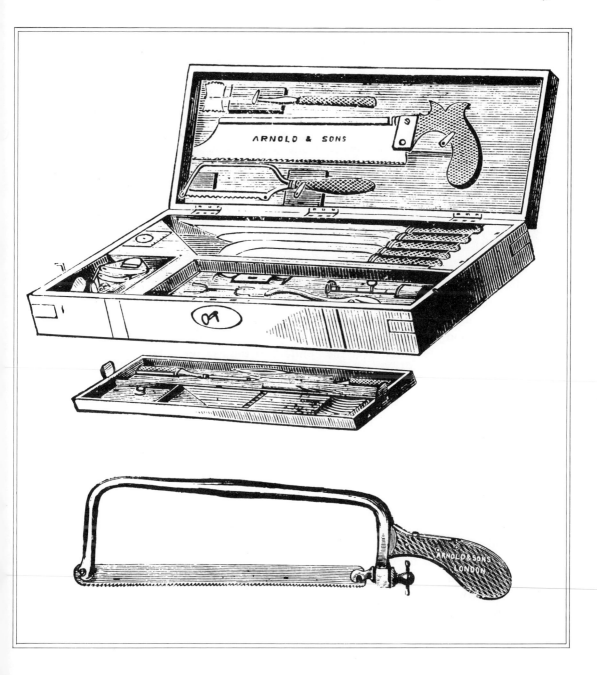

a heap on the floor. He was picked up, placed in his bunk, it being then about 8 am, but before 10 he was a dead man — poisoned, burnt, positively burnt everywhere the acid had touched the skin — and that by the carelessness of a fool of a young doctor, who could not attend the old man, as he was himself indisposed.

Undoubtedly there were more conscientious men among the surgeons than poor ones; indeed, one has only to read the journal of Dr Lightoller in this book to realize the great load a dedicated man accepted. By 1892 instructions to surgeons exceeded eighty pages[8] and one is left feeling that the holder of the office needed more than mortal powers to carry out his duties. Below are listed a few of the regulations that bound him:

The Surgeon is to understand that he is not only charged with the Medical care of the Emigrants, but that on him devolves also the maintenance of discipline among them, and consequently the enforcement of regulations for securing cleanliness regularity, and good conduct . . .

. . . it will be his duty to watch over the conduct of the Master, Officers, and Crew of the Ship in all that relates to the Emigrants — to see that the proper allowance of food and water is duly issued to them — to protect them from ill-usage or interference, and expecially to prevent, as further explained hereafter, communication with the single women, whether on deck or in their own apartment below . . .

The Surgeon will carefully examine each emigrant before embarkation, and not allow any person to go on board the ship who may be suffering under any disease dangerous to others, or likely to be aggravated by the voyage, or who may be unsound either of body or mind, or in bad health . . .

The people ought to be berthed according to their natural connexions, and so as to place in the neighbourhood of one another those whose relative circumstances and habits render it most likely that they will agree. Women advanced in pregnancy should be placed in the lower berths . . . The names of the occupants should be affixed to each berth . . .

The Surgeon will appoint one Constable, who is to be either a married man or a married woman, for each three Messes of the single women. The duties of these Mess Constables will be to receive and to carry to and from the galley the provisions of the Mess, and to clean the Mess utensils after each meal. The object of this arrangment is to deprive the young women of any pretext for resorting to the galley or fore part of the ship ...

The Surgeon, in case of need, can appeal to the Captain for his aid and co-operation in enforcing the requisite discipline on board, especially where the crew are concerned. The law invests the Captain with large punitive powers over the Crew, and with larger powers over Passengers than have been confided to the Surgeon ...

No unmarried female Emigrant is on any account to be allowed to act as servant or attendant to the Surgeon-Superintendent, Captain, or Officers of the ship, or to enter their cabins. The Surgeon-Superintendent should bear in mind that one of his most important duties is the care of the morals and the protection of the single women, and he should prevent the association of single men and women who are not immediate members of the same family ...

The Emigrants should be encouraged to bathe as much as possible — the males in a bath provided for the purpose and in tubs in the fore part of the ship; the females in the bath room prepared for their use. He should take care to prevent indecency and practical jokes ...

Great care should be taken to preserve dryness between decks. For this purpose all washing must be strictly prohibited there, and holystones and dry rubbing alone used to clean the deck. The swing stoves and hot sand should be used frequently, and wherever damp may appear ...

The Emigrants should have every encouragement to take the air on deck. The Surgeon-Superintendent should promote Music, Dancing, and every harmless means of combining exercise and amusement. But the Officers and Crew of the ship are not to dance with the Emigrants or to associate with any of the single women . . .

The Emigrants are not to be molested crossing the line . . .

Gambling, betting, or smoking between decks must on no account be permitted . . .

. . . it will be the duty of the Surgeon-Superintendent, with the aid of the Teacher, to give as far as possible a profitable direction to the [emigrants'] occupations and amusements . . . he will endeavour to form reading and listening classes, in which those Emigrants who can read most fluently should in turn be encouraged to read aloud to the rest when not otherwise employed . . .

As soon as the single women have gone below for the night, the Matron will lock the door of the apartment and keep the key . . .

As a measure of precaution, the Surgeon when visiting single women professionally is to attend them in the Female Hospital or their own berths; but in either case the visit is to be made in the presence of the Matron, or of some discreet married woman . . .

The Surgeon will not interfere in any way with the navigation of the ship, but he will note daily the latitude and longitude at noon. Between the 1st of April and the 1st of October the Ship is not to be navigated in a latitude higher than 47° south; nor, between the 2nd of October and the 31st of March, both inclusive, in a latitude higher than 53° south. If, however, on the approach of the ship to these high latitudes the Surgeon finds the health of the Passengers to be endangered by the cold, he will not fail to make a proper representation to the Captain on the subject . . .

. . . The Surgeon's remuneration will consist of a payment per head on the Emigrants landed alive, at a rate to be agreed on between the Agent-general and himself, but not to exceed 20s. per head. In every case the payment will be contingent on the good conduct of the Surgeon, and on the Government being satisfied that he had discharged his duties zealously and efficiently . . .

These regulations represent a small part of the document which surgeons were required to sign. It was, of course, one thing to frame far-reaching regulations, quite another to be sure they would be observed. Given a speed-obsessed master like 'Bully' Forbes, no surgeon could be sure the ship would not exceed 53° south. Some masters kept the ship's whereabouts a secret between himself and the mates who took the noon sights. Again, every ship had its gamblers, indeed, some gamblers seldom stopped, except to sleep or eat or have belongings auctioned to provide further capital. On many ships one reads of smoking between decks. Most ships lacked facilities for steerage passengers to bathe — in any case, the Highland Scotsmen, the Irish and the lower orders of English had marked

Daily sick parades brought the surgeon-superintendent 'an aggregation of human suffering'. Early in the voyage he was just as likely to be afflicted by seasickness as his patients were.

aversion to overall washing. As for a surgeon turning back emigrants suffering 'any disease dangerous to others', tragic occasions have already been mentioned of passengers, especially children, embarking on ships while harbouring infectious diseases contracted in the emigrants' depot itself. Again, there were many ships' officers who did much more than dance with single females. In some cases officers entered into a state of cosy domesticity in their cabins with an emigrant of their choosing — and this with the connivance of the surgeon.

The voluminous regulations did not apply to foreign ships, but then, few foreign ships were bringing emigrants to Australia. An exception was the relatively small number of German ships. Until the inquiry held in Sydney in 1858 these ships were notorious for avoiding the expense of carrying a qualified surgeon, or for meeting several other standards demanded by Britain. At the inquiry the Health Officer of the Port of Sydney, Dr Alleyne, said in evidence:

One or two of the German ships have brought out people capable of taking medical charge, but generally speaking, they are persons who ought not to be trusted on board ship; they are usually of no efficiency whatever. In a ship that arrived, I dare say about twelve months ago, or not quite so long, the captain was acting as surgeon, and a day or two before making the port had a very difficult case of accouchment, which he succeeded, almost miraculously, in bringing to a successful termination.[9]

Often these 'surgeons' were no more than barbers, practised in the niceties of blood-letting. At the same inquiry, H. H. Browne, Agent for Immigration in Sydney, said in evidence:

... the so called doctors on board them [are] usually men who after they leave the ship are often to be found in Mr. Scholtz's establishment, cutting hair and shaving; many of them have I seen there.

A properly qualified German surgeon, Dr C. F. Eichler, made two voyages to Australia, one as an emigrant, the other to return to Germany to marry. Questioned at the inquiry he said:

I did not intermix much with [the emigrants]; I was quite private. I had not the superintendence of the people in the same way as the doctor has on board an English vessel ...

Had you any power to enforce sanitary regulations?

No; but I tried the best I could do with the captain; if he did not do what I wished I could not help it.

In point of fact, did the emigrants arrive in as good health as when they embarked? ...

Some that were flourishing in appearance when they came on board looked miserable when they arrived here; they would not be able to work immediately, I am sure.

To what do you attribute that change in their condition?

It arose out of sorrow, and want of food, and the ill effect of the whole management of the ship.

A further witness, J. Molitor, a German builder, had lost his wife during the passage to Sydney. Asked if she had received medical attention he replied:

Yes; but the captain took the power from the doctor, and would not allow the doctor to give her what she wanted; she got so well once that she could sit up, and then the captain took the delicate victuals away, and from that time she sank; being in the family-way she had no strength to carry the child any longer, and it was born too soon; the child died first, and two days after she died.

Even on the government-supervised British ships, keeping men and women free of venereal diseases and single women free of pregnancy was battle enough for surgeons. William Harbottle, emigrating on the *Scotia* in 1849, a ship chartered by the Commissioners to carry 224 emigrants, 'for the most part agricultural labourers', wrote of its problems with a degree of cabin-class disdain:

... some of the single females have been detected cohabiting with the sailors — which cannot be a matter of surprise to anyone as most of them have seen *life* in London or been sent out by their friends for delinquencies at home. The Commissioners cannot expect otherwise if such are sent out. Capt. Strickland says that twenty-four hours in the Deptford Depot was sufficient

A medical chest of 1885, late in the era of sail. It was essential for the chest to be lashed down if the jars and bottles were not to be smashed in storms.

to contaminate the most virtuous — that the single of both sexes were indiscriminately herded together or at most some tattered piece of canvas formed the only barrier.

Undoubtedly the most important person responsible to the surgeon-superintendent was the matron. Her range of duties was wide — from instructing the young women in household duties to examining their heads for lice.

With a view to prevent any irregularity [in the sleeping quarters] you are authorised to muster all the unmarried young women at any hour you may deem necessary for the purpose; but you will be responsible for exercising this authority with descretion.

A woman with such authority was bound to be resented — the young men were not the only ones hankering to meet the opposite sex. Into the bargain, many of the matrons seem to have been tyrants. Such a one was encountered by Mary Anne Bedford:

... you never heard such a noisy woman in your life. She goes up and down shouting like someone out of her mind ... There is no one on the vessel that likes her. They have told her they would put her in irons many a time.

One can only suppose the woman to have been deranged. In the tropics she became worse — one is left astonished by the lack of firm measures from the master of no less a ship than the Black Ball *Champion of the Seas.*

... There has been the greatest row with the matron today. She was near having a fight with the first mate. Then one of the young women had a fight with her and two men that were serving out the water parted them. This afternoon she got a brush to one of the girls to hit her with. So another girl got some water and threw it over her. Then about a dozen got round her and beat her. There is never a day passes without some of the girls having a row with her. The Captain came down but he holds with neither side. He always laughs it off if they tell him anything. All that he said [was] he thought that he would have to come and be the Matron himself. They all had a good laugh. The mates often tell the girls they should beat her. So they have been trying it today. She always tells them she could master six of them and I believe she could ...

Dr R. Scot Skirving was obliged to take over one morning from the matron on the *Ellora*, with amusing consequences:

Miss Acid (I'll call her) ... a lean, vinegar-faced woman well in her fifties, with a tongue like a rasp ... reported that the girls refused to get out of their bunks to dress and do the usual domestic chores very properly required of all emigrants. Miss Acid had made several previous voyages and was no novice to the arts of these wild girls.

... I got the pump rigged and the hose passed down the companion, at the foot of which I stood nozzle in hand. I then addressed the rows of young women, mostly in the supine position. 'Girls,' said I, 'this caper won't do, you'll have to show a leg.'

'Ah, go along with you, Doctor, we'll just be lying here as long as we likes' — I'm afraid it is usually the Irish who make shindies of this sort; they make a kind of hobby of raising Cain.

'Ah, no,' said I, with my best bedside manner. 'Young ladies, there is no attraction in bed for you on a fine morning like this, so out you'll get like the perfect dears you are.'

'Ah, to hell wid your flattery! There is nothing on this boat but worrk and that old cat's tongue fur us when we do bees get out of them harrd beds. Anyways we're stoppin' in them till we're rested.'

After a few more interchanges of shot I said: 'Well, girls, I don't want to make your beds wet and damp your pleasant faces, but I swear by the great hook-pot that if you are not out by the time I count twenty I'll turn this very hose on you.' I squirted a little to show that it was in order.

There was a pause as I counted, and then a sudden upheaval took place all about, and they shot out of their beds — fat legs and fatter bodies — just a parabola of half-naked young women poured out on the deck. They had to come out like water out of a spout, endways, because the only egress from most of these bunks was from their ends.[10]

A matron on the ship *Kate* in 1854 seems to have been much above 'Miss Acid' in personality. The grateful surgeon-superintendent referred to her as:

... our excellent matron, Mrs. Grieves, whose kind, firm and dignified deportment with her cultivated intellect and superior habits, presented a model for imitation, which I am afraid rarely falls to the lot of an Emigrant ship.[11]

The voluminous instructions to surgeons concluded with several appendices. Number 1 listed 'surgical and Midwifery Instruments which the Surgeon-Superintendent must possess':

A pocket Dressing Case, containing Scalpel, two Bistouries (blunt-pointed and sharp), Gum Lancet, Tenaculum, Forceps, Spatula, Scissors, two Probes, Silver Director, Caustic Case, Curved Needles of different sizes.
Lancet Case with at least Four Lancets.
Case of Tooth Instruments.
Midwifery Forceps and Trachea Tube.
Set of Silver and Gum-elastic Catheters, including Female Catheter and some Bougies.
One Amputating Knife and Catlin, one Amputating Saw, one Hey's Saw, Tourniquet.
Cupping Apparatus.
Silk of different sizes for Ligatures and Sutures.

Desirable Additions.
Trocar and Canula.
Trephine and Elevator.
Craniotomy Forceps, Perforator, and Blunt Hook.
N.B. — The Surgeon should be provided with the British Pharmacopoeia, published by Authority of the Medical Council.

Suture needle, full curved

Suture needle, half curved

If this list highlights the state of surgery at the time, Appendix Number 2 — 'List of Medicines &c. Required to be Put on Board for every 100 Persons' — does so even more clearly in the medical sense. It has drawn interesting comment from Jean M. Manning, a researcher into nineteenth-century drug usage.[12] She viewed the list as 'a very comprehensive one for the time; not wasteful, not cheeseparing'. The drugs were provided by the Apothecaries' Company who 'could be relied upon to make sure that they were properly packed for the voyage. Also they would be drugs of the best quality and fresh-ness . . .'

Mrs Manning places the drugs in four main categories:

1. Those for the treatment of diarrhoea. (Diarrhoea was very prevalent because of lack of preservatives, refrigeration and lack of knowledge of the cause of putrefaction.)
2. Those for the treatment of constipation. (Constipation was considered to be widespread. Also, the treatment for almost all non-specific illnesses — debility, headaches, anxiety, rheumatism etc. — was considered to be 'a good purge'.)
3. Those for the relief of pain. (At this time there were no sedatives — e.g. bromides — or analgesics. The only drugs available were opium and its active principle, morphine.)
4. Those for the relief of coughs and colds, bronchitis and tuberculosis.

Some of Mrs Manning's comments highlight the medical practices and prevailing attitudes of the day. *Cretae Praep* (prepared chalk) she describes as a 'very cheap and very effective anti-diarrhoeal agent for "gumming up the works" ', but the more palatable *Pulv. Aromat* (aromatic chalk powder), used for the same purpose, was evidently reserved for cabin passengers and officers, as a very limited quantity was carried. *Calomelus* (mercurous chloride) was provided for 'teeth-ing difficulties in children, but it was also a purgative' — as was the familiar castor oil (*Ol. Ricini*) and the considerably more drastic croton oil (*Ol. Croton*). *Pulv. Ipecac et opia* (powdered ipecacuanha with opium) — better known as Dover's Powder — was used for relief of fever pain. There was no form of anaesthetic, chloroform not being in general use until late in the era of sail, consequently surgery had to be performed rapidly, the patient usually being given spirits or mor-phine then held securely. Amputations were carried out in a matter of minutes. Tincture of opium, plus aromatics, was regarded then,

Dental instruments. As it was unusual for a dentist to be carried on an emigrant ship, extractions were performed by the surgeon-superintendent.

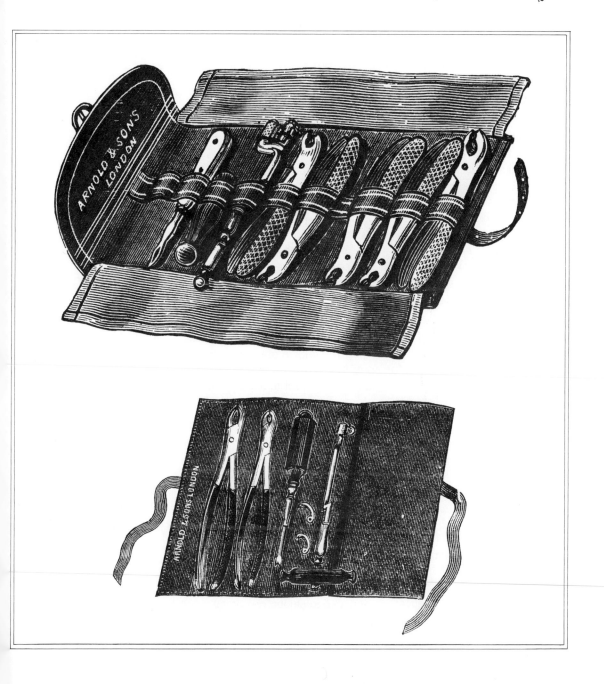

as now, as an effective treatment for coughs. There were numerous alternative cough remedies: the familiar cod-liver oil, camphor, creosote, oil of peppermint, to mention a few, but as some of the coughs had a tubercular origin, there was no hope of the treatments giving anything by comfort or temporary relief.

The only drug listed which could be used for VD (apart from mercury) was copaiba, an oily plant resin. Possibly each migrant was examined for VD before being accepted — hence no additional drug was carried. (Not that the drugs used for VD at the time did much good!)

The list of disinfecting agents is interesting: 2 gallons of chloride of zinc would almost certainly be a 5% solution, as this was used for 'syringing out offensive pus cavities, sinuses, foul ulcers'. (ref. *Squire's Companion to the British Pharmacopoeia*). 'Half a hundredweight of chloride of lime': this was an early name for chlorinated lime, used as a disinfectant from the time of its discovery in 1788; it was officially accepted in 1836. The amount carried was a liberal and very wise choice for the times.

To turn from Mrs Manning's comments to the general state of medicine at the time: it should be remembered that almost the entire era of sail pre-dated Lister's findings on the prevention of surgical sepsis. Worse, there was no realization until 1909 that typhus was spread by body lice, although it was obvious that it occurred where people were crowded together in dirty conditions — a fact that led to its various names: gaol fever, ship fever, camp fever. An advisory tract for emigrants[13] simply said of it:

Recollect that this, like all fevers, is a complaint that will last its own time; that there is no such thing as cutting it short; and that the game you have to play is to get the patient to *live on* till the fever leaves him.

Get him to 'live on'! Typhus *began* with a breakdown of the will to live. Then,

. . . disinclination to mental and physical exertion, heaviness of the eyes, yawning, disturbed sleep. With the onset of fever there was shivering and the pulse might become rapid and weak or intermittent in its beat . . .

In the second stage the patient was reduced to stupor. He lay muttering in low delirium, and the tongue was usually dry and heavily coated.[14]

At this stage the rash generally appeared and the skin began to

Dr Francis Workman (1833-97) came to Australia as surgeon-superintendent on the *Sobraon* in 1883. He had in his charge many passengers suffering from tuberculosis and was among the first doctors to question the efficacy of a sea voyage for the disease. He practised in Melbourne until his death.

Artery forceps (Luer's)

darken — a symptom that gave typhus one of its names: 'black fever'.

Dangerous symptoms, heralding the approach of death were: dilation of the pupils, early delirium, the occurrence of hiccup and suppression of urine.[15]

The link between cholera and contaminated drinking water was not realized until 1848. Even then, ships continued to draw drinking water from rivers at ports of departure. The medical instructions of 1864, from which much has already been quoted, lay down a requirement that 'Emigrant Ships will always carry a Distilling Apparatus for converting salt water into fresh'. Many ships not under direct government control did not do so and frequently the equipment on government ships broke down completely.

Throughout the entire era of passenger-carrying by sail it was supposed that a sea voyage benefited a person suffering from 'pulmonary phthisis', that is, tuberculosis. The supposition was based in part on the belief that vomiting helped the consumptive patient — a belief dating back at least to Aulus Celsus, born in Rome some forty years before Christ.[16] Celsus went so far as to produce a rocking bed to benefit his patients. Belief in the benefits of a sea voyage persisted at least until the 1880s, nor was there any suspicion that tuberculosis was communicable. As a result, tubercular emigrants were not isolated from other passengers. Some of them survived and benefited later from the Australian climate; others died at sea; many undoubtedly passed the disease to fellow passengers. Some tubercular patients booked for the round voyage and continued home via Cape Horn after dropping emigrants at Australian ports. One of the ships carrying such patients was the *Sobraon* — 2131 registered tons; 317 feet long and 42 wide. Her tubercular passengers were accommodated two to a cabin, the cabins measuring only nine feet by six and a half feet, under a six-and-a-half foot ceiling. The surgeon, Dr Francis Workman, spoke out strongly in 1884 against the supposed benefits of such voyages:

... the patient passenger [is] committed to such a novel course of treatment, to last nearly three months, from which there is no withdrawing, however much he may hate it, or however little it may suit him. Australia or death is the word. Once the anchor is weighed at Plymouth no land is touched at, perhaps not sighted, till the anchor is dropped off Melbourne.[17]

On Dr Workman's voyage the *Sobraon* languished in the doldrums for ten days.

A great part of each day the ship lay with her head pointing anywhere but her course, and the sails flapping in melancholy fashion against the masts and the vertical sun shining through the misty atmosphere on the glassy ocean, rolling sullenly ... the air was saturated with moisture.

Workman could hear the sufferers 'coughing and spitting all night'.

... the ventilation was imperfect, the atmosphere became something I shuddered to go into.

In the cabin of one patient he described the air as 'saturated by his emanations from sweating and spitting'.

I listened to many bitter lamentations from people, who had they at all known what they had to go through ... would never have dreamt of coming.

But well-intentioned relatives urged members of their families to take the sea cure for years after Workman's address was published. Many were doomed to his conclusion: 'A ship is a most wretched place to die in'.

Even among well-informed emigrants, standards of hygiene were primitive — as witnessed by the reluctance of many cabin passengers to use the 'patent water closets' in preference to chamberpots. The device was admittedly no more than a flushable chute to the sea, with a leather flap to protect the posterior, but at least it kept odours from living quarters. Add to these odours those of the livestock carried on the deck above and the result boggles the imagination.

The smells were, of course, among the most notable feature of life on board. The combination of animal and human excrement, foul water from the bottom of the ship below pump wells which never came out, the remains of old cargoes and the perpetually rotting wooden structure of the vessel herself must between them have produced a dreadful stench, unrelieved by any kind of ventilation system in the ship. People were accustomed to this ashore in towns and villages which stank like an Oriental slum today![18]

Lousiness on board ship was scarcely to be avoided; even if one were a cabin passenger, lice were waiting in every crevice for the embarkation of fresh victims. Their first attacks occasioned great surprise and disgust. In a diary intended for his brother, George Tucker wrote that two of the single men on the *Northumberland* were found to be lousy:

... They were made to strip by the steerage passengers, and their shirts and under flannels examined: lice in any quantity were found, and the captain communicated with, who threatened them that he would throw their beds, bedding, etc. overboard if they were not properly washed, cleaned, and thoroughly overlooked. The threat has been since carried out, and they are thrown on the mercy of the doctor or captain whether they will have a bed or clothes for the rest of the voyage. I have no doubt they will be provided with them, as it is now very cold at night and not much better in the day.

Within two days George Tucker was confessing:

A good piece of news I can acquaint you with is that I, and, in fact, all the steerage passengers are getting gloriously lousy.

Even Dr Scot Skirving, sailing as late as 1883, could not defeat lice:

Dr Robert Scot Skirving in 1899, aged forty. At twenty-four he had been surgeon-superintendent on the emigrant ship *Ellora*. Although young for the position, he had already qualified not only in medicine, but as a master mariner. Until his death at ninety-seven, he was notable in Sydney both as a medical practitioner and a yachtsman.

I am sorry to have to admit that lice and bugs were a veritable plague. It was useless for angry viragoes, with arms akimbo to shout taunts of lousiness to their nextdoor bed-mates. Ah no! For all shared the attention of parasites of the best-known brands. I solemnly declare that when the sweeping of the 'tween decks took place, I have looked into the line of dust and seen mobs of our little guests crawling about. I encouraged the men to have their hair cut very close; but with the women the days of bobbed hair had not yet arrived, and I fear that 'glory of womanhood', long locks, made fine coverts for these little brothers of the poor and dirty.[19]

Dr Skirving was recalling the voyage as an old man who had long known the truth about lice. He added:

We had no epidemic of any kind, but if one case of typhus had occurred, what an outfly of that evil disease might have followed with all these body lice about to spread the glad tidings . . .

Some passengers didn't much care about lice or filth generally, as Edward Snell was to find on the *Bolton*:

A row between the Doctor and 11 Mess about their dirty habits. The contents of their mess shelf carried on deck and flung overboard consisting of 7 or 8 allowance of beef and pork, about half cwt. of bones and fragments, an old candle box . . . grease, dirt, old rags, enough to breed a fever in the ship. Many of the passengers lousy . . . Jack Braithwaite in very bad health, all over sores, having brought a present with him from the Plymouth ladies.

Even for people intent upon personal cleanliness, 'sea-soap' and saltwater were an inadequate combination. In any event, the only chance of using them was on deck behind temporary canvas partitions. Not all surgeon-superintendents afforded steerage passengers this opportunity. William Thompson, the *Meteor* Scotsman whom we met earlier, described an 1854 alternative for cabin-class males:

This morning we have begun cold Bathing, but not Stark as

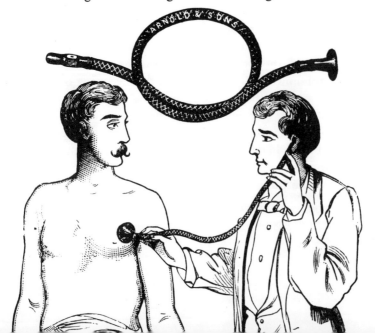

Stethoscope, flexible clinical (Reid and Morison's)

it would Certainly shock the Morals of our Feamal community ... Mrs. Clark has taken pity on us and has Constructed 2 pair of *Trunks* with which we cover our Nakedness. With these extraordinary inexpressibles we sally on Deck and souce ourselves with Buckets of salt water ...

Many women, even in cabin class, seem to have sacrificed cleanliness to Victorian modesty. On the *Meteor* Thompson wrote:

Bathing on deck. This was almost wholly restricted to males. Restrained by the prudery of the day, married steerage females often remained unwashed for long periods. Unaccompanied females, segregated from *all* males, might fare somewhat better. (An illustration by Edward Snell from his diary.)

Miss Henderson has turned her head where her feet should be in Bed and unfortunately the window was left open. Ramsay in passing saw as he thought a pair of shoes sticking up & Curosity led him to look a little more minutely as he ammagined the person must have gone to bed with ther shoes on, but low and behold the Black things turned out to be a pair of veritable feet & Covered with a thick coat of filth. Quite enough to turn a Man's Belly upside down such a sight meeting his eye in the morning. The Capt Certainly ought to erect a Temporary Bath a place covered in so that they can wash themselves from the Clew to Earing.*

The era of sail was also the era of patent medicines. A typical concoction was the famous Holloway's Pills. Thomas Holloway, a young Cornishman, purchased in 1828 the recipe for a patent herbal medicine from an Italian. He persuaded the senior surgeon at Middlesex Hospital to recommend it and then launched an advertising campaign. The success of this venture turned his mind to other quack medicines. He and his wife concocted a laxative pill, which contained castor oil and ginger. This they sold very profitably at the docks to people setting out on long sea voyages. To this they added Holloway's Ointment, advertised as 'the cure of gout and rheumatism, inveterate ulcers, sore breasts, sore heads, bad legs etc. 1/1d., 2/9d., 4/6d., 11/-, 22/-, and 33/- per pot'.[20]

Some of the home remedies mentioned by diarists sound as if they might have been no worse than the bought potions. F. W. Leighton for example, listed several before he left home:

*Terms applied to sails: 'clew' the lower corner, 'earing' the upper corner.

For seasickness — Take a few fresh figs, reduce them to a pulp and mix them with a little rum or Champaign wine diluted with 10 or 12 drops of lemon juice. Let the seasick drink of it and they will speedily recover.

For a cold — Dissolve Narbonne honey with the juice of a lemon. Take a spoonful night and morning.

A single does of 3 or 4 grains of sulphur arrest the most melignant attack of cholera.

To prevent the scarlet fever — 10 drops every night and morning (during exposure) of a solution of 4 grains of the extract of belladonna in a half an oz. of distilled water for an adult, 5 drops for a child 4 years old and upwards and 3 drops for an infant.

Important — We have ascertained that 1 oz. of carbonate of ammonia (smelling salts) put into a peck of flour will render bread perfectly sound be the wheat ever so much grown. — The way to use it is to dissolve it in the water used for making the flour in paste before the yeast is added.

While Leighton's last entry does not fall into the category of a home-health remedy, it mentions a substance no family — or at any rate, no female — neglected to carry: smelling salts. Swooning and going into hysterics were common among Victorian women both ashore and at sea. Granted that at times there was enough on the voyage to cause hysteria among both men and women, one is drawn to the conclusion that swooning and hysterics were expected of the 'fair sex' of the time. Gallant gentlemen were forever rushing to their aid. An occasion described by Oswald Bloxome, when a wave had broken through a cabin porthole on the *Florentia* in Bass Strait, is typical:

I ran instantly and a pretty scene presented itself — there was Miss McLeod fainting — Mrs. Hopkins in Hysterics, Henrietta supporting Mrs. Tingcombe and looking a picture of despair.[21]

Surgeons frequently went to the women's quarters to calm the occupants, but one of the most alarming cases of hysteria involved men and women alike and showed the men in considerably the worse light. It occurred on the *Selkirkshire*, bound from Glasgow to Rockhampton in 1882 and was recorded by Frances Thomson, young wife of the surgeon-superintendent:

Amputating knife (Liston's) single-edged

Saw, skull (Hey's)

Tonight a dreadful scene took place, such as I hope I may never see again. The people were having a concert and all was going on very nicely, when a man rushed into the midst of the peoples crying ship on fire. At once dreadful *panic* took place, men, women and children rushed madly about, shrieking and crying. The noise was deafening, women fainting on all sides, little children neglected by their mothers, went about with their little hands clasped, begging someone to save them. About fifty of the single men at once tore the covers of the lifeboats, and got into them ready to save themselves. Happily it turned out after all to be a false alarm. One of the sails had fallen down that was all. They found the man who gave the alarm, and put him in irons. [After an inquiry, he was kept in irons for a week.][22]

It is evident from Frances Thomson's account that fear of catastrophe was never far below the surface of passengers' minds and this is hardly surprising.

One can only admire the fortitude of countless women who gave birth to children at sea. They lacked anaesthetics and they knew it was distinctly possible that either they or their infants would not survive; frequently both were lost. Yet listen to Sarah Docker emigrating with her husband in 1828:

Frid. 27th [June]: Nothing particular occurred during the week. I still continued very sick and became so weak that I could scarcely sit up. About 6 o'clock this morning I became very unwell and had the Doctor and Mrs. Davies called up, and a little after six Mary-Jane was born. She was so small that I was inclined to think she was born too soon, but the Doctor thought that it was owing to my having been so very sick ... After my confinement I was never in the least sick and should have been up in a day or two but the weather was exceedingly stormy and the Ship was very much tossed.

As for her husband at this time:

Mr. D. was so very unwell that he almost thought he should not survive the passage.[23]

By Dr. Scot Skirving's time, chloroform had come into use. To read his account of a confinement on the *Ellora* in 1883 is to wonder what it might have been like a few years earlier. He was obliged to induce labour when a young woman was so exhausted from continual sea-sickness that he doubted she would survive unless delivered:

Labour began in due course, and so did a hard westerly gale. I had the patient in the so-called hospital, the half-deck where in other voyages lived the apprentices. Seas came on board, the decks were full of it, and there was often quite a lot of salt water in our precious lying-in chamber. We had, of course, to keep the patient in an upper bunk to keep her out of the wet. Labour progressed piteously slowly, and I felt that if I waited till Nature completed it, her feeble vitality would surely flicker out. So I made up mind to deliver her with high forceps.

Picture the scene — a dark deck cabin with plenty of water about and plenty more spurting in through the chinks at and about the weather-boards of the door. A couple of dim lanterns swung from hooks, and the gloomy interior was resonant with ceaseless thunder of the gale and the creaking of the straining ship . . .

I removed the lee-boards of the patient's bunk, but how was I to get purchase to deliver her while I was standing up and struggling to balance myself to the roll and pitch of the vessel? However, I managed somehow, and got a good steady strain on the forceps. There were worried and uneasy moments. A well-meaning, ample-bosomed, ignorant young woman (it would not be wholly incorrect to call her an experienced virgin), who said she 'was a bit of a nurse', and who told me in a hoarse aside as I pulled, that 'she knew a thing or two, as she 'ad 'ad herself a love-child larst year', assisted me, not inefficiently, while another dame, also of experience in such matters, gave an occasional whiff of chloroform. I finished the labour instrumentally. The child, a little mite of a girl, was taken below to the married quarters, where there were several women with babies at the breast, and mothered by one of them . . .

My poor little fragile patient was in a sad state of collapse, but what could one do under such circumstances? All hands and

Cupping Instruments

the cook, especially the cook, did their best, and the long night wore away.[24]

A reader familiar with the mortality rate for childbirth on emigrant ships, waits now for the loss of mother or child or, more probably, both. But no —

The vomiting ceased and she retained what 'invalid comforts' our stores afforded — and I landed them both alive in Sydney 126 days after leaving Plymouth.

Then something even beyond this:

Some years ago I had the pleasure of getting a letter from the mother ... She and her husband were both well and had prospered moderately, and the child, born in such hard circumstances, had in due season given my patient 'two grandchildren', which she said, 'were the joy of her life'.

Dr Skirving was twenty-four on the *Ellora*. It is not surprising that he was an ornament to his profession until his death at ninety-seven in 1956.

For a conscientious surgeon there was little respite, especially if there was an outbreak of children's diseases. Dr Thomas Wilmot, of the *Irene*, bound from Liverpool to Sydney in 1852, diagnosed measles on the first day out. By the end of the voyage, despite his endeavours, thirty children had died — an average of one every three days. As well, he lost four adults. He never flagged in ensuring that the emigrants exercised, got plenty of fresh air and were kept clean. In addition he carried out all burials and christenings. He well deserved the emigrants' vote of thanks to him.[25]

Bad though loss of lives on the *Irene* had been, it was by no means among the worst ships. The worst were the overloaded three-deckers used during the gold rush to move large numbers of emigrants to Melbourne. Because the rush of so many men to the goldfields had resulted in a disastrous shortage of labour, restrictions on family emigration were eased. Until 1852 there had been limits on the numbers of children accepted for emigration: a couple could not receive an assisted passage if they had more than three children under ten years of age and two under seven. In the belief that a family man was less likely to go to the diggings than a single man, these restrictions were removed. Numerically the removal did in fact have the desired effect: many more couples with young children sought to emigrate. But the demand for ships occasioned by the rush, led shipping firms to raise their charter rates. The government responded by selecting the lowest tenderers — those with double-decker ships. On the Atlantic double-deckers had carried emigrants with less loss of life than smaller ships, but on the long run to Australia there was a tragic reversal.

To his report for the year 1852 the Victorian health officer appended damning figures:

Ticonderoga	811 passengers	96 deaths on arrival
Marco Polo	888 passengers	53 deaths on arrival
Wantana	796 passengers	39 deaths on arrival
Bourneuf	754 passengers	84 deaths on arrival

In the body of the report he wrote:

... the impulse given by the Gold Discovery and Assisted Immi-

Burial at sea of a crew member of the *Loch Tay*. A Union Jack usually covered the canvas-wrapped body during the brief service. Crew members most frequently died as a result of falls from aloft. Their belongings were quickly auctioned.

gration has been very great, no less than forty-two ships, conveying in all 15,477 souls, having cast anchor in our [Victorian] waters in 1852. Of these Immigrants, 5007 were adult males and 5345 adult feamels, the remaining 5125 being children.

I regret to state the number of deaths which occurred on the voyage amounted to 849, forming a large percentage of the whole. This result I attribute, in great measure, to the practice recently adopted of embarking large numbers of from 600 to 800 people on board two-decked ships, as it will be seen that in only four ships, *Bourneuf, Marco Polo, Wantana* and *Ticonderoga,* the united deaths amounted to no less than 356.*

It is gratifying to remark, however, that during the current year, and since Her Majesty's Colonial Land and Emigration Commissioners have abandoned this pernicious system, and refrained from sending out more than 350 souls in vessels of moderate size, the per centage of mortality has very much decreased ... I consider vessels of 700 to 900 tons burthen are those best adapted for the purpose, with a view to the preservation of the health and discipline of the Immigrants ...[26]

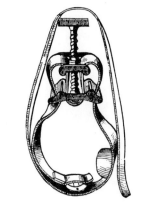

Tourniquet (Petit's spiral)

The Health Officer's report showed that the change of policy had reduced the death rate for arrivals in Victoria to 541. It was considerable improvement, even so, one in five of those under the age of twelve months perished, and one in thirteen of those between twelve months and fourteen years.

By far the heaviest losses occurred among assisted emigrants. This was so for two reasons: firstly, they brought with them many more young children than did independent emigrants; secondly, the colonial governments primarily assisted people of low-income brackets who tended to have scant knowledge of hygiene and strongly resisted attention by the surgeon either to themselves or their sick children. Scores of them might have been saved had it been acceptable to apply to free people some of the discipline that ensured cleanliness on convict transports.

Major J. H. Welch, in his *Hell to Health*, stresses 'the insurmountable objection of the Irish and Scottish parents to any form of medical treatment for their children'.[27] The *Marco Polo*, sailing under government charter in 1852, carried among her 811 passengers, 661 Highland Scots, most of them travelling in families. When she reached Melbourne sixty-eight days later — an extraordinary reduction of time — the newspapers were so excited by her passage that they gave little attention to loss of life on board. After extolling the hard-driving 'Bully' Forbes, the Melbourne *Argus* of 21 September merely added: 'Fifty-three deaths occurred on board, out of which there are only two adults.'

---

*Included in this figure are those who died in quarantine.

Forbes himself remarked that births had balanced out the deaths. At the emigration depot at Birkenhead the children of one family had been obliged to sleep in a bed vacated that morning by children suffering from measles. Measles subsequently broke out on the *Marco Polo* and spread rapidly, probably exacerbated by lack of co-operation on the part of the parents. The ship had been grossly overloaded, even a five-foot high section of the upper deck being used as accommodation.

The *Ticonderoga*, worst of the Australian 'plague ships', was carrying a preponderance of Highland Scots. Her ninety-six dead on arrival were increased by eighty who died in the hastily established quarantine station at Point Nepean. When she entered Port Phillip flying the yellow flag, those who boarded her were confronted by an appalling scene.

The ship, especially the lower part was in a most filthy state, and did not appear to have been cleaned for weeks, the stench was over-powering, the lockers so thoughtlessly provided for the Immigrants use were full of dirt, mouldy bread, and suet full of maggots, beneath the bottom boards of nearly every berth upon the lower deck were discovered soup and bouille cans and other receptacles full of putrid ordure, and porter bottles etc., filled with stale urine, while maggots were seen crawling underneath the berths, and this state of things must have been prevalent for a long time as the 2nd Mate describes the ship to have been in the same state when he supervised the cleaning of her by the Captain's order five weeks previously.[28]

Major Welch wrote of this voyage:

It appears that from the commencement of the sickness, the majority of those on board were so prostrated and miserable that all feelings of decency, propriety, and self-preservation were abandoned. This was in spite of great efforts by the various ship's officers who were indefatigable, yet powerless to cope with such states of mind.[29]

It was later stated that Captain Boyle, master of the *Ticonderoga*, was the only person on board not attacked by typhus. Boyle was commended highly by Lieutenant-Governor La Trobe:

... Had it not been for his personal exertion, firmness, and self possession, it may really be doubted whether the unfortunate vessel which toward the close of the voyage became little more than a floating pest house, would ever have reached its destination . . .[30]

Twelve years after the losses on the *Ticonderoga*, the Victorian government proposed closing the quarantine station at Point Nepean and using instead a hulk in Hobsons Bay. This drew swift and effective attack from the Chief Medical Officer, Dr W. McCrea. After pointing out the non-infectious nature of typhus 'in these climates' if those who contracted it were kept in the fresh air, he added:

> I have had sixteen years' experience in the British navy, in the cleanest and best regulated ships in the world, and if there is one thing more than another deeply impressed on my conviction, it is that a ship or hulk is the very worst place in which three or four hundred passengers could be placed for such a purpose . . .[31]

Terrible though the case of the *Ticonderoga* was, one's mind reels before the prospect confronting the Canadian authorities at Grosse Isle, in the St Lawrence. The hospital at the quarantine station there had accommodation in 1847 for 200 patients; an estimated 20,000 descended on the place. All the staff were ill or exhausted; there were scarcely enough people to bury the thousands of dead.[32] All in all, Australia's suffering was light, though fearful for many afflicted families.

Official reports of illness at sea make melancholy reading today. Had there been as many diarists among steerage passengers as there were among those travelling cabin or intermediate, one can imagine the poignancy of their stories, especially those who travelled on the three-decker ships of 1852. There exist revealing diary entries from less notorious voyages. Mrs Thomas Hinshelwood wrote on 16 June 1883:

> I was awakened this morning by a poor woman laying her trembling hand on my shoulder saying 'will you come M'am, my baby is dead'. I went with her and prepared the little one for its watery grave. She bore up bravely but broke down terribly after the funeral; that makes two within twenty-four hours.

And Jessie Campbell, going to New Zealand in 1840, writing of her dying child:

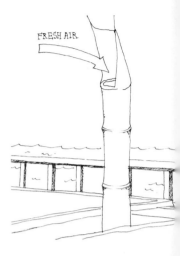

The windsail. Used both at sea and in gold mines, the windsail directed air to places where ventilation was poor. This, in ships, was usually the orlop deck, which was too close to the waterline for scuttles to be opened in any but the calmest seas.

Dear little lamb she likes so much to have me beside her in bed, even during the day. She gives me her little hand to hold or sometimes puts it across my neck ... [The child died a week later.] ... she resigned her breath as quietly as if she were going to sleep without the slightest struggle. What would I give to be on shore with her dear little body, the idea of committing it to the deep distresses me very much.[33]

Sarah Allingham, bound for Melbourne on the *Marco Polo* in 1855, wrote of a newly born infant dying through being 'overlaid' in a shared bunk. 'The dear little thing was thrown over without ceremony after it was dark.'[34]

When young men kept diaries, their entries on the personal tragedies about them tended to be laconic. Thomas Small, irrepressible Scottish bootmaker, made entries on successive days in 1863:

5/6 One poor girl who was a little weak in the mind when we left Liverpool has turned fair mad. They have got a straight jacket for her and a wooden box shaped like a coffin with a hole in the lid to allow her head to get out.

6/6 A child died at 8 o'c. & the father passed us with the little corpse in his arms going to put it out at one of the portholes on the quiet.

The father's forlorn action was, of course, irregular, but seems less heartless than the official treatment of a suicide:

The passenger who was ill committed suicide by cutting his throat, was committed to the deep in an hour afterwards without any prayers, this event gave rise to reflections not of the most pleasant nature.[35]

The twenty-one-year-old Arthur Manning, bound for Sydney in 1839-40 recorded in tragi-comic terms the death of a Miss Waugh. At her parents' wish the girl's body had been placed in a coffin rather than sewn in canvas.

While we were at tea we were startled by a report that Miss Waugh was quite warm, and therefore could not be dead! She was immediately taken out of the coffin, and the doctors were sent for. They soon discovered that there was not the slightest life in the body; so she was nailed down ...

Although Miss Waugh proved to be dead, one wonders how often mistakes were made. Take the evidence of Otto Sutor, given at the 1858 inquiry into emigration from Germany.

Thirty-four persons died on board the ship with typhus fever. I, being the only person who spoke English on board, attended every morning, in Hobart Town, where a number was taken to hospital, — to go with the physician to hear their complaints. He attended so little to his duty that one old woman was actually being sewn up in canvas to be thrown overboard who turned out to be still alive.

Had the medical man not made any examination in that case?

He never visited her. The same afternoon the woman really died.

Do you state that they were actually sewing her up?

Yes, and she opened her eyes and asked what they wanted with her ... I spoke to the physician afterwards; we were rather vexed about it, because so many died that we thought there might have been some others who had not actually been dead when thrown overboard.[36]

In this case the German physician was qualified!

Given the standards of the day, the record of health on the long run to Australia was relatively high. It is a record that obviously owed much to experience gained in the transportation of convicts and to the continuance of government surveillance. For all that, a passage wholly safe for infants was to remain beyond the reach of nineteenth-century medicine and travelling conditions.

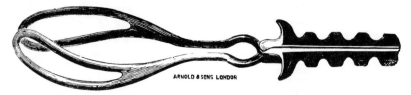

Midwifery forceps (Anderson's)

Surgeons-superintendent were just as responsible as ships' masters for bringing emigrants safely to the new land. Overall their most important function was to be champion and protector of their charges, to care for the weak and to discipline those who were troublesome to others, to demand the best possible diet and treatment from masters. They needed as much skill in human relations as they did in medicine. Undoubtedly there were many unworthy surgeons, but perusal of more than a hundred emigrant diaries suggests that most of the men appointed to the task were conscientious and humane. Most voyages would have been intolerable without their arbitration, and losses of life would have been very much higher without their devotion.

10 *Messing and Dining*

Some hae meat, and canna eat,
And some wad eat that want it —
From the 'Selkirk Grace'

Nothing led more surely to discontent at sea than poor rations, or rations poorly prepared. And yet, even when there was every cause for complaint, some emigrants from impoverished homes found themselves faring better than they had ever done before.

Until the great exodus of families began after the Napoleonic Wars, the only human cargoes transported in large numbers over long distances had been soldiers, slaves and convicts. The dietary scale of soldiers and sailors led to the dietary scale of convicts transported to Australia. Charles Bateson wrote of convict messing: 'From the outset the scale of rations was based on the allowance in the Royal Navy, the convicts receiving two-thirds the naval ration'.[1] He went on to list the ration for each mess of six men. It is worth looking at both the convict rations and their messing system, for emigration based much on transportation: 'by 1812 each mess received (weekly) 20lb.of bread, 12lb. of flour, 16lb. of beef, 6lb. of butter, 8oz. of rice, 1½lb of suet, 3lb. of raisins, 6 pints of oatmeal, and 4oz. of sugar.' To this was added pea soup four times a week and gruel with sugar or butter in it each morning. Bateson commented that 'the provisions furnished for the convicts were no worse, and probably better, than those aboard most men-of-war, and certainly were superior, in quan-

Steerage passengers at their table. The two mess captains have brought in a rare treat — buns, to be enjoyed with a cup of tea. Had a full meal been served, the outcome would have been considerably worse. Rough seas could continue for days, sometimes weeks.

193

tity as well as quality, to those on many of the early emigrant ships'. He is referring here to emigrants travelling steerage — as the vast majority did. Cabin passengers were provided for on a very much better scale, as shall be seen later.[2]

Although the dietary scale was precisely laid down for emigrants and was improved over the years, the quality of rations for all classes varied considerably from ship to ship.

A mess form was issued to each adult government emigrant; thus he knew his rights — at least, as far as quantities were concerned. But between his rights and his mouth were various obstacles: the rapacity of some provisioning firms and shipowners — some ships supposedly provisioned for the entire voyage were in fact forced into intermediate ports for additional supplies; the filching of supplies by unscrupulous officers at sea, either for their own consumption, or for future sale; the inexperience of some emigrants — especially among the single men — in preparing dishes; the frequent crankiness of the cooks whose job it was to cook what was taken to them. As for the 'biscuits', which figure so largely in the dietary and in emigrants' complaints, these were 'four inches square and at least an inch thick. They were baked very hard, presumably as a way of preserving them, and that made it impossible to bite them.'[3]

On convict transports mismanagement, dishonesty and poor preparation of dishes could be dealt with more effectively than on emigrant ships. Bateson has it that on the transports:

> The surgeon-superintendent was made solely responsible for the rations. He had to see that each convict received his due share, without any deduction, that the food was properly cooked, and that it was served at the appointed meal hours . . . Every cask of provisions was to be opened on deck in his presence, and, having noted the state, mark, number and contents of each cask in his journal, he was to see the beef and pork placed in the padlocked harness casks [A cask holding food for immediate use].[4]

It is evident from emigrant diaries that well-intended safeguards of a similar nature often failed, even on government-chartered ships; on the other hand, most emigrants had one distinct advantage over convicts in messing: they were able to bring supplementary provisions with them from home, indeed, shipping companies reckoned on them doing so. Preserved eggs were brought, ham, pickles, sugar, jams, and much else besides. There was exchange of these additional foodstuffs and, all in all, private supplies made steerage fare endurable

Scale of victualling. Although this was a better dietary scale than many steerage passengers were accustomed to at home, the Scots preferred a greater ration of oatmeal and many of the Irish were not familiar with tea. Mess captains had to watch the issuing officer carefully in case he held back the full measure of their supplies.

A PROPOSED SCALE OF VICTUALLING AT SEA.

PER MAN.

PER MAN FOR	BEEF.	PORK.	FLOUR.	SUET.	PLUMS.	POTATOES.	RICE.	PEAS.			COFFEE, COCOA, OR CHOCOLATE	TEA.	SUGAR.	MUSTARD.	VINEGAR.
	lb	lb	lb	oz.	oz.	lb	lb	Pint.			Morning.	Evening			
MONDAY	...	1½	...	...	...	...	...	¼			1 oz. per Man daily.	¼ oz. per Man daily.	1 lb per Man weekly.	¼ oz. per Man weekly.	½ Pint per Man weekly.
TUESDAY	1½	...	...	...	...	...	½	...							
WEDNESDAY	...	1½	...	...	...	...	...	¼							
THURSDAY	1½	...	½	1	...	...	...	...							
FRIDAY	...	1½	...	...	...	...	½	...							
SATURDAY	1½	...	...	...	...	...	...	¼							
SUNDAY	1½	...	½	1	1½	...	...	...							
Per Week of 7 Days	6	4½	1	2	1½	...	1	¾			lb. 0 oz. 7	oz. 1¾	lb. 1	oz. ¼	Pint. ½
Month of 30 Days	25¾	19¼	4¼	8½	6	...	4¼	3¼			1 14	7½	4¼	1	2
2 Do. of 30 Do.	51½	38½	8½	lb. 1 oz. 1	12	...	8½	6½			3 12	15	8½	2	4
3	77¼	57¾	12¾	1 9½	18	...	12¾	9¾			5 10	22½	12¾	3	6
4	103	77	17	2 2	24	...	17	13			7 8	30	17	4	8
5	128¾	96¼	21¼	2 10½	30	...	21¼	16¼			9 6	37½	21¼	5	10
6	154½	115½	25½	3 3	36	...	25½	19½			11 4	45	25½	6	12
7	180¼	134¾	29¾	3 11½	42	...	29¾	22¾			13 2	52½	29¾	7	14
8	206	154	34	4 4	48	...	34	26			15 0	60	34	8	16
9	231¾	173¼	38¼	4 12½	54	...	38¼	29¼			16 14	67½	38¼	9	18
10	257	192½	42½	5 5	60	...	42½	32½			18 12	75	42½	10	20
11	283¼	211¾	46¾	5 13½	66	...	46¾	35¾			20 10	82½	46¾	11	22
12	309	231	51	6 6	72	...	51	39			22 8	90	51	12	24
15	386¼	288¾	63¾	7 15½	90	...	63¾	48¾			28 2	112½	63¾	15	30
18	463½	346½	76½	9 9	108	...	76½	58½			38	135	76½	18	36
24	618	462	102	12 12	144	...	102	78			45 0	180	102	24	48
36	927	693	153	18 18	216	...	153	117			67 8	270	153	36	72

Bread, as much as they can eat, without Waste, not exceeding 1½ lb each Man, per day.
Water at the rate of One Gallon each Man, per Day.
Each Sailor to provide a Spoon and a Tin Quart Pot.
Mustard and Vinegar to be considered as Extras, and served out in Tropical Climates only.

SUBSTITUTES, IN CASE THEY SHOULD BE FOUND NEEDFUL.

Molasses in lieu of Plums, at a proportionate rate.
1 lb of Po[illegible]atoes or Yams to be considered equal to ½ lb of Flour and Suet, or Peas or Rice.
1¼ lb of Soft Bread, or 1 lb of Rice or Sago, or 1 lb of Flour—equal to 1 lb of Biscuit.
1 lb of Sago, 1 lb of Scotch (Pot or Pearl) Barley, 1 lb of Rice—equal to each other.
1 lb of Rice, or 1 Pint of Culvaranes, or 1 Pint of East India Dholl—equal to 1 Pint of Peas.
1 lb of Rice—equal to 1 Quart of Oatmeal.
1 lb of Butter—equal to 1 lb of Sugar.
2 lb of Cheese—equal to 1 lb of Chocolate or Cocoa.
¼ lb of Onions, or ¼ lb of Leeks—equal to 1 lb of other Vegetables.

At 1½ lb. of Beef or Pork per Day, one Man consumes about one-twelfth of a Tierce of Beef, and one-tenth of a Barrel of Pork per Month.

By the Act 7 & 8 VICTORIA, *the Rate of Provisions must be fixed by Agreement.*—It is now imperative that, in cases of all Vessels of the Burthen of 80 Tons and upwards, the Quantity of Provisions to be served out to each Man during the Voyage, shall be fixed by Agreement between the Master and Seamen; but a **daily supply of Lime Juice** and **Sugar is indispensable**—(*See Act.*)

London:—Published and sold by C. WILSON, at the Navigation Warehouse and Naval Academy, No. 157, Leadenhall Street—1847.

for the average emigrant. Those unfortunates who lacked supplementary supplies faced a hungry voyage; usually they were people who had suffered hunger for much of their lives, consequently they did not complain to the degree one might expect. As these were likely to be the same people whose clothing was inadequate for the climatic extremes of the voyage, it is little wonder they often suffered excesses of misery.

Of course, storage of supplementary foodstuffs in cramped steerage quarters was a constant problem. An entry in Samuel Shaw's diary illustrates the hazard it imposed in rough seas:

> The ship rolled very much all night. About five tins of molasses were placed on the side of the ship above the beds, and through the night they spilled on top of the beds. One fellow got it all over his head, but he never woke up until morning, when you may guess he was ready for a wash.

The term 'mess', in the sense of 'a company of persons eating together', goes back to the fifteenth century. In later times it was used when troops were being transported overseas: the men were formed into 'messes' because there was insufficient room for each soldier to draw and prepare his own rations individually. By the time of the convict transports, Bateson relates that each group of prisoners messing together, elected their own 'mess captain'. 'Besides drawing the ration, he was responsible for the maintenance of tidiness and for the orderly conduct of his messmates.'

As a convenient means of feeding large numbers of people at sea, it had much to commend it over the free-for-all that so often prevailed on the Atlantic, where weak or seasick emigrants often starved because they were unable to fend for themselves among those physically stronger. Sizes of messes varied.

> Owing to the various sizes of families, and the mixture of children of different ages, it is impossible to fix the same number for every mess.

Thus the emigration commissioners in 1838.[5] They set the most desirable number as six adults, or the equivalent of six if children of various ages were included; twelve was regarded as the maximum. But messes were not limited to family units; often they consisted of groups of friends from the same neighbourhood, the same church, the same factory. In the single men's and the single women's quarters individuals were less likely to know each other and mess members might begin the voyage as complete strangers.

Each mess elected its own captain, much as convicts did, but single women were not permitted near the galley — and so into the company of men. Taking prepared dishes to be cooked was a man's job. In the married quarters each male took his turn as mess captain, but occasionally one person would accept the task for a long period on payment of a small fee by the other members. A prolonged period as mess captain could prove a sore trial. F. W. Leighton resigned from it with relief:

It is a task of no honor and very great difficulties from the various tempers you have to please.

The mess captain's function of collecting and distributing food was well described by E. Cuzens, who, as a boy of ten, travelled out with his family on Dr Dunmore Lang's *Travancore*. The Cuzens' mess consisted entirely of members of their own family:

The rations were served out once a week, and meat twice a week, by the Chief Officer. At this function the family was not a name but a number. In the mate's book was entered the quantity of each article to be supplied, and when the number was called out some representative of the family was expected to step forward and take what was coming to them. In the case of meat the following plan was adopted: the casks in which the meat was packed were about the size of ordinary beer hogsheads, and the head being removed the officer arrived with a long three pronged fork and brought up a joint of meat. Each piece was bound with string or wire in which was attached a metal disc about the size of a postage stamp on which was impressed a number and the weight in pounds and ounces. If the joint was too large or too small for family No. 1 the mate would cast his eye over the list until he found the family it would suit, and handed it over to them, impressing on everybody the necessity of remembering the number of their joint so as to claim it again from the cook at dinner time. This was repeated until all were supplied, frequently the first being last and the last first. The next step was to carry the meat to the galley which was presided over by a big negro who threw them altogether into the boiler and left them to stew till dinner time. At about half past twelve forty or fifty people assembled at the galley, each with a tin dish for their dinner meat, when the Cook also arrived with a big three pronged fork thrust into the boiling mass and brought out a joint, called out the number on the disc, which was quickly claimed, and so on until the boiler was empty.[6]

Antoine Fauchery found this one of the most entertaining times of the day. The cook he watched on the *Emily* was not one of the usual negroes:

He is an ex-caulker with little, pointed eyes, broad shoulders, hands black with tar. To pay his passage to Australia, the most difficult and dirty work has been imposed on him. Well, he is

The galley was usually on the main deck. In very rough weather it was not uncommon for the fire to be put out by the sea. A high proportion of cooks were Blacks.

no less cheerful for that; he is always laughing heartily, with a laugh that goes from ear to ear. He is obliging, active, always on the go, and sweats fat and resin through every pore. To say that he takes meticulous care in the execution of his work would be to credit him with secondary qualities for which he does not give a fig; — it is not his job to cook. — And so we sometimes find in our *aliments* a knife-handle, the lid of a snuff-box, a waist-coat button; but after all, what does that matter? For those whose delicate stomachs refuse to digest hard substances it is sufficient not to muse too much as they eat ... As for bits of rope, bits of thread, everything that goes with the material of navigation, good Lord! all that is general, universal, its everywhere, and we cannot but find a little of it on our plates every day! Never mind, we shall not worry our cook over such trifles.[7]

John MacKenzie, a cabin passenger, sometimes amused himself by watching the steerage messes from the vantage point of the poop deck:

... there is never-ending cooking going on and a rush to the galley each for their own ... like so many dogs in a kennel let out to get food. I have a fine view of them from the poop, all spread over the deck and divided into messes, tearing away at Stirabout, Port or Soup and Bouillie, interspersed with children at every group whining to get shares of whats not good for them. While some are picking their scraps from the galley among the rest ...[8]

Another cabin passenger, Edward Stamp, was one day watching the steerage passengers when he saw 'a Scotch woman combing her hair in a Tin dish in which she had just eaten her dinner from'. The sight led him to erupt into doggerel:

> For what purpose I cannot say,
> But such gigantic crawling prey;
> In numbers fell, from out their Lay
> And came spilling into the Tray.

His disgust then outstripped all rhyme and rhythm:

> From Scotland this person came

> It seems the custom of the claim
> Dirty, filthy, wretched creatures
> Worse than all countries put together.[9]

Diaries abound with descriptions of dishes prepared by steerage passengers — some results comic, some pathetic, others showing the ingenuity of some passengers and the helplessness of others. In the married quarters the task of preparation fell mainly to the wives. The greatest range of botched dishes was undoubtedly produced by the single men. One wrote to his mother soon after his arrival:

> You would have been quite amused to see us make pies, puddings and cakes. I asked an Irishman who had just put some dough in a tin to be baked whether he had greased the tin, he said no. I replied You must do so or the cake will stick; and believe me the fellow actually greased the outside instead of the inside, in perfect ignorance, there's a specimen of Erin's Sons.[10]

The young Irishmen, so many of whom had subsisted on a potato diet at home, were probably the most confused of all the bachelors; few were even acquainted with tea — Terry Coleman, in *Passage to America*, mentions that some put it in their pipes and smoked it! Thomas Small was one of a youthful group of Scots who formed a mess with some Irishmen:

> ... Had a splendid dinner cooked of potatoes & beef, & lo' when we sat down to eat it we could not & the reason is this: — some of our Irish friends had been getting their hair cut, & whether they had thrown or put some of the cuttings in the dish I could not say, but, however, it spoiled our dinner & nearly spoiled his head that had got his hair cut as the dish was in the hands of James Logan to throw about him.

Among the single men travelling second class on the *Bolton*, Edward Snell found some who considered themselves above preparing their own meals. 'Many of the "gentlemen" are too lazy to cook their rations, they live on what they can cadge from other messes at meal times.' One mess, he said, had prepared a pudding which proceeded to run like soup all over the oilcloth table cover; what was left was pitched overboard.

Haircutting. This was carried out either by a friend possessing scissors or by a shipmate seeking to make a little money. Short hair gave men some protection against lice; the women's hair, on the other hand, made fine coverts for these 'little brothers of the poor and dirty'. (An illustration by Edward Snell from his diary.)

Fauchery seems to have been one of the few people not dispirited by the quality of food — either that, or his irony was intended for his Parisian friends:

Each week our provisions allow us, and more than allow us, to have three or four meals a day if we see fit. In the morning, salted beef with dried potatoes; at noon, salt pork with rice; at two o'clock, dried potatoes with salted beef; at four, rice with salt pork. — Lord bless you, if we wanted it, we could at eight o'clock have both salted beef with potatoes and salt pork with rice! — Ah, it is not quantity that is lacking; there is on board enough salted food for two years.[11]

Emigrants were distinctly better off for food in the earlier years, when calls were made at intermediate ports. At that time surgeons were given an express instruction to obtain fresh food:

While in port, and for one or two days afterwards, if practicable, one pound of fresh meat, one pound of soft bread, and one pound of potatoes per adult are issued with a suitable supply of vegetables, in lieu of the salt and preserved meat, and of the flour, suet, raisins, rice, and peas.[12]

In those leisurely early days a ship might call at the Canary Islands, or the Cape Verde group, or even at Rio de Janeiro, or, at the other extreme of longitude, Tristan da Cunha. Masters of ships not under charter to the government had comparative freedom in determining their calls, provided, of course, they abided by company directions. In 1839 Anne Drysdale wrote of a decision by the master of the *Indus* to call at 'Port Praya' [Port Praia in the Cape Verde Islands] — at least, 'the captain *thought*' this to be the port they were approaching. His assumption proved correct and they left with an abundance of fresh food.

Turkeys, fowls, pigs, sheep, oranges, Bananas, Pumpkins and Pineapples. The cabin is all hung around with oranges, besides each passenger having their private stores, being in their own berths.

But it was, of course, the cabin passengers who could afford to buy freely — and they were the ones in least need of an improved diet.

After the gold rush, government-chartered ships bound for Eastern Australia had to carry sufficient provisions for a non-stop voyage of 140 days.[13] All reputable ships, chartered or not, abided by this, but there were some which ran so low in food that they were forced to run for a port. Few, though, can have matched the *Norway*, which, in 1853, was obliged to send her boats for food to the island of Bravo, in the Cape Verde group; had then to call at Simonstown for both repairs and food, and finally was again short of food in Australian waters. She was fortunately only carrying ten adults, six of them couples with children. Among the single men was twenty-three-year-old Henry Nicholls,* a lively journalist, who took part in the hair-raising landing on Bravo in a leaking boat. Nearing Australia he wrote:

We are now without sugar, butter, suet and almost without treacle, only having about half a pint each. We are in training, like a well-known horse, to live on nothing. We shall not want many luxuries in Australia . . .[14]

The Dives and Lazarus contrast in foodstuffs on most ships inevitably led to pilfering. If steerage passengers were caught, they could expect little mercy. Arthur Manning, a cabin-class gentleman of twenty-one, wrote indignantly:

. . . a woman was tried, and found guilty of stealing bread out of the oven. The bread was the property of the Cabin passengers, who had no idea of letting the *fair culprit*! get fat upon *their* scanty allowance, and therefore sentenced her to three days solitary confinement on biscuit and water! There is a kind of prison built between decks, where we confine offenders. We have given it the name of 'Coldbath Gaol', from its being in such a position that when any sea comes over the ship it *must* wet the 'Sinner in quod' and cool him by a lotion to his head.

---

*Henry Nicholls, born in London in 1830, was involved in radical journalism before he left for Australia. In Melbourne he became editor of the short-lived *Diggers' Advocate* and was soon afterwards a leading gold-fields radical. Following Eureka he was one of the members of the Local Court set up in Ballarat to deal with mining cases. In 1860 he was largely responsible for far-reaching revision to mining regulations. A leading reporter on the *Ballarat Star* for twenty-five years, he joined the Hobart *Mercury* in 1883 as editor, a position he held for thirty-nine years until his death in 1912.

Live provisions for first-class passengers being taken on board the *Indus*. Pigs travelled better than sheep and the crew tended to make pets of them, usually dubbing them 'Dennis'.

(Manning was writing in 1839. Trial of steerage passengers by their betters still sometimes occurred years later and even on government-sponsored ships. Edwin Bird, in his *Marco Polo* diary of 1853, tells of the 'Court Martial' of an Irishman — in this case for threatening the mate: 'We found him guilty was sentenced to 9 days in Irons and kept on Bread and Water . . .'[15]

Manning wrote of the 'scanty allowance' afforded cabin passengers. How did they, in fact, fare? Of course standards varied greatly (discussed in chapter 7), but cabin passengers, who sat at the captain's table generally had no need for private provisions. On the *Eagle*, in 1853, for example, the first cabin was 'provided with three stewards and a stewardess, who attend on the passengers exclusively; and they are provided with fresh provisions daily'.[16]

Meat, milk and eggs were generally provided fresh at the captain's table. The head of livestock carried was astonishing — the *Sobraon* had on board three cows, ninety sheep, fifty large hogs, a number of sucking pigs and between 300 and 400 fowls, ducks and geese. Usually a goat or two were carried as well — they proved good sailors and could even consume the carpenter's shavings.

Mr Tait, passenger on the *North Briton*, bound for Sydney in 1837-8, gave as good a description as any of the ship's ark:

On either side of the poop extends a double row of hencoops full of chattering fowls which emit rather a disagreeable effluvia but sometimes supply [us] with fresh eggs and often with fresh meat ... Beyond the main mast on the steerage side are two large rowing boats the one turned upside down on the other and the lowest being raised up a little from the deck by supports. In the lowest boat there is a level board put in so as to form accommodation for 8 sheep which are fed on hay and corn, and have been reduced to two since we left. Before preserved milk was introduced they took out a cow in this apartment. Under the lower boat is a pig sty with 10 or 12 little pigs which are fed on the refuse of our kitchen and occasionally supply us with fine fresh pork. In this part of the vessel there is rather a disagreeable odour, but as the deck is frequently washed, we feel little annoyed by it.[17]

One can imagine the scene had these boats been needed for their proper use!

For description of cabin fare we can turn to the diary of an unidentified passenger of 1842:

People ... load their stomachs with the most incongruous mixtures. At dinner, for instance, after rich pork they will take roast duck with boiled ham, currant jelly and perhaps pickles, with boiled fowl, currant jelly and caper sauce: or roast mutton with tongue and pickles, plum jam; to say nothing of several sorts of vegetables, etc. .... Rich tart or plum pudding, often a plate full of both, follow these simples, which just leave a corner in the stomach for a piece of new bread and strong cheese, thus preparing a foundation for rather a larger plate full of almonds and raisins or another desert ...

The diarist declared that such a dinner would probably have been preceded by a 9 o'clock breakfast:

consisting of something like a pound of rich salmon immersed in butter, ham, five hot rolls, a plateful or two of boiled rice smothered with marmalade; to say nothing of a slight noontide refection of bread and cheese, Brandy, Port wine and porter

... It is not really surprising that people feel queerish at sea when several weeks have passed on the water.[18]

For many the rich cabin-class diet palled after a few weeks. Several requested a switch to salt beef for dinner, since they were 'tired of fowls and ducks', but they soon found the beef to be 'horribly hard and salt'.

John MacKenzie, who likened steerage passengers at meal times to 'so many dogs in a kennel let out to get food', wrote of his own fare:

Breakfast is substantial, always cold meat — fish — a ham rasher — with potatoes, eggs, coffee (without cream) ... Dinner ... always soup, and different sorts [on] alternate days ... corned beef and sometimes pork also, vegetables, potato biscuit, sometimes a pudding and never without cheese. Port or Sherry Wine always at dinner ale to choose, and if required brandy in any way you like ... Tea at 6 o'clock has always a dish of meat for those who like ... biscuits and tea (without cream)

It would falsify the picture of cabin standards to exclude some less attractive descriptions — one of E. Lloyd's, for example, telling of poultry dishes:

Our fowls, reduced in number to some dozen and a half, and in person to skin and bone, were pent up in their narrow coops till they trod one another down. As they fought and struggled for their pittance of daily bread, some one poor creature would every day sink under the pressure of its misfortunes, crouch down in the bottom of the coop, and allow the stronger ones to trample it down under foot in their scramble to the trough, as if all desire were gone and life and death a matter of indifference. It is needless to say that these objects of pity fell under the hands of the cook just before they yielded up the tribute of nature, and paid a diurnal visit to the dinner table; where, as the knife attempted to sever their joints, they fell almost spontaneously apart ...[19]

And here is Robert Corkhill, travelling cabin on the *British Trident*:

I have frequently seen pigs and sheep which died of disease (I believe a great proportion died in this way) doped up by the butchers and sent to the cook and ultimately found the way to the saloon cabin dining table as *fresh pork & mutton.*

Cabin passengers on the *Asiatic* must have retained nauseating memories of a turkey dinner:

After prayers come dinner, as the Cabin passengers sit down to that meal, it is discovered that the Butcher dressed the Turkey without having taken out the entrails, it is discovered by the Captain while helping a lady to some of the stuffing — queer Stuff — the dish is taken off the table, and sent forward, and the inside taken out, and the precious morsel is sent back to the Cabin on the Principle I suppose of better eat late than never. The said entrails are put aside for the Butcher to eat and accordingly after the Captain has dined, he is as good as his word with the Butcher, and sends for him, and the entrails, and actually forces the bones and the offensive parts into the poor devils mouth. I am in common with many of the people in the ship surprised at the Captains conduct, particularly after reading prayers in the morng.[20]

Although the livestock was carried for the use of cabin passengers, other classes were permitted on some ships to buy a little meat. William Deakin, father of Alfred, Prime Minister of Australia, did so on his passage to Adelaide in 1849-50 after wearying of the other fare available:

The potted meat called Bouille is wretched. We cannot eat it at all and the beef we can do nothing with, consequently if we had brought nothing with us we should fare but badly. A considerable portion of the Bouille was in a putrid state, and I should say made from the flesh of diseased animals and those which died from natural causes. Our sheep are now getting poor, and I can now and then get a chop for a change for 9d. 1 lb.[21]

Mishaps to stock occurred on numerous voyages, but none can have been more extraordinary than the fate of one of the *Marco Polo*'s cows:

If the weather were fine and mild, steerage passengers ate their meals wherever they could on the cluttered main deck.

[She] had not been attended properly and had been left to roll about with the ship, consequently the thin partition of her house gave way, which is just above the hatchway into the 2nd and 3rd cabins. She fell first through an incredibly small place into the 2nd intermediate which, of course, broke her fall. She then fell from there into the 3rd Cabin. You cannot imagine the awful fright it gave some of us. I thought the ship had struck a rock and the bottom stove in, others thought the ship was on fire but thanks to the Father of all our Mercies neither of these things had happened ... Was surprised to find in the morning that although the cow had fallen through an aperture of only 18 ins. yet the poor animal was not either killed nor were any bones broken although she groaned very much. She is still in the 3rd Cabin and I suppose will continue now until the end of the voyage.

The diarist was Sarah Allingham. Although she referred no more to the cow, her descendants understood that the unfortunate animal had to be left among the passengers for the remainder of the voyage. As they suffered the complications of her company, it is to be hoped that '3rd Cabin' rather than '1st Cabin' received the benefit of her milk.

While there were great differences throughout the era of emigration by sail in the quality of food served to cabin class and steerage passengers, this did not always apply to the quality of water. Water was always a problem. Even on the strictly controlled convict transports, it was drawn from rivers not far upstream from the crowded English ports. Bateson says that it was often foul before Cape Town was reached — [It became] 'very offensive in smell as well as taste and deposit[ed] a copious, dark, peatlike sediment on the bottom of the cask. Thames water was so unreliable that many masters and surgeons preferred to call at Teneriffe to complete their water.'[22]

The surgeon-superintendent of an emigrant ship in 1839, on removing the bung of a water barrel, was able to ignite the escaping gases.

[They] went off with a tremendous flash and report. All water, after being at sea a length of time, decomposes and forms gas; but if that be permitted to escape, and the free circulation of pure air act upon it, it becomes speedily purified.[23]

Water was supposed to be filtered before being taken on board, filtering being carried out with a colander-like device which allowed droplets to fall for a distance through the air. Either the equipment was not always used, or it was inadequate for the purpose, or perhaps the water was beyond this rather crude means of purification. Curiously, filtration by these means came into use much after the introduction of distillation of sea water; in fact, a distillation process was submitted to the Dutch East India Company as early as 1624 and the Royal Navy began distilling fresh water from sea water in 1776.[24] It has already been mentioned that numerous emigrant ships carried distilling equipment, but, even when it was working properly, it failed to provide water in sufficient quantities and complaints about the drinking water were made throughout the entire period of sail. One finds emigrants regularly using lime juice and other additives to render it palatable.

On ships making the direct voyage to Australia, very large water tanks were carried — those on the *Matilda Wattenbach* held 700 gallons — so there was little prospect of relief if this supply was tainted.

Cabin passengers did not, of course, wash their own dishes or, for that matter, their own clothes. Steerage passengers washed both in salt water, consequently a downpour of rain brought them streaming onto deck with tubs and dishes. Although the water had a flavour of old canvas from the sails, it was much to be preferred to the ship's water even for drinking.

Despite the state of the water, the emigrants seldom thought of foregoing their mugs of tea or coffee. Antoine Fauchery watched the steerage rush for tea water with Gallic amusement:

Hot water! cries the cook from the depths of a little sentry-box erected in the middle of the deck, between the mainmast and the mizzen-mast; inside it there burns incessantly one of those enormous cast-iron stoves invented in America, which would suffice to serve an army, — provided that the latter did not eat from the menu.

At the cook's call you see gushing forth from fore and aft, through the two companionways between decks, two human waves armed with coffeepots of all shapes and sizes, that fuse into one at the door of the galley. There, they jostle, tread on each other's toes, burn their fingers, form echelons on each other's shoulders; it is worse than a handful of ha'pennies would be, thrown on the roadway to chimney-sweeps. Decidedly, our neighbours across the Channel take things seriously where tea is concerned ... Often I have seen sailors abandon a half-made knot to run for their mugs, and consequently I have wondered whether, in a grave situation, hot water would not take precedence over a desperate manoeuvre! I believe and fear so.[25]

Usually water was collected in a 'hookpot'.

This was something like a tin jug with a lid and holding about 2 quarts. The side opposite the handle was flat and furnished with 2 iron hooks about 2 inches apart, and, if the cook had no hot water, you filled this hookpot with cold water and hung it on the bars of the galley stove until boiled. It often happened that in your hurry the hookpot and hot water were on the lower deck before you — hence arose the saying 'Scaldings below'.[26]

Cabin-class passengers were, of course, served their tea or coffee in the dining saloon, but the plunging ship remained no respecter of classes; its violence fell on cabin and steerage alike. John Ramsay, emigrating cabin class on the *Loch Sunart*, wrote home:

You would get a good laugh if you saw us seated at meals when the ship is rolling and hear us reminding the boys to watch their delf — 'Willie hold on to that plate. John hold that jug, or Janet come to table, sit down and hold your dish, or watch that teapot, or mind that sugar bowl.' Table cloths are rolled up like a stick or rope and laid lengthways from end to end of the table, one at each edge and two at equal spaces between to keep dishes in their places, but for all that we require to keep a sharp look-out and even with all our care an odd dish gets smashed.

Steerage passengers had no stewards to come to their aid. William Johnstone, travelling cabin to Launceston, watched the *Arab*'s steerage passengers staggering up onto the deck with their bowls:

The cry of 'Tea-water!' brought steerage passengers flocking on deck. On this ship, going out to Australia early in 1849, space on the main deck appears to have been very limited. Steps to the poop deck may be seen in the background.

The cook [was] dealing out pea-soup to those of the Emigrants who were well enough to fetch. The heavy seas broke over the side occasionally extinguishing the fire, or pouring into the coppers by way of seasoning the soup. Their salt beef is boiled in seawater or they would have suffered much more from this cause. In endeavouring to walk from the galley to the hatchway with their bowls in their hands, three out of five were thrown down, by which they not only gained a complete ducking, but lost their dinner as well . . .[27]

All of which sounds good entertainment for one viewing it from the dry confines of the poop deck.

Today one wonders why there was not outcry against the inequality of messing conditions, but, once at sea, who could protest to the shipping company? What, then of the master? It is worth hearing Herman Melville: 'A passenger might as well go to law with the Czar of Russia as with a ship's captain.'[28] Nevertheless, many half-starved emigrants did protest to ship's masters. Such an occasion occurred on the *Lightning* while she was under the command of 'Bully' Forbes. William Greenhalgh wrote that a third-class passenger had brought pea soup 'similar to dishwater' to Forbes. When he began complaining, Forbes was 'much annoyed and said he would put the man in irons if ever he took such a liberty again'. But then a whole group of third-class passengers banded together to take up the issue.

They placed their cans in a row when the ship gave a tremendous roll on one side and sent cans of soup and passengers rolling first on one side then the other, all amongst the pea soup [which] spoiled all their clothes [and] caused fine fun and laughter.

Fun anyway, for Greenhalgh and the other cabin-class spectators. Another such case — surprisingly, it occurred on one of Caroline Chisholm's ships — was described by Mark Amos years after the event.

During the voyage a serious mutiny broke out amongst the passengers, owing to the insufficiency of proper food and water; the captain's authority was disputed, and his orders were disobeyed. He then took steps to stop the trouble. The hatches were closed, the sailors armed with cutlasses and muskets, and stationed so as to prevent egress of any person from below. This continued for 24 hours, and only two or three persons were allowed to come on deck at a time. On the second day the ringleaders were discovered, placed in irons, and confined in some

out-of-the-way place for two or three days, by which time peace
was restored. The offending ones were subsequently released
on promising to conform to ship's discipline.[29]

Miserable though these scenes are, they do not reach the depths
of hunger and despair suffered on the Atlantic or on German vessels
bound for Australia. The deplorable accommodation and lack of medical care on the German ships has already been described. Dr C. F.
Eichler, a witness at the 1858 inquiry into German immigration
answered questions on the emigrants' health and diet:

... the people kept up pretty well; they were poor and miserable,
but still they were well; there was not great disease on board
the ship. People can bear a good deal in this way. They eat anything they could get; I know that sometimes, to get something
to eat, the children picked out what was given to the chickens,
frequently.

Was that from sheer hunger?

I should think so. Some of the women, I have been informed,
to get something from the sailors, carried on an improper intercourse with them ...

This evidence was supported by witnesses from two other ships,
one witness being F. J. Lander, formerly director of a school at
Frankfurt-on-Main. The question asked him related to the behaviour
of the young women:

You have said that the intercourse which prevailed with the
women was chiefly on the part of the sailors, and not of the
passengers — do you think that these women were bad characters, and sought for this intercourse?

Want of food drove them to have the communication with the
sailors.

How do you say that?

No one had sufficient, and these girls that lent themselves to
the sailors were supplied with victuals by them so well that they
had abundance, and could give it to others ...

Is there anything else you wish to tell the Committee?

On one occasion we received water in such a state that we

could not use it, and had to be twenty-four hours without any drink. That water was used for tea, coffee, and cooking the food, and we could neither eat the food nor drink the water, and had to fast for twenty-four hours ... A respectable young man who was sick asked the cook for some warm water to make a cup of coffee for himself; when the cook struck him with a piece of iron on the head, which inflicted a large wound — no notice was taken by the captain ...[30]

Poor though the messing of British steerage passengers was, it is fair to remember that conveying large numbers of men, women and children over vast distances was a new field of human endeavour. Since it would have been impossible to carry livestock enough to feed hundreds of people, calls at intermediate ports, rather than obsession with speed, would undoubtedly have brought improvements in messing, but speed was demanded by the emigrants themselves in answer

Soup being dished to steerage passengers on the main deck of an emigrant ship. The impedimenta limiting the deck space include a signal cannon, a cabin trunk and tackle erected at an open hatch.

to the lure of gold — and at least it shortened the period of hardship. Of one thing we can be certain: had the government not set standards of victualling for chartered ships, but left the matter to owners, steerage passengers would have been infinitely worse off than they were.

It is interesting to look closely at the exercise in group co-operation that working in a mess on board ship involved. Six, or eight, or a dozen people took a wide variety of tasks in turn. Most steerage men took their turn at being mess captain, and so received rations for all. This was a position of trust. Even if a man and his family were not by nature trustworthy, they dared not take extra food for themselves, for soon it would be the turn of one of their shipmates to be captain. Married women prepared meals which were shared with other women who, next week, would take their own turn. Both men and women took turns in cleaning the communal table and floor after the mess had eaten together. The married men took in turn the thankless task of cleaning waterclosets; of taking the role of 'constable' to patrol the married quarters at night as a safeguard against fire or theft or anything else untoward. Again and again one reads of an unco-operative member of a mess being pulled into line by his messmates. So the lesson in co-operation went on for anything from three to five months among all who emigrated steerage. And, while it went on, these people were segregated from those they regarded as their 'betters'. When at last they reached Australia they were accustomed to the advantages of group effort and turned to it readily in the strange and often inimical new land. Thus the voyage played its part in shaping the Australian ethos.

11   *Pastimes and Consolations*

Day after day, day after day, the same;
A weary waste of waters, still the same;
Waves beyond waves, the interminable sea.
                                             Southey

Two or three or five hundred people, most of them shut between decks, very few of them accustomed to ships or the sea, all confronted with a voyage to last three or four or five months. Even though this was an age before man had made time a tyrant, when whole days equated with what we now fit into hours, the superfluity of time inflicted tedium beyond belief. As weeks crept into months the ship seemingly lay at the centre of the same circle of sea, sometimes turbulent, sometimes calm, always gaoler.

We are getting very tired of each other ... We do indeed find it a tedious journey. No one could form any idea of it.

This diarist, Anne Gratton[1], lived in the relative comfort of cabin accommodation; conditions were infinitely more tedious for those below deck. Time was broadly structured for them by the ship's routine: their hour of rising was dictated, their hour of cleaning quarters and of inspection by the surgeon-superintendent, their hour of lights out.

Confined though steerage conditions were for married couples, they still found space to dance. The unaccompanied men and women, segregated at either end of the ship, were limited to dancing with their own sex, though segregation was sometimes relaxed during dances on deck.

Mrs Thomas Hinshelwood, bound for Rockhampton in 1883, adapted to the routine quickly:

... We rise before six, get the children bathed and ready for

school, and our bed folded up on hinges* by half past seven; breakfast at eight. We wash our dishes, while the husbands sweep our floors, and we are all expected on deck by nine o'clock for the day. We have a free library, and read and chat till one — dinner time. Tea about five, then comes time for getting ready for bed our little ones, who are all very merry.

But, adaptable though she was, Mrs Hinshelwood wrote two months later:

It is a month today since we passed the Canaries, and have seen nothing but sea and sky ever since. I sometimes don't even know the day of the week.

James Robertson remembered in later years that he had started the voyage enthusiastically enough, but in the Indian Ocean everyone's enthusiasm had waned.

By this time, two months at sea, salt junk and idleness had so deteriorated the bearing and mental character of the passengers that they had sunk into milksops, and found languid amusement in small practical jokes that a child would be ashamed to be diverted at. Day after day they looked upon a vast expanse of ocean, unbroken by a footstep of land ... there being only one beautiful woman to excite scandal, she was altogether insufficient to supply tittle-tattle to 300 tongues dying of inanination for a sensation ... this lethargy, partly broken by cards, chess, draughts and backgammon, would not have been so enervating if a man could have settled himself composedly, without disturbance, to read or study, or to cheat his neighbour and fly the country. None of these devices could have been pursued successfully.[2]

William Kingston, who compiled *The Emigrant Voyager's Manual*, urged uneducated passengers to use the abundance of time to improve themselves[3]:

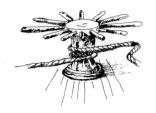

Capstan with bars in position, ready for use by the crew. When not in use, the bars were removed. On Sundays the capstan head was covered with a Union Jack and from there a clergyman of the Church of England conducted the service. In the absence of a clergyman, it was usual for the captain to read the service — one declined 'because he sometimes cursed'.

*Hinged beds were a late development, one favoured by Caroline Chisholm. Bunks made up into settees.

You will be well supplied with books, and I should advise you to make as much use of them as you can, and to take full advantage of the lessons the instructor is ready to give you, remembering always that you may never again have so excellent an opportunity of improving yourselves as you now enjoy.

It was sound advice. Teachers were appointed from among the passengers and many emigrants learned to read and write during their months at sea. Kingston continued:

I wish particularly to impress upon your minds the advantage and amusement to be derived from keeping a journal of the occurrences of each day ... If the weather is very bad, and you cannot have the ink-bottle out, write it up in pencil.

Of the thousands of diaries written, hundreds are still cherished by families in the old world or the new; most, alas, have vanished over the years.

Kingston also urged physical exercise: ball games, drilling, boxing, skipping, dancing, music — music; ah, there were risks here!

... let me urge you to avoid singing any frivolous, much more indecent songs; if any of your companions commence any ribaldry, stop them at once; stop them by every means in your power. Do not let such sounds pollute the ship. Remember, that on that very night a fearful storm may arise, and you may all of you be called into the presence of your Maker. Think how awful it would be to stand before the great Being with such sounds still ringing in your ears — sounds hateful and detestable to Him.

Religion was the great consolation of most, but, as the tone of Kingston's words conveys, its piety was often stifling, stifling at any rate, to the ears of later generations. On board ship, the services broke the daily routine and involved the people in the pleasure of singing. On Sundays Divine Service was conducted according to the rites of the Church of England. If no Anglican clergyman were travelling on the ship, the master was expected to read the service and perhaps also read a sermon from an appropriate collection. Some masters declined — one 'because he said he sometimes cursed'.[4] The capstan was covered with the Union Jack — which evidently sanctified it — and the emigrants attended in their best clothes. Indeed George Tucker declared divine service to be mainly a fashion show:

It is just the same here as on shore: it is only those have good clothes to put on who attend, and they are principally women, dressed up like so many peacocks, in all the colours of the rainbow, looking as devout and meek as it is possible for them to look, with their bible and prayer-book in their hands, and wondering what was the price of this or that person's bonnet; and if any of them have decked themselves out more gaudily than they have, looking and feeling quite spiteful . . .

Many of the working-class steerage passengers were non-conformists of various persuasions and no objection was raised to their holding separate services between decks. At these the perils of the voyage added intensity to the extempore prayers.

We commenced by singing the well known Hymn 'Where two or three with sweet accord' &c — after which I was called upon to offer the first prayer which I did with trembling — but was much assisted — a pious Scotchman (a carpenter) prayed next — After which a young man from Lancashire (a bricklayer) read the Parable of the wise and foolish virgins — Made appropriate remarks — and closed with Prayer — And although we were surrounded with Papists and unbelievers — not the least indecorum or opposition was manifested . . .[5]

Irish 'Papists' were not always afforded 'sweet accord'. When Charles Gavan Duffy was on his way to Australia in 1855, following his turbulent career in Ireland, he interceded on their behalf.

On the first Sunday at sea I may be said to have begun my Australian career. The bell was rung at ten o'clock in the morning and the captain read passages from the Book of Common Prayer to the bulk of the cabin passengers. When he finished I came out of my cabin and asked him if there was an Established Church on the *Ocean Chief*. 'Certainly not', he said. 'Well, have the goodness to have the bell rung again, and I will read prayers

Bonnets similar to those worn by first-class passengers during their promenade on the poop deck.

for some hundred Irish Catholics in the second class and steerage. The captain complied and I got through the business fairly well, and continued the practice till the end of the voyage.[6]

It reflects equally on the times that Gavan Duffy found it necessary to absent himself in his cabin during the captain's reading. Few of the Irish Catholics had such an advocate as he; more often they were subjected to jibes which goaded them to retaliation. Thomas Small, a steerage bachelor, typified some of the young Scots.

... a few of us all Scotchmen, were sitting laughing when the Catholics began prayers, so after they were done they told us if we did not keep quiet the next night they would smash us up, so six of us went to the Captain and told him. He said we had done what was right in coming to him and promised to look after it.

There was a to-do on the *William Metcalfe*, bound for Melbourne in 1839. At the centre of it was a man destined to become very well-known in Melbourne — W. F. E. Liardet.[7] The name of the diarist, J. B. Were, is familiar in Melbourne business circles to this day.

One of our steerage passengers who has his wife and some of his children in the Intermediate Cabins, a Mr. Liardett, has given much trouble and annoyance to the Captain and Officers of the ship, and on being required to desist playing the flute by the Doctor O'Mullaine while prayers were being read ... Mr. Liardett refused and was otherwise insolent and on being remonstrated with that he was an impudent fellow, he gave the Dr. a blow or two and pulled his nose. This of course was a very great insult and the Captain being called, we had quite a scene ...[8]

As Liardet was himself a gentleman, obliged to emigrate after having drawn rather too heavily on his fortune, he was probably smarting in his lowly quarters.

Excessively pious though the Victorians were, they showed less pretence when faced by death than we do today, when the subject is as taboo as sex was to them. Of course, death was a common visitor to their families and it usually approached more slowly than

Crinolines and bustles coincided with the later decades of emigration. To don such dresses in the confined space of a bunk was impossible. Most dressing and undressing by women had to be done in view of shipmates.

it does in the age of heart diseases and road deaths. When its approach was recognized, there was usually no equivocation within a family, even if the doomed member was youthful. Robert Poynter, emigrating with his family in 1854, realized when they were in the chill latitudes of the southern Indian Ocean, that his daughter Jenny, an asthmatic girl in her teens, was nearing her end.

She asked me this morning if I thought she should live to reach Melbourne. I told her I thought she could not, she then said I hope I am prepared,'God's will be done, not mine' — I do not wish to live suffering as I have done lately. She called for most of the passengers and bid them all goodbye, also Capt. and mates, steward and ourselves ...

If it sounds to us extravagantly morbid, we cannot deny its courage and its lack of dissembling. The girl died three days later.

... whilst the service was being read, her remains were lowered into the sea which was raging at the time most furiously ... It was hard to part from her and to dispose of her remains in this way, but it was necessary to do so, and it matters not where the body is we trust her gentle spirit is in heaven ...

Deaths at sea, on the way to an unknown country, were more than usually desolating; the burial service on the open deck was stark. Unless the bereaved family could afford to have the ship's carpenter make a coffin, the body was wrapped in canvas and weighted at the feet; this the sailmaker stitched up. It was placed on a grating at the bulwarks on the main deck and covered with a Union Jack. Often the ship's bell was tolled, but the ship itself raced on. A clergyman or the captain read the service; the grating was tilted and the body launched into the sea.

Mrs Hinshelwood wrote feelingly of the death of a Scotsman:

One of the finest looking highlanders on board who used to amuse us by playing the pibroch in the moonlight, was seized with inflammation during the night and died at noon. Poor fellow, he was only twenty-nine, and his young widow is terribly distressed. They were only six months married. The funeral was at dusk, and she insisted on being present. The body was sewn in a canvas coffin and carried aft, with the Union Jack for a pall. The poor woman stood with her hands on his breast while the service was being read, and few of us shall forget her cry of anguish which followed the dull splash of the heavy body into the twilight sea.

Most burial services were conducted with decorum, but Robert Corkhill told of the funeral of a child on the *British Trident* at which:

our chaplain (the Capt.) appeared to labour considerably more under the influence of brandy than under the influence which usually attend or *ought* to attend those who take upon themselves to commit the body to a glorious resurrection.

If a deceased person's next-of-kin had little money, it was usual for some of his belongings to be auctioned and passengers were often generous in what they bid. Inevitably, these auctions themselves were something of an entertainment, though not as much so as auctions held when unsuccessful gamblers had to recoup their losses by selling off some of their belongings. On some ships these auctions were necessary every few days. Heavy drinking and heavy gambling were endemic in the single men's quarters. Sophy Taylor wrote:

I cannot tell you how many sales by auction we have had, for when some of the unsteady characters have spent their money in drink and want to raise more, they have a public sale of whatever they can best spare. One young man sold a coat for 7/- which cost 24/- when he came on board.[9]

The single men's quarters were usually the least settled part of the ship. Fortunately there was fairly regular alleviation of segregation when single men and women were released for dancing on warm evenings. A programme that survives from an 1855 voyage lists the dances: '1. Country Dance; 2. Polka; 3. Quadrille; 4. Country Dance; 5. Waltz and Galop; 6. Polka; 7. Quadrille; 8. Reel or Schottische.'[10] The larger ships often carried a German band, but its services usually went to cabin passengers. 'Sometimes', said the *White Star Journal*, 'three distinct parties may be seen each dancing their own measure to their own music: Quadrilles on the poop, polka in the waist, and a rattling Irish jig before the main-mast.'

The parties were 'distinct' because they were divided into shipboard classes. Robert Corkhill referred sarcastically to the 'great condescension with which they [the cabin passengers] were allowing us use of the poop for the ball.' When cabin passengers held their own ball 'the poop was partitioned off by rails suspended so as to prevent the vulgar gaze of the common passengers'.

The dances of the era were vigorous and the surgeon-superintendent urged his charges to fling themselves into the measures energetically. Dancing under the moon on a tropic night provided one of the pleasantest memories of the voyage; pleasant but tantalizing, for those who hoped to slip off with a partner, as, when time for lights out approached, segregation was strictly enforced: all males and females over the age of twelve were conducted to opposite ends of the ship.

Segregation was regularly relaxed between parents and their older children. Mrs Hinshelwood wrote:

It is an eager gathering of mothers to see their daughters on

Bachelors listening to a fiddler between decks. The bunks in the background are tilted towards the centre of the ship. The weather is sufficiently fine for a porthole to be open.

deck every day, as they are strictly forbidden to leave their part of the ship ... [I] felt sorry for the girls who had no friends on board.

A month later Mrs Hinshelwood was ill:

I have received another great kindness from Dr. Eccles today, for which I feel very grateful. He sent Lizzie down from the young women's quarters to nurse me and look after the children. This is quite an unusual indulgence, and she had to promise to carry no letter or parcels between the young men and women.

There was no segregation among cabin passengers, but then there were relatively few unattached women amongst them — and, in any event, it was supposed that they would behave as ladies and gentlemen. Of this class Edward Snell remarked:

I don't know what to make of the ladies, one or two of the Miss Brindons are not amiss the rest appear to employ themselves principally in sitting on the cabin skylight or Hencoops each with the head of a young man in her lap and eternally wanting someone to sing though they never sing themselves. I've sung 'A Life on the Ocean Wave', 'The Pilot', 'Minute Gun at Sea', and the 'Battle and the Breeze' at their request at least 40 times each day.

Despite the solace of resting his head in a female lap, Snell declared:

... if I find the folks in Australia the same stamp as the passengers on board the *Bolton* I think when I get out there I shall just 'about ship' and get it back again.*

The day after this entry he wrote wryly:

Nothing to be seen but the same eternal blue circle around us and now and then a sail at a great distance. All the songs are used up and we feel rather at a loss for amusements.

If the young men incarcerated forward had been granted Snell's female company, they would probably have delighted in it. On one

*Snell, in fact, became the engineer responsible for the laying of the Geelong–Melbourne railway.

ship two of the single men managed to reach the single women's quarters by inching their way down a ventilator. Their apparent success turned to disaster. The girls might have proved pliant could they have been approached singly, but encountered *en masse*, each a witness to the response of others, they became unexpectedly violent. They stripped the intruders, lashed them to the bunks, called the surgeon-superintendent and, while waiting for his arrival, pelted their hopeful Lotharios with anything to hand.

Opportunities for conducting affairs, or even having a voyage mistress, were very much easier for senior officers than for passengers. Robert Abbott, emigrating on the *James L. Bogart*, wrote of two 'passably young ladies about whom a strange report is afloat — the Men's Hospital having been fitted up for their use and now used for other purposes by James (1st mate) and others.'[11] The captain and the first mate had such a violent altercation over the first mate's favourite that the captain ordered a sailor to put the mate in irons, whereupon the mate drew a dagger and also threatened to blow out the captain's brains. But as the ship neared its destination the mate evidently began to think of his share of the bounty and of the harm to his reputation when it came time for him to sign on for later voyages. He tried to cajole passengers into signing a petition that they had 'seen nothing immoral in the conduct of Miss Bale and Miss Britten and that the hospital has not been used for any improper purpose'. Abbott added: 'Great reluctance on the part of passengers to sign.'

'Bully' Forbes was alleged by the passengers of the *Schomberg* to have 'kept a woman in the second cabin'; in fact, to have had her in his own cabin shortly before the ship was stranded off the Victorian coast.[12] Similar allegations were made concerning the surgeon-superintendent. Although the allegations came from immigrants incensed by loss of their possessions, their stories tallied closely.

An emigrant ship was very much a man's world. Women were never afforded opportunity for sea bathing, no matter how hot the weather. Men, on the other hand — especially men of cabin class — were sometimes rowed beyond the range of susceptible female eyes on calm, hot days and allowed to swim, or trail by a rope. One man who ought to have known better — the surgeon on the *South Australian* — dropped overboard from the ship when it appeared to be becalmed. As he rounded the stern he realized that the vessel was actually moving forward more rapidly than he could swim. His life was saved

The 'wandering albatross' (*Diomedea exulans*). An inhabitant of the southern hemisphere, it sometimes has a wing-span exceeding eleven feet. With scarcely a movement of these wings, the albatross will soar behind a ship for weeks on end. It only touches land once a year for breeding purposes.

Although Coleridge's Ancient Mariner expresses the fearful consequences arising from killing an albatross, no superstitions prevented crews and emigrants from 'fishing' for them. A small triangle of wood baited with meat was trailed astern. The bird's hooked beak would catch in one of the angles of the triangle. Hauling in one of the larger albatrosses was a task for two men.

when he grasped a trailing rope and was hauled aboard. In a book of advice to emigrants that he subsequently wrote, he recommended bathing in a sail lowered from the ship — but it is scarcely conceivable that he would have countenanced this for women.[13]

Nor was shooting a sport for women. Many of the gentlemen brought their guns with them and, although these had to be given into the keeping of the master, they were readily released for sporting occasions. Frequently the marksmen fired at bottles suspended from the yardarms. Occasionally someone managed to sever a halyard, to the extreme annoyance of the crew. But this was small harm in comparison with the wanton shooting of sea birds. Louisa Meredith, in her *Notes and Sketches of New South Wales* wrote feelingly of the shooting of Cape pigeons, also called 'passenger's friend'.

Had the *sobriquet* been '*passenger's victim*', it had been far more appropriate, for it appears the universal custom — shame on those who make it so! — to massacre these poor harmless and really beautiful birds for the mere wanton love of destruction. Every one possessed of a gun, powder, and shot aids in the slaughter, or at least does his worst; and besides the killed, I have watched many and many a poor wounded bird, disabled from flying or procuring food, float helplessly away to perish in pain and starvation, because some heartless blockhead had no other resource to kill time than breaking its leg or wing.

The Cape pigeon was not the only victim; 'fishing' for albatross was as popular with passengers as it was with the crew. Mrs Meredith wrote sensitively of this noble-looking bird:

The great white albatross (Diomedia exulans) fully realized all my ideas of its grandeur and solemnity. I never saw it without thinking of Coleridge's wild and wondrous tale of the 'Ancient Mariner'; nor can there possibly be any creature more fitted to take its part in such a dread and ghostly narrative than this melancholy, grave, and most majestic bird. It soars along with widely-expanded wings that often measure fifteen or eighteen feet between the tips, with an even solemn flight, rarely seeming to stir, but as if merely floating along. Now and then a slow flapping motion serves to raise him higher in the air, but the swift movement and busy flutter of other birds seem beneath his dignity. He sails almost close to you, like a silent spectre. Nothing of life appears in his still, motionless form, but his keen piercing eye ... [14]

The albatross generally sailed clear of gunshot, but passengers soon learnt from crews the skills of catching it with the triangular 'hook' (see chapter 8). Numerous diarists related that they were mounting the head of yet another albatross. This 'fishing' was done from the stern and seems to have been one of the few occasions when crew members and passengers of both classes mingled.

The rigging was regarded by the crew as their own domain. The first time any adventurous young man attempted to climb into it, he was immediately pursued. Most were soon captured and a payment was demanded for their 'footing'. Moses Melchior, a Danish emigrant, found himself required to pay in liquor:

The other day I climbed the mast for the first time. One of the sailors followed me and tied a rope around my feet and the mast so that I could not move, and he would only let me down again on my promising him a bottle of brandy. It seems to be the custom when anybody goes up the rigging for the first time, he has to pay his way down again.

The crew were probably well aware that Melchior was bringing out three hogsheads of Danish brandy.

Robert Mitchell, coming out on the *Malabar* in 1852, was involved in a hair-raising game of follow-the-leader in the rigging, when all other forms of entertainment had palled:

... a passenger (a sailor) who had been at the Californian gold-fields, took the part of leader — and a good one he made — ran up the rigging to the mast-head, down into the coal-bunkers, from flying jibboom to rudder chains Peter went, followed by a few adventurous spirits. Up on the forecastle, off with shirt, shoes and cap, out on the sprit-sailyard, and with a spring he went head foremost into the depths of the Southern Ocean, another and I being so foolhardy as to follow him. After disporting in unknown depths, I made for the ship, which I imagined

Steerage passengers passing time on deck. Some of the younger ones (centre) are being taught to read; other emigrants (background) are drawing water.

was sailing away from me. On looking up I was appalled at the
vast height I had sprung from ...

Their frolics were cut short by the sighting of a shark and they were
quickly hauled on board. The shark was soon afterward caught and
hauled up by windlass.

... some 16 feet long, one of several which were now swimming
around us ... With his great jaws he got hold of the strong beams
that go out upon the bows ... and to these he held.[15]

They had finally to tear the shark and portions of the timber away
together.

The passengers often derived amusement from the crew's singing
and dancing and, more particularly, from their mime at the end of
their first month at sea. For this month they had been paid in advance
to cover kit, but usually the money was spent on grog, or fleeced
from them by crooked boarding-house keepers or waterside harlots.
Since most of them began the voyage broke, they contended that
they had worked a month for nothing and this they rejoiced to have
behind them.

This evening the sailors buried their 'dead horse'. That means
the month's pay they received in advance is worked out, and
they celebrate the occasion by making a sham stuffed horse, a
sailor on its back, dressed in jockey's clothes; and the rest of
the crew dressed in masquerade attire, such as a doctor, to find
out the cause of the horse's death; an auctioneer to sell his
carcase after death, and policemen to keep the crowd back. The
signal is given by seven bells being struck, and then the boatswain
and his two mates commenced blowing their whistles; that done,
the boatswain, in a stentorian voice, shouts, 'Now, boys, out with
that old dead horse.' At this a rope, manned by all of the crew
who are not otherwise engaged in the ceremony, commence pulling very slowly and singing the same as they do when a sail
is being hoisted. After they have pulled it the length of the vessel,
the horse is supposed to die, and a dreadful struggle appears
to take place between it and the jockey. It is all of no use, and
the heartbroken jockey is bound to admit at last that the noble

animal has succumbed to grim death. But still he will have the opinion of the doctor as to the cause of his death, and the doctor is accordingly found. What his verdict was I did not hear, but, after expatiating on the merits of the noble steed through life, the auctioneers produced and the dead body disposed of (after a lot of laughable badinage between the bidders and the auction-eer) for the paltry sum of £3,000 on condition that the purchaser is to see him take his great and unparalleled leap. He is then dragged under the yard arm, whence he is hoisted; when he reaches the top, as far as he can go, blue fire is lit, and that, with the light of a full moon upon the scene, made the effect grand. When the fire went out, the old horse took his leap from the yard-arm into the sea, amid the shouts of both passengers and crew. They wound up with hurraying for about half-an-hour for the captains and others, and then spliced the main-brace — which means some rum. Dancing and music after to finish the evening.[16]

The lid was really lifted from fo'c'sle life during the horseplay that marked crossing-the-line. Passengers were supposed to be immune from attention, but often they were doused. The ceremony Robert Poynter describes on the Dutch *Cornelis Gips* was more typical than he realized:

... then commenced the foolish and cruel mummery of shaving by Neptune and his attendants. They were all dressed up for the occasion in the most grotesque manner and painted in various ways some half the face white and the other half Black, one darkie nearly naked painted in various devices all over, and hardly decent for females to see. Neptunes Frow had a cap on belonging to my wife and which they certainly did not come by in a very honest manner... Captain seemed to have no power over his crew or else he sanctions their proceedings and did not display his gallantry by allowing the ladies to [be] treated much worse than the gentlemen. Water was thrown over them till they were completely drenched ... they did not interfere with us finding that we should resent it ... with the crew 3 or 4 who had not crossed, were used brutally, they were handcuffed and blindfolded and marched round the deck and ropes were tied across to throw them down while pails of water were placed every 2 or 3 yards apart, and thrown into their faces as they went by, they were then set on a board over a tub of water and the process of lathering with a large brush and pot of tar and grease and when they gasped for breath, the brush was pushed into their mouths. They were then ordered to say something through the speaking trumpet which was held tight over their mouths and when they attempted to speak, water was poured down the trumpet and nearly suffocated the poor devils, the board was then taken away and he was soused into the tub and his heels held up and water poured on to him by pails full. It was most brutal and the whole affair reflects anything but credit to the *Cornelis Gips* or any one connected with her . . .

Feelings between Poynter and the Dutch captain remained strained for some days.

. . . More arbitrary power displayed than gentlemanly feeling or good sense, but he is not an Englishman and we must make allow-ances . . .

In fact, crossing the line on British ships was every bit as bad, though admittedly some masters forbade the 'ceremony' entirely rather than risk it getting out of hand.

The large emigrant ships, with the morale of hundreds to be reckoned with, had a good deal of organized entertainment. In writing his *Colonial Clippers* Basil Lubbock researched shipboard concerts.

[They] were generally pretty numerous during a passage. As a rule each class had its own; then, to end up, a 'Grand Monster Concert' was organised, in which the talents of saloon, house on deck, and steerage were pitted against one another . . . Looking back over the old concert programmes, I find that negro melodies . . . were even then very popular, amongst which figured 'Nelly Bligh', 'Poor Old Joe', 'Stop dat Knockin' ', 'Oh! Carry Me Back' and others. The rest of the programmes were generally filled up with the old familiar Scots and Irish folk-songs, some well-known English choruses, the usual sentimental ditty, and amongst the sailor songs I find

'A Life on the Ocean Wave', 'Cheer, Boys, Cheer', 'I'm Afloat', 'The Pride of the Ocean' and 'The Death of Nelson'.[17]

Reports of concerts always appeared in the ship's newspaper, which usually came out weekly. Some were handwritten, some printed. Despite the efforts of the voluntary editors, most of these papers give a pale picture of life at sea when read today; perhaps this is so because their main aim was to create a cheerful, patient atmosphere on board. The humour was drearily heavy, thus, on the famous *Lightning*, a riddle: 'Why is the Commander of our ship like an electric wire? Ans. — Because he is a lightning conductor.' Letters to the editor were occasionally more revealing of conditions on board:

... Sponging with a little salt water may go on within the limited space of a cabin, but it is a poor substitute for a bath.[18]

During the first days at sea, many of the papers' columns were filled with explanations of the ship's routine and it was usual for the captain to report each week on the progress made — or lack of it. Lotteries were run — there was always one to allow passengers to estimate how long the voyage would take; auctions were announced and hours of church and Sunday school were given. If a ship was encountered that was fairly recently out of a port, the 'latest world news' would be given headlines. At the time of the Crimean War the fall of Sebastopol was being cheered at sea for months after the event.

The greatest pleasure at sea was meeting a homebound ship. The occasion was not only exciting, but offered opportunity to send letters home. At first the two ships would sight each other at a distance and for a time neither would know the identity of the other; there were even fears, early in the century, that the stranger might prove to be a pirate. At a distance the ships exchanged signals.

There is something rather singular in a conversation between people ten miles distance from one another. The ship upon the horizon, her hull scarcely visible, and the unaided eye scarcely able to distinguish anything like flags, asking questions and receiving answers almost with as much ease as a verbal conversation would be carried on ... This is all managed with ten flags, and by a transposition of them according to the code ...[19]

If the stranger proved to be a British ship, the two would draw together if sea conditions allowed, until they were within hailing distance through 'speaking trumpets'. Edward Snell described the procedure:

... every voice on board is hushed but our Captain's that we may hear the questions he asks through a trumpet, and the questions and answers through the same medium from the other vessel.

Snell recorded a typical opening exchange: 'What ship is that?' 'Bolton of London.' 'Where bound?' 'Adelaide.' 'What are the French doing?' and a typical parting piece of information to be taken home: 'Report us well and increasing in numbers.'

Mrs Clacy conveyed the excitement of a meeting vividly:

Early in the morning a homeward-bound sail hove in sight, and as the sea was very calm, our captain kindly promised to lower a boat and send letters by her. What a scene then commenced; nothing but scribes and writing-desks met the view, and nought was heard but the scratching of pens, and energetic demands for foreign letter-paper, vestas, or sealing-wax; then came a rush on deck, to witness the important packet delivered to the care of the first mate, and watch the progress of the little bark that was to bear among so many homes the glad tidings of our safety. On she came — her stunsails set — her white sails glittering in the sun — skimming like a sea-bird over the water. She proved to be the Maltese schooner *Felix*, bound for Bremen. Her captain treated the visitors from our ship with the greatest politeness, promised to consign our letters to the first pilot he should encounter off the English coast ...[20]

If two ships were becalmed, it was common for officers and a few cabin passengers to exchange visits, each group happy to see new faces. Such an interchange even took place when a New Zealand-bound ship overtook a convict transport bound for Van Diemen's Land:

Spoke a ship this morning the *Woodbridge* with 250 female convicts on board. In the afternoon the mate ... and two or three more went on board her and she came near enough to us for

An episode on a ship crossing the line, 1854. This quaint oil painting depicts a blindfolded sailor being lathered by the 'barber' before being tipped into the pool behind him. King Neptune looks on from below. Officially emigrants were not to be molested during this horseplay – they appear here as spectators – but often the prohibition did not stop sailors dousing everyone with impunity.

the capt. to hold conversation with our capt. We could very plainly see the poor wretches, they looked happy. Those who went on board told us they were all exceedingly clean — they had a clergyman, two Drs. and a schoolmaster and mistress, two pianos and other musical instruments in the cuddy. As they were going from us one of the men played several airs on the key bugle which sounded very pretty and pleasing to us.[21]

Early on the morning of 9 March 1854, Nathaniel Levi tumbled out of his bunk, as the chief mate had called that there was a chance of getting mail off to England.

... alongside [was] a boat from a vessel called the *Mohawk* which had been to Wooahoo in the Sandwich Islands* and now returning home to Nantucket in Massachussets New England. One of their crew I think the Chief Mate was on board of us ... He had been out 46 months and just returning home. There were four of the crew in the boat that brought him. Our Captain gave him some newspapers and some fruit, so also did other passengers for the *Mohawk's* Captain's wife and two children which had both been born since leaving America in 1850. The man seemed lost at seeing so many living beings about him and no wonder considering the length of time he has been out. He told us he

*Oahu the main island in the Hawaiian Group. At Oahu this whaler had been only 4500 miles in a direct line from home, but had to make the long journey around Cape Horn to get there.

was married and had received but one letter from his wife in all the time.

Very occasionally, in the North Atlantic, a Portuguese slaver was encountered, the fearful effluvia from her strong on the wind, but once the Cape of Good Hope was astern, no ships bound for home were met, as their route lay eastward around Cape Horn. Often a fast ship overtook a slower one bound also for Australia or New Zealand, but the seas of the high latitudes seldom allowed exchange visits and, if the winds were favouring them, few masters chose to stop. Many a ship did not even see another sail during this long haul. These were the latitudes of greatest tedium and greatest danger. Rough seas often caused concerts and dances to be cancelled, or led to preachers, auctioneers, dancers, debaters and the rest being pitched together, whereupon all would roll helplessly across decks suddenly steep and malevolent. Indeed, the greatest consolation in these seas was calm after storm. Nathaniel Levi emerged on deck after a fearful series of storms had died:

All is mute, the very ocean itself is still, not a ripple to be seen. The crew are doing nothing and a solitary passenger here and there may be noticed walking steadily up and down as if in communion with itself. Life seems to be extinguished from everything, no flapping of sails nor shouting out of orders, but still and peacably we lay without feeling the slightest motion. A whisper might nearly be heard from one end of the ship to the other.

For those confined 'tween decks, the light was often too poor, far south, for the literate to read, but some passengers played musical instruments and so there was often singing and limited dancing in the passageways. Among 200 Swiss emigrants coming out in 1855, forty formed 'a singing crowd':

... and we did sing I can tell you all the way, all young and happy full of hope of making a fortune in Australia and then go back home again.[22]

There were times when the passengers wished the singers would be silent and that the musicians would put their infernal instruments away. Even the easy-going Edward Snell could become testy:

One young man is employing himself and annoying others by attempting one of Wragg's duets played as a solo on the flute while another not far from [him] is exercising himself on the violin.

Consumption of alcohol, especially among the bachelors, was often prodigious. One young man, who declared in his first diary entry that he had only been drunk once in his life, recorded that he and the six others of his mess had consumed a dozen bottles of ale before dinner and seventeen bottles of wine after it — this to celebrate the supposed imminent departure of Wilson, one of their number, who, disconsolate without his wife, proposed returning by the next passing ship. Wilson, however, was still with them when the seven celebrated the crossing of the line by drinking a dozen bottles of sherry in three quarters of an hour; indeed, he was still with them at the end of the voyage.[23]

Because people were packed so closely, it was inevitable that fights would break out. Aggressiveness increased, of course, with drinking, but fights themselves were often regarded as welcome diversions, even when wives were trying desperately to separate husbands. No fight could have been viewed by steerage passengers with more enthusiasm than one between two intermediate women:

... so exasperated were they that after being separated for some time [by their husbands] and when one would have supposed they would have been quite mortified and ashamed they again rushed into it like so many dogs and it was with difficulty and to *their* great displeasure they were finally separated. The steerage passengers were quite delighted at having so good an opportunity of throwing off the stigma which rested upon their character as being the most unruly part of the ship and on the strength of it gave a hearty cheer for the intermediate passengers.[24]

Despite the inevitable quarrels between decks, most time was spent in reading, knitting and laying plans. Undoubtedly the chief pastime was endless yarning. Nostalgic recollections were shared; hopes and fears for what lay ahead. Many people developed friendships that lasted for the rest of their lives in their adopted country and led to reunions of passengers till old age ended them.

TT ST, SHIP "SOBRAON" CIRCULAR QUAY, SYDNEY N.S.W.
FEB. 1871

12   *The New Shore*

Shipboard existence had become a life within a life with its own rules and priorities and its order of social precedence. Although the home-land receded further and further with each wave cast aside, the ship remained an extension of the life that the emigrants had known there. It had other subtle links with home: on these very decks emigrants had embraced and spoken last words to those they were leaving behind; over these rails they had waved farewells and then had seen faces blur and the land itself vanish.

For all its discomforts, the ship offered a degree of security: one had few decisions to make, there was no isolation, no need yet to force a way for oneself. Among steerage passengers life was probably closer to a welfare state than anything known until that time.[2] They were assured of beds, assured of food, assured of a degree of medical care. For everyone, shore life was suspended. One had only to submit to shipboard authority — and for most, submission had been an accepted way of life at home. The familiar class system, which had continued after a fashion on board ship, was soon to be fractured forever, but this was yet beyond imagining.

Well before the new shore was sighted, the crew began to spruce the ship up with holystone and paint; the anchor was positioned for use; the best suit of sails was hoisted. Testimonials were circulated by cabin passengers extolling the good work of the master and the surgeon-superintendent. As may be imagined, many declined to sign

Journey's end: the *Sobraon* after arrival at Circular Quay in 1871. Constructed of teak on an iron frame, the *Sobraon* was the largest composite ship ever built — 2131 tons — as well as one of the fastest. Its shortest passage was sixty-eight days to Melbourne.

them. Villains and laggards there undoubtedly were among masters and surgeons, but there was probably never one who pleased all his charges. Passengers were given final access to their trunks to enable them to change from old clothes worn during the voyage into the best they had. Some, of course, possessed little to change into. Uneasy excitement began to pervade the ship; a fuller realization dawned of what it meant to cut oneself off from the mother countries and venture into the unknown. Like individuals in an army invading a strange shore, many began to wonder anxiously what would follow the landing.

> ... we shall be at Port Phillip on Saturday ... Although glad to see dry land, I shall bid adieu to my snug little berth with regret — as long as I am in the ship I feel in Old England. How then can I say farewell without a tear when the last link be broken which binds me to the land I love?

The diarist, whose name we do not know with certainty, was writing on the *Caledonia* in 1842.[3]

The last issue of the ship's newspaper was put out:

> Last! — a sad word that! a little sad even for us, though it means the conclusion of the voyage, — a rest to some — hopeful labours to others, sweet meetings of long parted friends ... In but a few hours our company will disperse, probably to meet no more. And so nothing remains but to say adieu, and throw down my pen ...[4]

There was watch for land long before it was due to come in sight and mounting impatience with adverse winds. '. . . it is three months since we sailed', wrote Mary Anne Bedford, 'and we are all getting very tired and longing to see land.' Some of the single women about her were in a state of wild excitement:

> The Irish girls are so glad with the thoughts of landing that many stayed out of their beds of a night and are running up and down throwing things about that we can get no sleep for them and the rats running over us.

Well before land showed over the horizon, there came scents and signs of it. William Howitt, a well-known Quaker journalist, travelling to Australia in 1855, thrilled to them while still ninety miles out to sea:

... on opening the scuttle in my cabin, I perceived an aromatic odour, as of spicy flowers, blown from the land; and going out to announce the fact, I met a gentleman coming into the cuddy, who said, 'Come on deck, and smell the land!' People could not at first believe it; but there it was, strong and delicious ... The wind is blowing strong off the shore; and the fragrance continues, something like the scent of a hayfield, but more spicy. I expect it is the yellow mimosa [wattle], which my brother Richard said we should now find in flower all over the valleys ... This evening another sign of our approach to land — a hawk, for all the world like an English hawk. It is wonderful what excitement so small a circumstance occasioned after three months' absence of land.[5]

Soon there were other signs. James Robertson, watching among the wearied company of a ship that he does not identify, saw sudden animation stir them:

... this inert mass of cooped up beings became galvanized into a new life by — a butterfly. This brown, dusky-colored, fragile-winged messenger was viewed with ecstatic admiration by 300 pairs of eyes. It was no inhabitant of the sea; it bore the olive branch of land.[6]

Even though blessed with scents and signs of land, ships bound for the eastern colonies still had the final bogey of entry into Bass Strait. The masters' great fear was King Island which, they hoped, lay forty miles to starboard. In 1838 Samuel Rawson was among emigrants on the *Florentia* who actually sighted the island's notorious shores:

Heavy gale, about 10 a.m. land in sight, proved to be King's Island which the Captain supposed we had passed 8 hours before, there is a reef here which runs out about 2 miles from the island on which the *Neva* female convict ship was lost and nearly every soul perished ...*[7]

---

*The *Neva* was transporting female convicts and their children from Cork to Sydney in 1835, when she struck the Navarine Reef off Cape Wickham. Of 241 passengers, fifteen survived.

By 1848 the great landfall light had been erected at Cape Otway to lead ships into the strait. Even so, masters still regarded the entrance as hazardous, especially if they had had no sighting of land since leaving England. When the *Kent* sighted the flash of the Otway light, 'there was a stunning shout. The captain said, "Thank God! we have made no mistake then." ' [8]

How many emigrants might have cried 'amen' to that! The formal lines of the white shaft contrasted with the inimical sea and cliffs and was a sign that those who had come earlier were holding out a reassuring hand. And yet, after the fields and cottages of home, how forbidding the scene was.

> ... It appeared dull, dark and uninviting, huge cliffs rising out of the ocean, the surf breaking on them with a great roar, and on their summits, stretching inland, appeared forest of dull, sombre-tinted looking trees. Not a field to be seen as we sailed along, nor the least sign of habitation.[9]

But it was land. After months of trial by sea, few would have chosen to continue with the ship back to England by the Horn. The trials of some had been great indeed. On the Black Ball clipper *Netherby* over 400 emigrants had struck storm after storm in the winter of 1866.[10] At one stage they had been battened below for fourteen days, emerging to find that the ship's decks had 'the appearance of a wreck'. As they approached land their surgeon-superintendent expressed the hope that the now fine weather would continue. '. . . Though some may be weakened by the voyage, a few days on fresh meat and vegetables in the delightful climate of Queensland will set them all right again.' But as they neared Bass Strait, cloud obscured the sun for three days. The emigrants were at dinner when the ship struck the west coast of King Island in darkness, not far north of the spot where the *Cataraqui* had lost 399 lives thirty-one years earlier.

An amazing rescue ensued. Although the *Netherby* was rolling heavily, the waves breaking over her seaward side, she survived the night. At daylight two resourceful officers took a line ashore by lifeboat and fastened it there. The boat returned to carry women and children ashore. A second lifeboat joined it. Despite the seas running and the maze of reefs, the two set up a shuttle along the rope and before dark all 451 passengers were safely landed — the most extraordinary mass 'arrival' in the history of Australian immigration!

The first person seen by emigrants reaching the colonies in the normal way was the pilot. As they had usually not seen a new face in months, no man could have been more closely scrutinized than he was; he might have been a courier from another planet. E. Lloyd inspected the Port Jackson pilot 'all over with a fierce curiosity, down to his very buttons'.[11] During the gold rush William Howitt heard the Port Phillip pilot bear the first spate of inquiries from an eager crowd of men:

. . . a tall, grave-looking personage steps on board, and is instantly surrounded by the eager passengers as by a swarm of bees.

Passengers departing the emigrant ship *Jerusalem*, 1871. The destination is probably Sydney.

A hundred questions are put to him at once. 'What of the Diggings? Do they keep up? Is there plenty of gold? Are they likely to last? Do people really make fortunes in a few weeks? How are the holes? Can we get easily up the country?' etc. etc. ... The news oozed out rapidly ... Abundance of gold; — New Diggings discovered; — High market price of gold; — Wonderful instances of good luck! Hurrah followed upon hurrah.

Then came inquiries about the price of provisions; of freight; of carriage; of horses and bullocks; and all looked blank with consternation. Horses which had been declared in English newspapers, quoting former prices, worth from £10 to £15, selling at £70 and £100; pairs of bullocks, said to be worth £5, selling at £40; and so on! Freight to Melbourne from the bay £3 per ton. How in the world were many people to get out of the ship even! Now was felt, in all its horrible force, the mischief of making floating grogshops of passenger ships, in defiance of a dozen stringent Acts of Parliament. Where was the money of scores and hundreds of intermediate passengers, which would have carried them with ease through this costly Melbourne and up to the Diggings? All vanished in rum, beer, and tobacco-smoke! Where were those valuable orders on Melbourne banks which careful parents had entrusted to uncareful sons, so that they might not be able to spend their all on board? Cashed by the captain, and all evaporated in smoke and alcohol too! ...

Anon shall these prodigal sons be seen opening their boxes and exposing to sale on the knee-deep mudbanks of Melbourne their shirts and their best clothing for cash to carry them on their needful journey.[12]

Howitt was an intolerant individual — but he was right. Many a remorseful man at many an Australian port not only sold some of his belongings to raise cash, but had to abandon articles he could neither sell nor afford to have transported.

After all they had endured on the long journey, what were the newcomers' first impressions of the ports that received them? There was not much about Melbourne by the time of the gold rush to commend it. 'Scenery: mud and swamp, swamp and mud', wrote Mrs

Charles Clacy, 'like the Lincolnshire fens must have been before draining.'[13] William Rayment arrived in the summer of the same year: 'Clouds of dust rising from Melbourne so thick as to impede the view of the background.'[14]

One can understand the feelings of Baron Alexander Caesar Menyanszky, when he saw Melbourne in 1848 and assessed the rest of the country by it:

> The flat shore — the town marked out, and not yet built — the temporary huts — the naked landscape without vegetation or water ... During my stay, I could never get rid of the idea I conceived from the first, that the work of creation had stopped short in Australia, for everything seems but half emerged from chaos, and life to be scarcely developed. It seems to me that Australia, the youngest child of Nature the work of her exhaustion, was born prematurely.[15]

It was Melbourne's ugliest era; trees had been felled for miles around and there were yet no buildings or streets to please a European eye. Earlier, during its first decade, the Port Phillip settlement retained some of its pristine beauty. The anonymous female diarist who had expressed such melancholy when about to leave the *Caledonia* in 1842, must have been one of the last to write impressions of a yet-unspoiled scene:

> About 10 o'clock got on board the *Governor Arthur* steamer to proceed on our way to Melbourne 9 miles up the Yarra Yarra — This is the most beautiful river I have ever seen, even the ever-winding Wye with all its natural attractions sinks into insignificance compared with it — As the bay disappeared I became transfixed with admiration at the transcendent beauty of this highly favoured land — No language can convey a correct idea of its loveliness. — The untrimmed trees present to the eye three distinct generations. — The tender plant just springing from the ground — The full grown budding and blossoming, and the forest tree of years almost branchless and leafless bearing its whitened head far above the whole ...

Although this was early in Melbourne's history, Sydney had already

been established for over sixty years. Only it and Hobart burst on the emigrant's eye as places of beauty and civilization, not only because they were the oldest settlements, but because they were deep-water ports with superb natural settings. Young Thomas Mort, before many years to become pre-eminent in organizing Australian wool sales, called at Hobart in 1837 on his way to Sydney:

In the late 1830s Port Adelaide was known, with some justification, as Port Misery. The water close to shore was too shallow for loaded boats, hence the predicament of these new arrivals.

I am afraid to attempt a description of the scenery ... I can confidently say it outrivals all I ever did see, and I have seen some of great beauty in Old England. At 7 o'clock we got into port and immediately landed — imagine, if you can, our delight! I am sure the inhabitants would think us mad. The first thing I remarked were the beautiful hedges of geraniums, all in full flower, extending for ½ mile in length, and which you were allowed to pluck with impunity. There were also the low-roofed, single storey houses, which had a very singular appearance to a stranger, covered with tiles instead of slates. Here and there you might see a two-storied house, but very few. Nearly the whole of them had verandahs supported by pillars and covered with rose-bushes, vines, and geranium trees.[16]

When Mort reached Sydney he declared he would have 'pronounced Port Jackson the finest spot on the face of nature' had he not first seen the Derwent.

For all that, it was Port Jackson that drew the most rapturous comments. E. Lloyd arrived there in 1844, after 136 days at sea:

Gently sloping banks, wooded to the water's edge, dotted here and there with handsome stone villas, like any watering or suburban place in England. The water a beautiful bright green ... scarcely disturbed beyond a slight ripple. The bright yellow-coloured sand upon the shore, boats moving about, and mooring up, and lying high and dry on the beach, artisans working and hammering away, and the shore fluttering with signs of animation; all presented such a scene of life, activity, and bustle, to which for nearly five months I had been a stranger, that, added to the ecstatic thought that this after all was Sydney, was Australia ... gave me the impression of being in a delightful dream.[17]

Eleven years later William Adams arrived when Sydney was celebrating the Queen's birthday:

... the Place is all Decorated With Flags and Bands of Music and One Man of War Fired a Royal Salute that was 21 Guns quite Close to us and it Shook the Ole Place and Was answered be the Battery the Same and it was Mos Noble ... People speak English the Same as Being in England and it is Considered to be the Fines arbour in the World and is a Beautiful Town and all Lighted up with Gas and illuminated and we ancord in 50 Fathoms of Water and We are Within 100 Yards of the Shore

and the Fire Works Look Splendid and a Bird just Like the king
Fisher Come and Lit on our Rigging . . .

When ships reached the more recent settlements — none of them
blessed with Sydney and Hobart's natural environment — women particularly felt the harshness of the new scene. The sisters Fanny and
Bessie Bussell arrived at the Swan River in 1832 to join their brothers
who had been pioneering since 1829:

. . . The coast looks very flat, we can discover some houses, or
rather wigwams, tho built of stone, as the habitations. It rather
reminds me of Stonehenge . . .

My first sensation was that of desolation. Capt. Stirling was
absent, we knew no one in a strange land, we will not go on
shore, we will stay in our own ship which has been hallowed
by Mama's presence.[18]

They had been preceded by Mary Ann Friend who had come to
the Swan River on a ship commanded by her husband. The young
wife conceded that the country was as 'beautifully undulating and
thinly wooded' as it had been described.

. . . but alas the soil is nothing but sand. The town of Fremantle
strongly resembles a Country Fair and has a pretty appearance,
the pretty white tents looking much like booths — at present
there are not above five or six houses . . .[19]

The men tended to look first to the prospects the new land offered
in gold or crops or stock. By 1850, when William Deakin arrived in
Adelaide, there was much about it to encourage him:

The Port . . . is very similar to a thriving English village near
London, although some few things give it a foreign aspect, such
as bullock drays, the difference in foliage and the prevalence
of straw hats and pipes and a kind of Yankee independence of
manners, but is undoubtedly a thriving place . . . The general
appearance of the locality indicates great sterility to a stranger,
but yet when you get into town you wonder where all the fine
fruits come from, grapes, tomatoes, plums, peaches, apples etc.

etc. . . . They say when hot winds prevail it is very bad, but we arrived in time to escape it, and the winter just coming on will prepare us for the next season. We have not found it at all unpleasant excepting the dust in the roads being of such a light sandy character is thrown up by the traffic on it.

Over twenty years later, on the other side of the continent, Richard Watt arrived at the mouth of the Brisbane River in the *Young Australia* and was brought upstream by the steamer *Settler*:

. . . The river . . . suddenly sweeps sharply round and as it has steep rocky banks which are overgrown with large evergreen trees, it could make a capital picture for artists who I am sorry to say are not appreciated in this country . . . The town was in full view by the time we came to our landing place, and I confess that it exceeded any expectations by far. It is large and straggling, connecting up North and South Brisbane . . . At the landing stage all was confusion and bustle, excited passengers hauling up their luggage to the wharf, each trying to secure the best places for fixing it. Then the meeting of long-departed friends, or the disappointment of others who had come out expectant, and learned for the first time (as in two cases) that their brothers had met a cruel fate . . .[20]

The arrival procedures, indeed the voyage by sail itself, changed remarkably little over the decades. Always there was the boarding by the pilot; always interrogation of the surgeon-superintendent by the resident health officer; always a filing before the immigration officer. So it went on for generations of newcomers. As late as 1883 Mrs Thomas Hinshelwood, describing her arrival in Rockhampton, wrote in terms little different from diarists who had preceded her by half a century.

Mon. 20 Aug.: A busy day getting our boxes up for the last time. We have put away all the clothes we don't require, and taken respectable ones to go ashore in . . . The gay dresses displayed are something marvellous.

Thurs. 23 Aug.: It is exactly three calendar months today since we left dear auld Scotland, and we are rapidly nearing our

desired haven. About nine o'clock we reached the entrance to
Keppel Bay . . .

Sat. 25 Aug.: We reached Rockhampton at four in the afternoon, and proceeded straight to the depot, where we were supplied with bread and tea. We were very tired and glad to be
on shore, even amid our strange surroundings.

Tues. 28 Aug.: Rockhampton is a thriving, but strange-looking
city to European eyes. The houses are all wooden erections, some
spacious and handsome buildings with verandahs running round

Railway Pier, Port Melbourne, in
the 1870s shortly before steam
began to overtake sail on the run
to Australia.

both stories, shaded by creepers and tropical plants and flowers or green gauze curtains. The roofs are covered with tin or zinc, shaped in sloping hollow ridges, so that the water may run off. Every house, however small, has a zinc water tank for rain water which is carefully kept for drinking. The whole town has the appearance of a place unfinished, but still in progress ...

Edward Webster, writing in 1857, captured a scene known to thousands:

... a steamer came and took us with our luggage up the Yarra to 'Cole's Wharf' at Melbourne ... It was an amusing sight to see us all assembled on the Wharf our luggage around us looking for all the world like so many birds who had escaped from their cage, and did not know where to fly to: each stood asking advice of his neighbour, one proposing this thing and another that.[21]

There we leave them, some to succeed, some to fail, all with conflicting doubts and expectations, most hoping to make money enough for a trip Home, but few ever to realize it. It was to be a long farewell indeed, generations long. Only with the coming of the jet airliner would the descendants of these people have easy access to the lands that were once home.

The Diaries

The

LIFE &

ADVENTURES

OF

E. SNELL

from

1849 to 1859

Diary of John Fenwick, 1854

Lively and informative though his diary is, little is known of John Fenwick. The diary was published by the Geelong Historical Society in 1969 from a typescript which had been in the keeping of the late J. J. Cary of Geelong. Cary had been secretive about the sources of material he held; added to this, his house was rifled after his death. Fortunately the diary survived.

From the passenger list it is known that Fenwick was a merchant aged twenty-nine years who was emigrating with his wife Ella, aged twenty-seven. A second diary, believed to be his also, tells of a journey with cattle in outback Queensland in 1863. All else about the Fenwicks remains conjecture.

Not only is the diary a delight — alert and good-humoured as Fenwick was — but it gives a vivid picture of one of the most famous clipper ships of all, the *Lightning*, racing out under the command of the equally famous James Nicol ('Bully') Forbes, who was then at the peak of his career. On the return voyage from Melbourne to Liverpool, Forbes was to set a record passage of sixty-three days, a time never to be broken by sail.

The title page of Edward Snell's amusing diary of his voyage out on the *Bolton* in 1849. As an engineer, Snell was to be responsible for the laying of the Melbourne-Geelong railway.

(Part II title page) Edward Snell's record of letters received from home after his arrival in Australia.

It is evident that when Forbes turned 'to run his easting down', he was secretive about his latitude: '. . . there are two statements of Latitude', says Fenwick, '39S and 49S . . . The fact is we are kept in the dark for some reason or other.' The reason was in all likelihood a desire on Forbes' part to go as far south as he dared without giving rise to complaints; also he was one of those masters who did not care to have his route freely known — such was the rivalry of the times.

Both the *Lightning* and Forbes were to meet disaster. The *Lightning* burned at her moorings when loading cargo at Geelong in 1869; Forbes, the year after Fenwick's voyage, lost the magnificent British-built *Schomberg* off Curdies River, Victoria, on her maiden voyage. The circumstances were such that he was never given another first-class command. (See chapter 3 for greater detail.)

The *Lightning* was carrying 452 passengers, the great majority, of course, steerage. It is evident that Fenwick, although only a second-class passenger, was respected even by Forbes.

1854 — Sunday 14 May — Ship *Lightning* towed from the Mersey — a tug on each side and one ahead — as we took our departure at noon. Guns were fired from the Shore and the *Marco Polo**, and returned by us. Band playing 'Cheer boys, cheer'; many joining them in chorus; flags flying — many full hearts leaving their native Land for ever — away we go. During the aftn. one tug leaves us, taking the Owners, Clerks, etc. back to L'pool. Divine service in our Cabin — and ditto after Tea — too much ranting & praying — we cannot get fresh air for the crowds who attend. The wind is too light to give us any assistance. We get our meals in great discomfort & without order — everyone for himself & many are very rough & rude. Hilly land all the way to our left.

15 May: One of the tugs left us & took a large mail from the passengers. The English coast has disappeared & we progress behind the remaining Tug. Several sails are set but there is no wind to fill them. Made a complaint to the Doctor about some

---

*The *Marco Polo* was Forbes' former command, the ship in which he had set a record of 68 days to Melbourne two years earlier.

filth — his senseless saucy reply proves him one fool to begin with. P. M. off Tuskar light, S.E. coast of Ireland. Only Saloon passengers are allowed on the poop — a promenade 90 feet long by 35 feet for 50 people — a much less space is left for 500 of the others! My wife and the other females of ours were invited up by the Captain when they please. The rest of the deck is a dense crowd of men, women & children — ropes, luggage & confusion of all sorts — some read, one knits, others smoke, & most are idle. The Deck house, Hatchways and forecastle leave very little room in the main deck.

16 May: The last tug left us somewhere before breakfast, off Cork. Wind very light, sea smooth, every sail set, a fine appearance we must have. Now & then we see the great backs of porpoises rolling along. Some of the 'Firsts' had their guns out for their benefit; they, however, neither hit them nor the divers. 6 p.m. a Barque *Queen of the Ocean* City Point (Virginia) to L'pool passed us. The Capt. jumped in to the Quarter boat & hailed her. There was barely time. Gave the name of each, the other asked the Longitude & news. '9 at noon', & 'War has begun' was all the extra & we separated, giving them a tremendous cheer. This event made a great excitement on board ... There are at least 80 people from Jersey and Guernsey; they speak (besides English) a lingo I can make nothing of. The majority of them are bound to the Diggins. There are too, numbers of Welsh and Cornish people — 3 or 4 Frenchmen. The rest are made up of English, Scotch, with a sprinkling of Irish. Water has been served out to us, one quart each — the remaining 2 quarts are kept back for the Tea Coffee & cooking. The purser is regular stupid fellow, knows nothing of his duty, & attempts to conceal all under a mask of importance. His not serving out our rations keeps us very piggish at our meals ...

17 May: Going on as usual — people getting dissatisfied with the purser — the burnt rice — the beastly fat pork, about 2 oz. to each person, is enough to exhaust anyone's patience. We met together on the subject. I wrote a note to the Captain — all signed it — and down came the purser in a rage to know what the Devil we wanted & threatened all sorts of annoyances to the signers. I told him at last with my most authoritative air to hold his tongue & hear what I had to say. I said we were to a man determined to have our proper allowance of everything without further delay. He then softened down & said the things had been so badly stowed away, that they were not to be found at once, but in another day or so all should be in order.

18 May: ... The Captain says we must set every yard of canvas, and if that does not make her go, we must put up our Shirts. It is amusing to observe his anxious watchfulness — every step or two he looks up at the sails & whistles for a wind. Then he orders a pull at this & a stretch at that. But to see him seriously whistling — that's the joke ...

19 May: We have had an escape last night from one of the most fearful of all accidents — A lady in the saloon who wished to hide her lamp after 10 o'clock, had covered it up and either gone to sleep or forgotten it. The State room was very much burnt & one of the deck beams had hold before it was extinguished. The rule had hitherto been for the Carpenter to go round at 10 p.m. & see that all passengers' lights between decks were extinguished. The result of the accident is that all our lanterns were collected & taken charge of by the Capt. Two of the ship's lanterns [are left] burning in the body of the cabin until 10, when one is extinguished. The Lucifers were collected and thrown overboard. It is very well the lamps are all away; the little inconvenience we suffer is amply compensated by the decrease of risk. One little wretch of a boy had previously been throwing lighted papers about the berth when his parents were on deck. When the Steward discovered him the lights were all flying about. The Officer of the Watch goes round the Ship every hour to see that all is right. Today I got the people into Messes — the purser had made three attempts & failed. People now have their flour, &c, and feel contented. A spell on the poop in the evening is very pleasant now the climate is so mild. The Band plays at intervals from 6 till 9 — at noon, and from 3 till four. The 'first's' dance till they are tired. The Captain's sister, Miss Forbes,° appears a very nice girl. The lady who set the cabin on fire has been generally disliked from the first — she is considered very bold & noisy, & wears spectacles — goes about without either bonnet or shawl. Every one at once guessed that she was the delinquent . . .

20 May: Saturday. Today we had some excellent pea soup — only it was burnt & that spoilt it. Some one complained to the Captn. and if he did not rate the 2nd cook, it is a pity. The cook said he did his best, but that would not satisfy the Captn.; he threatens to flog him if there are any more complaints. This matter was hardly settled till the other (1st) cook kicked up a row. The sailors could not get their tea & the fellow threw hot water at them when they came to scold him about it. He was quite drunk, one of the men flew at him, blacked his eyes, & then the officers came up and were bringing the cook aft when the Captn. saw him near the main Hatch — He sprang off the poop & seizing the cook like a terrier, he dragged him into the saloon as if he had been a child. The man was put in Irons, hands & feet — he has got a caution I suspect. He has never been sober since we left. Many of the passengers have been giving him drink to get favours . . . We are now off the coast of Spain & a long way off too!

21 May: Sunday . . . After Tea had a chat with the Captain, who, by the bye, is the civilest man in the ship. He intends going as far south as 55°. This will be very cold, but a far better drier climate than 45° where many go — besides, he expects more favourable winds. As we proceed South the days become perceptibly shorter with little or no twilight. The Capt. says we shall have it dark at 4 before we get to Australia. Today, the covering over the Hatchway has been taken off & we get much more air . . .

---

*This was, in fact, Forbes' nineteen-year-old half-sister, Isabella Nicol, who, on arrival in Melbourne, married fellow passenger Blakiston Robinson. Their descendants live in Brisbane.

22 May: Monday ... Contrived a nice table for our berth; it is as useful as it is simple, & consists of a piece of Deal 15 inches by 30 & rests on the berth & a bead nailed on the partition next the cabin; it thus lies across & will slide from end to end of the berth, and when not wanted it is unshipped and kept against the partition by a Button — thus occupying no space. I have now several shelves up & feel nearly complete. Still we are very much cramped for space ...

Wednesday 24 May: ... The purser well nigh caused a row. One of our neighbours was showing a pistol to another on deck when the purser snatched it out of his hand & demanded his powder & Ball — this was of course indignantly refused. He then came down to the tween decks & told us that all arms, ammunition &c, must be given up forthwith; no one felt inclined to obey him, at least until the matter with the other young man was settled. The P. then went for the first mate who came down with half a dozen men to back him. He was told that the purser had exceeded his authority & we would resist until the pistol was returned; after that we would give up the arms, &c, on being civilly asked by the proper officer. The mate threatened to put everyone in irons who withheld their arms after his notice. I made mine ready in a parcel and there the matter ended. They never asked for them again. Had any force been used, it would have been resisted to the Death, the purser having made himself so odious ...

Friday 26 May: A dead calm. P. M. the Capt. took a trip in the life boat, and after he returned several of the cabin passengers went off & bathed ... The sea tonight was as smooth as glass and highly phosphorescent — any trifling thing thrown overboard sparkled like a thousand gems ...

Tuesday 30 May: The preparation of coffee we had this morning was the most curious any of us ever witnessed; in colour it was a muddy brown green. The taste was not quite so strange as the appearance. The pork at dinner was better than usual —

i.e. it was not quite so bad. I can dispense with Beef & pork very well when there is rice & treacle ...

Wednesday 31 May: Feels warmer today — 78° Fahr. down stairs ... Daily life on board begins about 5 a.m. & sometimes sooner — when preparations are made for washing the Decks; lots of men begin to emerge from the Hatchways of the Intermediate with wash basins & pails & from 6 until after 8 there is a goodly number busy washing themselves on both sides of the Deck house. The fires in the Galley being lighted before 5, many Messes are busy making Stirabout or Hemty pudding from 6 till 7. At 7 you may watch men, women & children issuing from their Holes with tin plates, frying pans, gridirons, &c, all making their way to the Galley to get them cooked — from the quantities of Ham & Eggs they bring up, one would imagine they don't care much for the ship's allowance. At ½ past 7 the chiefs of each mess go with every variety of tin pail & pan to receive their quantity of boiled coffee. In the second cabin our ablutions are performed below, & at ½ p. 7, one half being seated (this occupies the whole table), the stewards bring a tall pint mug of Tea or coffee. The Biscuits are placed on the table, each one taking what they require ...

Thursday 1 June: ... The Captain out of sorts and unwell all day. They had a concert in the Saloon. One of the Nobs says it was a miserable failure. The Tea today had been made partly with salt water — by someone's trick — Bless them! Made a great improvement in our Berth by raising the upper Bed abt. 1 ft. so that we have now room to sit up in Bed without Breaking our heads against the Bed above. We now sleep below, it being much more convenient for getting in & out. The Upper Berth we use as a store room & for keeping clothes, &c., in. This would also answer when you could trust your neighbours at the End & behind you — they could, if they pleased, even come over to us — all are for ventilation! ...

Saturday 3 June: Thermometer 83° in our Berth at starting ...

A French Brig & a Dutch Bark passed us in the afternoon — the latter we spoke — the *Marieanne* — Macao to Amsterdam — Altho' we were going almost smoothly along, the Brig was pitching Bows under, & the Bark very little better. Teevan [Andrew Teevan, moulder, aged 21 years], one of our mess to be described hereafter, is quite disappointed at this hasty way of speaking ships. 'There is no sort of conviviality at all about this speaking. I thought they would lay to for a day or so & have picnics back & forward — instead they do not give us time to say How d'ye do.' . . .

Sunday 4 June: Thermometer 84°. Weather alternately fine & squally. During Service, we heard the Captain's prompt orders — quicker than usual, & on being dismissed, saw that he expected something more than before. Men were stationed at several parts to 'let go' in a moment some of the smaller sails. All over to windward, the Sky was coming down towards us as Black as possible, and, immediately in advance, a line of white foam; gradually the Breeze freshened, &, as the Capt. watched us bending over with the increasing Blast, he every moment shouted to the Helmsman "No Higher", so that we might not be sailing too near to be taken aback — it was soon over — stronger than yesterday; but still nothing to frighten us. We did fly along whilst it lasted. After this, we had a succession of squalls & continued heavy rain. Quantities of water were collected in the awnings & carefully put into the cisterns, whilst numbers of people were out with pails & tins catching all they could. I got 2 gallons pure water; it had a smatch of sail certainly, but nothing to speak of. This was anything but a pleasant evening. A sail was over the Hatchway to keep the place dry — above we got wet — below we were steamed in a vapor bath at 84°. To add to our discomfort, we had now only one lamp for the entire Cabin. I composed a note to the Captain applying for the other; on being read, it was carried unanimously by the passengers assembled, and immediately granted by the Capt.

June 5 Monday: During the night a young man of 18 had been lost. The flapping of a sail knocked him overboard. Immediately on his shriek being heard, a rope was thrown & actually hit him, but he never attempted to catch hold. He then went down. Meantimes, they were preparing to launch the boat, but finding he had already sunk & that some minutes must elapse before it could be in the water, the attempt was abandoned. This was a pity as it looks as if something had been left undone, altho' there is no doubt it would have been useless. The lad had on a heavy suit of Oilskins & Sea boots; these burdens had no doubt prevented his floating. At the moment he fell, the ship was making scarcely any progress, it being during an interval of squalls, and it might very easily have happened that we lost a boat's crew as well. Another accident occurred this afternoon — One of the sailors fell off the Main Stay on his head; he is a good deal hurt but not dangerously. The evening was beautiful, the Moon tho' scarcely half grown, shone directly over our head, making it almost as light as day. The ship rolled along slowly & lazily, & the sails flapped to & fro — now flying out as if with a breeze, and then coming back against the rigging with a crack as if they were split. Numbers went to sleep on deck. Another batch of 20 or 30 were singing songs or listening, when I turned in at 11. Shortly after midnight, I was awoke by a general scramble; it had come on a squall, & splash came the rain like sheets of water; just imagine the sleepers awoken by this showerbath! I remained in my vapor Berth until 5 a.m. on

Tuesday June 6th: when I went on deck & enjoyed the luxury of a couple of buckets of water over me . . .

Wednesday 7 June: . . . In the evening a gruff voice hailed the ship. Soon the Owner of it came on board — a Hoary-headed old man attended by a 'Barber' & a lot of wretches armed with Handspikes. They made a progress round the ship & held a palaver with the Captain. They welcomed him into Neptune's dominions & Old Nep himself promised to take us safely across the Line that same night. There was a fine chorus of 'Rule Britannia'. Some of the men got groggy & there was an end of stupid ceremony. One Blue Light was fired from the poop. There were some very high words between some of the Firsts and the Captain. The Purser again the cause. Doctor & Purser might exchange places without the passengers being materially affected thereby. Many slept all night outside on deck, & a good many others on the floor of the cabin . . .

Friday 9 June: . . . The moon was shining with a splendour & brilliancy I never saw before — now & then it was dimmed as a squall or some of the white fleecy clouds passed over it. 1 p.m. White thick clouds rising — as they came on, the breeze freshened — it was deliciously cool — the ship was almost covered with sail, & as the breeze came stronger, she gradually bent herself to it, at the same time going quicker & quicker — then the rain came & more wind. Men were stationed at the Halliards & I went below to keep dry. There was letting go & easing off for a few minutes — the Captain had then come on deck & we were nearly on our side (i.e. the ship). 'Let go the Jibs.' 'The Jib Boom is overboard, Sir.' was the cool reply from the Boatswain forward — it went the same instant the order was given. The Capt. was on the forecastle in a moment & in another he was overboard with a rope to secure the wreck. Peter (a fat Austrian Bully; but one of the best sailors on board) had been before Hand with him. What a roaring of wind, thundering of flapping sails, dashing of spray, shrieking of orders there were before we were any way snug again. In half an hour, the carpenters were shaping new Jib boom & I went to sleep. 3 a.m. during the night there was another squall — much heavier than the last — but now we were in better trim — top galt, sails were taken in & the top sails reefed. The ship trembles very much when she dashes against a wave. There was no lack of fun below, notwithstanding — poor T sat in his water-proof with his head on his knees nearly all night. The German Band was standing hand in hand all round — determined to go together — many others . . . urging their friends to get up & come on deck to be ready for the boats.

Saturday 10 June: The Jib boom was out before 6 o'clock at night & by 12-24 hours after the accident — we had sail out on a new Jib boom! Some carpenters amongst the passengers had assisted or it could not have been made so soon from a quite rough unrounded spar. Teevan thinks we ought to petition the Captain to keep up less sail, for he sees very little difference between frightening a man out of his wits and killing him outright.

Sunday 11 June: Divine service as usual. The day was beautifully fine, and the effect of the ship dashing on through the clear Blue waves — everything so bright & glorious — was far more solemn & devotional than any of the artificial accessions got up in Cathedral on shore — not even excepting the deep thrilling of an organ . . .

Monday 12 June: . . . at 6 p.m. they made extensive preparations for a gale. 9 p.m. it came with a squall — we were soon under reefed Topsails & lower sails — one jib & a stay. As the sea rose, plenty of water came over the fore rigging. A good many dare not go to bed & they talked all night. Then every roll or pitch sent some crockery or tins on the floor; then the laughing at the accident, the noise of the wind, the rush and roaring of the sea — put all these noises & the rolling & pitching about in your berth, together, and you have one of the best anti-opiates ever discovered. Many got their beds so wet that they were obliged to sit up. In reefing the forestopsail, the yard was covered with men, you could not have stuck another on anywhere, & then it was no easy job.

Tuesday 13 June: Sea very high — very few on deck, and a good many of the sick ones sick again. 2½ p.m. Land on the Lee bow; run on till very near it & then 'bout ship. Till this order was given it was curious to see the anxiety with which every eye watched the Captain & then again looked at the near coast. The land was Belmonte just N. of Point Seguro, S. America. Noticed the Southern Cross for the first time. I saw it some days ago, but, expecting something much finer, did not know it. There are only 4 stars at no great distance from the others. Our Northern constellation, the Great Bear, is still visible, tho' not very high above the Horizon. 8 p.m. Many of the sails set today are taken in again — wind increasing to a gale — every now & then away goes a batch of crockery with a crash, or a lot of tins & pails with a rattle. Seas dashing over the Bows. It is well we are so high out of the water. Awoke at midnight, rather a fearful night than otherwise. Bottles, cans &c., &c., rolling to & fro on the cabin floor in grand confusion. The ship seems to twist like an old Basket & her trembling when struck by a sea is anything but pleasant. However quick the *Lightning* may be, she is certainly not a strong ship.

Wednesday 14 June: ... More sail set & we tear away as if we are to be strained to pieces. The Steward came flying down the Hatchway with a large Tureen of peasoup — nobody, only a female's dress, the worse for it ... Now & then a Batch of passengers pitched over to Leeward — some thrown out of their berths. Cooking goes on badly in this weather. ... Soup made of Salt water by mistake — our plum pudding raw ...

Thursday 15 June: Woke at 4½ a.m. by a tremendous bustle on deck — 'bout ship' in a tremendous hurry ... we are as near shore as possible before it was seen — the surf seen & heard ... 6½ Land ahead again — turned out to be Islands — expected to weather them but could not manage it, & so went to the Westward of them at ½ mile distance. The water had changed from the deep Blue to a fine pea green. I remarked to the Capt, that there could not be very much water here. — 'Oh! yes' he said, 'we have 7 fathoms — four will do for us!' This is running it rather fine — the ship draws 3 fathoms & there was a heavy swell. The Isles [the Abrolhos Islands]* ... were of group of 4, none appearing more than ¼ to ½ a mile long; they were quite barren save a furzy-looking stuff growing on the Slopes to the Rocks; against which there was a heavy surf beating ...

---

*The Abrolhos Islands lie only 75 to 80 nautical miles off the coast of Brazil. Forbes had been skirting the coast all the way south from the equator but began to turn away from it off Rio de Janeiro.

Friday 16 June: 6 a.m. All Hands up — a Brig close alongside. Everyone scribbling as hard as they can. 8. Capt & Doctor went off to her in a Life Boat with a Bag of Letters. She is a Brazilian Brig — Bahia to Rio Grande — out 18 days. They say yellow fever is very bad at both places. The letters may be in time for the next mail steamer which leaves for England in 10 days. Dead calm all day. Life Boat busy all day taking parties of 20 or 30 off to bathe. 2 sharks seen at the ship's side. 78° Fah. feels very oppressive.

Saturday 17 June: Still a dead calm — sea literally as smooth as glass, not a ripple on its placid surface ... [A shark is caught and the uproar annoys the captain who orders the line to be cut] — no sooner said than done & the great shark dropped again into the sea, with the pork, hook & 3 faths. of line. Peter's rope, however, had held him by the tail & he was hauled over on to the Main deck & dispatched ... During this time, the Mate° made a fool of himself, for he began to collar & cuff the passengers off the poop in a most blackguard style — he always picks out those who seem quiet or sick — there are several sturdy fellows who only want an opportunity to let fly at him — he has made himself completely disliked by all. He had, before the shark was caught, ordered me off & at the same time pulled me by the arm, but I told him in such a contemptuous manner not to touch me, that he swore he would give it me the next time he caught me there. I dared him & went again in the evening, but he took no notice. A lot of the fellows say they will go into Irons before they will see him treat me roughly. 4½ p.m. a ship coming rapidly in sight from the Northward — she brings a breeze with her & by the time she is abreast, we are under way too — she heads us — the flags are hoisted — she dips her Stars & Stripes 3 times, which means Goodbye — we are ryled! — on we go — we work to windward of her!! & soon are abreast — Ship ahoy! What ship is that? — A. the *Robin Hood* of Boston, California,

° 'Bully' Bragg — he was later to set some fast times as a master on the run to New Zealand.

32 days out. What ship is that? A. The *Lightning*, built at Boston,
L'pool to Melbourne. I know her; when did you leave? A. 30
days ago! (a stretch) [In reality 34 days] . . . I lost my Jib boom
the other night. In a squall? A. No! my back ropes broke (had
the chains not broken there is no doubt the Jib boom would
have stood). This was all that passed & the Capt. retired, when
an Irish lad — Paddy — jumped up & shouted as like the Capt.
as he could 'We caught a shark today.' This was such a burlesque
that the roars of laughter, drowned any reply which might have
been given. The Breeze died away & tho at dusk the stranger
was in sight, we were a long way to windward of him. When
the sail first appeared, she was so like the *Red Jacket* that the
Capt. offered to bet 50 dollars it was she. Until it was ascertained
to the contrary, every glass was in requisition, every eye was
strained to the utmost — a few dozens would have been drunk
that night if we had been up to the *Red Jacket.*

Sunday 18 June: . . . Divine service as usual . . . a stranger offici-
ated (from the Intermediate); he showed his ignorance & bored
us tremendously. Some of those chaps have far more vanity &
impudence than Religion, or they could never stick themselves
up & talk the nonsense they do. 2 knots an hour has been about
our rate. Sea as level & as smooth as a pond — still the ship
rolls & the sails flap to & fro with a terrible clatter . . .

Monday 19 June: Nearly calm — the Mate brutal again, having
kicked an Intermediate for washing himself on the windward
side. The water (drinking) tho' clear is exceedingly foul & offensive (they say). Thanks to my nose, I scarcely feel it and after
filtering, can drink my share, with a little lime juice in it, very
well. Had a pair of shoes soled & heeled by an Intermediate
— cost 4/6. I collected £1/1/6d in the Second Cabin for the
child born on board. The parents are not over well off &
comforts are not over abundant on board. Yesterday, there was
a terrible row in the saloon between some of the Gents. & the
Capt. They would go into the Drawing room to the Ladies
directly after dinner & the Capt. would not allow it. One of them,

who is a very great man & who managed the dispute, is ordered to be kicked out by the Steward if he persists. In the high words the Capt. said if he had known sooner that he [McCann] was a returned convict, he should not have come on board. Some of the others protested against this, as no one has any business with what McC. had been, so long as he conducted himself as a gentlemen while on board. 6 p.m. Breeze freshening a trifle. The Captain unwell. Lat. 23.30S. Off Rio Janeiro ...

Wednesday 21 June: A lad lost all the night & morning. While the Doctor & purser were making an Inventory of his effects, thinking him overboard, he was hauled into the Cabin by the Carpenter, who discovered him under the Long boat. Altho' everyone was glad he was safe, he was unanimously voted a rope's ending; nobody being willing to officiate, he escaped ...

Friday 23 June: During the night, a child died of Water on the Brain — put over board at 10 a.m. . . .

Friday 30 June: Sleet, cold disagreeable miserable, no such thing as comfort except in bed. Belough's Wedding day celebrated in our berth — 3 on the bed — 3 inside the berth — Franck & Memeitz at the door! ...

Saturday 1 July: ... Seas coming overboard now & then — showery — as uncomfortable as possible — wet on deck — our berth floor a perfect gutter by a leak above — everything conspiring to make one miserable — our neighbours behind have all their beds wet & that is several degrees worse than us. We had one roll that upset the gravity of everybody & everything in the ship. Our Berths slipped out & for some moments fastened us up in the room. The yardarm must have been in the water. Thermometer 47° on deck, in the cabin 52°. Yesterday the cold was bitter, but I did not measure it. At 8 a.m. it is scarcely light & at 4 p.m. it is dark — fine long nights — oh dear — and in England what pleasant evenings they will have.

Monday 3 July: ... we do tear thro & in a very uncomfortable position too. Working up the Deck to windward is no easy matter

& when you do get up, unless you have something to hold by, you have a good chance of sliding back again . . . Evening Wind much stronger . . . Midnight — did a little at 17 knots. Sometimes she jumps & rolls much.

Wednesday 5 July: During the night some robberies have been committed, 2 Hams, 4 Tongues, cheese, Butter & scones having been carried off. As these are likely to increase as we near our destination, we adopt the maxim — prevention is better than cure, & set a watch, in rotation, one to watch from 10 p.m. till 2½ a.m. & another from that time till the passengers are up. Feeling myself going to the cats for want of nourishing food . . . Ferguson makes us some stirabout every morning & this is really the best food I get, except Bread & Tea. We have no Milk & the nearest match we have is Sugar & Water — this is really good! — much finer than Molasses. By this attention, we often get Gruel for supper — all these things are treats aboard ship.

Thursday 6 July: 8 a.m. going E. by S. — very strong breeze — sea very high. Waves really magnificent — rising into mountains & then breaking at the top. We are now past the Cape of Good Hope & somewhere off the Mozambique Channel — there are two statements of Latitude 39 S & 49 S . . . The fact is, we are kept in the dark for some reason or other. [49°S is the more probable]

Friday 7 July: Have had a very squally tempestuous night — going at a fearful rate at times . . . 12 to 14 knots all night — all day weather ditto — Lee scuppers a long way under. Sea very high — many a heavy dash over into the Main deck — then the roars at every mishap — then an extra lurch & away fly 20 men from leaning against the weather side flying down to leeward — some on their feet, some on their sterns. 9 p.m. the ship seems to be going faster than ever — absolutely flying from under one — & every now & then dashing into a sea with a shock that makes every plank tremble. 10 p.m. Top gallant sails not yet taken in, altho' the Blocks 18 inches above the Lee Rail are frequently under water — the deck is on an angle of 45° to 50°, and you can only get along hand over hand by the Belaying pins on the windward side. The Second Mate, whose watch it is, says 'Now this is what I call carrying on' ... From 11 till ½ past 1, I was running about & lending a hand at every rope, sometimes hoisting up the sail to reef it, then hauling the yards. When running about that way, I found an agreeable tho' wild sort of excitement, infinitely more agreeable than being pitched about in bed or standing shivering at the top of the hatchway, watching the heavy sea. After I had made all snug on deck, I slept as sound as a top till 8 next morning. When the weather is fine & the sea calm, the *Lightning* is a very large Noble ship — everything about her looks large — In a storm what a change — she is then like a little boat & you can see a great mountain rolling away past — several feet above her high bulwarks. Then see the contrast between Man's mightiness and Grand Nature in her strength. *427 miles in 24 hours* [an average of 17.8 knots].

Saturday 8 July: 9 a.m. Had a very heavy squall & during the few moments it lasted the sea was a sheet of foam. 4 p.m. attempted to hoist the spanker, but the Gaff broke off at the mast, and came within 2 yards of us, Ella & I having got on the poop for a little fresh air & to see the Sea. The weather then came worse & looked more threatening than ever. The Mainsail was taken in & we had a very heavy wind till 8 p.m. & much rain. During these squalls the sea had risen considerably. The waves were tremendous and yet magnificent. The first really heavy sea came over about 7 o'clock — with a shock as if we had gone ashore — every light forward, and the galley fires were put out — then before 10, two more came over into the waist & down the Hatchway — & all the night the wind decreased & the sea lowered.

Sunday 9 July: A fine morning — calm all day — Divine Services as usual. The Captain has given up all hopes of being at Melbourne in 70 days now ... The Chief Steward (Saloon) comes down to our Cabin very often, makes himself a large man

& takes a good many liberties which do not agree with our conscience. On his going away, N. told him he better be off and not come back again as he was not wanted. He, of course, said he would come when he liked, but I & Frank said we would not have him on any account, & N. said if he did come back, he himself would kick him out (a fellow half as big again as himself). However, N. would have plenty of Backers. He then went out with a storm of Hooting. He has one or two females he goes & talks to, being the only exceptions. This scene gave the greatest possible delight to everybody in the ship where it was known all over in 5 minutes.

Tuesday 11 July: Roused up before 7 — a ship in sight — she lay to when we came up to her to speak — she turned out to be the *Monsoon*, L'pool to Portland Bay (Australia); left a day before us & has had fair winds & fine weather all the way. They have 3 more passengers than when they left England — a very light breeze & somehow or other the *Monsoon* is walking away to windward of us in a style rather astonishing & humiliating! This vessel was built by the same builders as the *Marco Polo* & is known to be a really good sailer . . .

Wednesday 12 July: Have gone on our course all night & left the *Monsoon* behind after all! Fine quiet breeze still continues & we have 4200 miles to go yet! Alas, for our quick passage! Nevertheless, it is not the ship's fault — have done well all this day & so steadily that is the beauty of it . . .

Saturday 15 July: . . . Having fought the purser till we are friendly, I had a long chat with him in the hold & got another tin of Mutton.

Sunday 16 July: . . . After an observation, course ordered to S.E. by E. Evening — going 15 knots. The Captain expecting to sight Kerguelen's Land during the night, the watch had to keep a good look out. Abt. 10, it was said we were only abt. 60 miles off the island. Abt. 11, the Fore top Stunsail Boom was carried away and almost immediately after LAND AHEAD was echoed along the poop. The carrying away of the Boom had brought the

Captain on deck, so that the misfortune proved our Salvation. The Land might be 1 or 2 miles off. The Helm was put up and the ship fell off, & by the time I was dressed & on deck we were coasting along — the land being to Windward of us. Hardly had we been assured that we were out of danger, when 'LAND AHEAD AGAIN, SIR!' put us all on the alert. There were a great many prompt orders from the Captain, & as quickly executed, for ALL HANDS were up. Again we seemed to be safe, when again 'LAND AHEAD!' & the Boatswain ran to the Captain, 'Land on the Lee Bow, sir'. 'All right,' said the Captain, 'Hard up the Helm'. Again more orders, and I, seeing the sailors alone & the Bulwarks on both sides crowded with people looking, but doing no good, I gave my feeble help to the ropes. Still the 'Land Ahead' shouting from the Forecastle. 'Land on the Port Bow!' A man in the Main chains, sounding & shouting to the Captain. He shouting to the Mate & Bos'un, they again to the men — at last the Crisis appeared inevitable — 'Breakers on the Lee Bow!' shouted the Mate. The sailors I was pulling with said, 'it's all up now by G—'. A great many were on the Forecastle with their Life Belts on — all waited for the shock — there was land on 3 sides of us & no room to turn, the wind blowing right aft. As soon as the Mate gave the last alarming intimation, the Capt. shouted at the pitch of his voice, 'Mr. Hodge!' (the Boatswain) 2 or 3 times — no reply. 'Pull quietly men and don't sing,' said the 2nd Mate to us; a long minute, perhaps more, passed — it seemed an age. At last, Hodge replied — 'ALL RIGHT, sir'. Then, 'Let go the Bunt Lines, Haul in the Main Tack — Yo, hoy'. 'Hurrah — We're clear!' It was news we could not exactly believe at first — in fact, it was not till after we were all clear, that we could exactly feel the danger we had escaped. They must have indeed been strangely constituted who did not lift up their hearts with Gratitude to the Merciful providence who had so signally preserved all our lives. The Coast was precipitous, rocky & covered with snow, & the night was very dark & very cold. How few could have reached the shore, and even there, How few could have survived on the Desolate & Barren Land in the depth of

Winter! Many who had been very frightened could now well afford to joke at the affair; some neither said or did anything, & nearly all seemed quietly to await their doom. One man who had bothered the purser about our danger was told by him to go to his Berth & keep himself warm there, for in ¼ hour he would be in a d....d sight hotter place. Another passenger came out of his berth, declaring if he had to be drowned, it should be in the open air & not in a damned hole like that, altho' he had paid £20 for it! The Boatswain, meeting one of the German Band, told them to rouse up & play 'Dead March to Hell', as half the passengers were going there directly. The Purser himself, who frightened everyone he could, appeared in full Uniform, &, calling another to him, said 'If we are to go to Hell, we may as well do in decent style from the Saloon, so bring us a quart of Brandy.' Anecdotes of an opposite character were not quite so current, but those I have given will show what some depraved hearts there are, even as they say when on the brink of Hell. The Captain said afterwards it was ridiculous of people to be frightened — 'Breakers on both Bows & Breakers under the Bows — they must imagine we dont know where we are — as if we were on an Exploring expedition — I just came to the place I steered for, and if I had missed it, you would have said I did not know my business.' If he wilfully came thro' those Islands & reefs on such a dark night, it was to say the very least, *highly imprudent*, a very little mishap would have cost us all our lives — many a ship has been lost in a much better position. Except the Capt. & Mate (whose real opinions we do not know), all the others thought it was a case. The probability, however, is that he merely intended to *sight* the Land in order to confirm his position, & that we were between the islands before he knew it. At any rate, he deserves some credit for his coolness & promptitude until we were out of the 'fix'. After getting thro', it fell nearly calm, and when I went on deck the next morning

Monday 17 July: before 6 o'clock, the little bit moon, altho' nearly obscured by clouds, gave me a pretty good idea of the fine Landscape Scenery of Kerguelen's Land. Hilly, some of the hills very high, rocky, uneven & covered with Snow. By 7 a fine breeze sprung up — by 8½ we were out of sight of the uncomfortable place which many, besides me, will never entirely forget. The Watch has orders to keep a good look out for another Island & Ice. The Island is said to have been seen last year by some Merchant vessel — its position is not certain & is not on any Chart. (Afterwards I heard the Capt. had steered full 20 miles clear of its supposed vicinity.) Catch him go out of his course if he can help it. The idea of an unknown island being *somewhere* near us made us all uncomfortable after last night's escape, & made one man say, 'There is no occasion for him to try to strike every island between England & Australia — it was not with his good will that we missed those last night ...' All this day, we have had a fine strong favourable breeze — another Fore top Studg. Sail Boom carried away, also 2 Stunsail yards ...

Wednesday 19 July: Favourable breeze still continues. Snow & showers of Sleet. Another child is born, being the woman's 7th — and all young uns. This woman tho' before strong & healthy has been an invalid ever since we got to Sea. — another in the same state keeps quite well. Evening — Blowing hard; d'ble reefed topsails — going very fast ...

Friday 21 July: Going beautifully. Snow & Battles with Snowballs — in July! Sea very high — long high swells rolling past — the ship going so fast that she appeared to chase them. The Ship rolls a good deal, but that's nothing so long as we are going our course so well. Eveng. Upper sails in blowing strong; going 18½ knots p. hour. — *432 miles the last 24 hours.*

Saturday 22 July: Everything on deck frozen hard — very cold but fine & bracing. Thermometer in the cabin 40° Fahr. Scarcely possible to keep warm except by helping the sailors to pull, & then the ropes are so cold & Icy. Everybody hoping to be in Melbourne before next Saturday. I hope we may; for there is no pleasure since the cold stormy weather came.

Sunday 23 July: Today, we are 70 days out & by this time I had hoped to have been in Melbourne. Still we have had no reason to complain of our voyage so far. Divine services as usual & well attended. A good deal of Snow at intervals.

Monday 24 July: ... At 7 & till 2 a.m. a most beautiful Arctic Aurora Borealis [*sic*]. The effect & appearance was unlike any I ever saw before ...

Tuesday 25 July: Everybody in high spirits. The Cables being got up, looks like our being near the end of the voyage. All day going beautifully with a fair wind. The sea very high & rolling after us like mountains to overwhelm us, but away flies the good ship on the Billow as lightly & as gracefully as a Seabird. Cape pigeons & Albatrosses are still following in numbers. Almost every day, some one or other sees a Whale or two, sometimes very near the vessel ...

Thursday 27 July: ... Capt. invited us into his private cabin, when we took wine & saw his charts. He declares that he saw land on the 16th & had his sister on deck looking at it fully ¼ hour before the Lookout saw it & before the Stunsail Boom was carried away. He also knew exactly that we would go between island, &c, &c, Anyhow, this is his proper policy to be so knowing on the subject, but I don't doubt the less that he found himself unexpectedly between the Islands.

Friday 28 July: ... The last 3 days we have been in delightful spring weather — if Australia in winter be no worse, they will be pleasant enough as far as temperature goes ...

Saturday 29 July: Wind light. 10 a.m. land seen, but nobody believed it, as it could only be seen from the Top. Went up & took a peep for myself. The masts certainly felt much higher than ever they looked when on deck. However, there the land was, like two little Islands, as we came nearer, we could distinctly see the Trees & hills on Capes Bridgewater & Nelson. 6 p.m. tacked ship & during the night, a good breeze took us right off the land.

Sunday 30 July: Gradually coming round to our course. 3 p.m. land on both sides. King's Island on the right & Cape Otway on the left — blowing very fresh & rainy — a nasty dark night — a good lookout kept.

Monday 31 July: 4 a.m. Land ahead; 'bout ship, — when day broke we could see the Sandy beach distinctly. We had passed the Heads; but soon got as far as the other side so as to enter, the wind obliging us to tack. The land tapers down to the Entrance, where it is very low ... The first appearance of the Shore was not so very inviting, even after being so long at Sea — it was sandy rocky & barren looking, altho' there was somewhat of Green & furzy looking hills. The lighthouse & fine white cottages of the Signal Station perched on the heights looked very pretty. After getting thro' the Heads, we appeared again as it were in the open sea ... No account of this Bay that I have seen is exaggerated — it is magnificent, both as to its scenery & capability — a fine fleet of large ships — the Elite of all nations were lying in it. The sides were beautifully wooded and studded with ornamental residences — in front lay Sandridge, the beach like a busy town — over its tops you could see the Steeples of Melbourne & rising again behind it the Dandenong Hills, upwards of twenty miles off. To the left lay William's Town — the mouth of the Yarra, with a fine stone lighthouse. Now & then, boats from the shore came alongside, & soon a Steamer. Many went ashore in it & more remained. Now we were actually at our destination & in the evening, it was very pleasant on deck — a fine Moon above us & the ship, notwithstanding the heavy squalls, as steady as a rock beneath us.

Tuesday 1 Augt: A steamer came off at noon & with it came John Tom Wright — clad in a glazed cap, w'proof coat & thigh boots — the garb of nearly all who came from the shore — altho' the variety of Hats, caps, Chinese & English wideawakes, was infinite ... He took ashore with him all the faymales, leaving Niemeitz & I to clear up & bring the cabin effects & luggage. That night we passed jollily ...

Diary of
Fanny Davis, 1858

Fanny Davis (1830-83), who left for Australia at the age of twenty-seven. She never fully recovered her health after her voyage on the *Conway* and died at the age of fifty-two.

Fanny Davis was born in England in 1830 and left Liverpool on the *Conway* when she was twenty-seven to follow other members of her family to Australia. The Sarah she mentions in her diary was a sister who had preceded her. Little is known of Fanny by her descendants beyond the facts that she married George Ingram Jones in the mid-1860s, lived in Ballarat, bore six children and died at fifty-two. Jones, a builder, had to spend a great deal of time away from home seeking work. After one long absence he was met at Ballarat station by three of his children, the eldest of whom was obliged to ask, 'Please sir, are you our father?'

The severity of the voyage greatly weakened Fanny Davis's constitution; she never again enjoyed robust health. When she first embarked she prized her berth 'at the bottom of the main hatchway', but as the voyage progressed she found that water entered it as readily as air and light. Nevertheless she remained remarkably uncomplaining and self-sufficient, even when her health was failing, and she retained an engagingly uncomplicated outlook. Her diary ends suddenly five days before the *Conway* reached Melbourne. The storms encountered during those days left her too exhausted to write further.

Thursday June 3: Having got all prepared to sail for Australia I go to the Depot at Birkenhead to prepare for embarkation, I think such a bustle was never seen. I expected to have found everybody looking miserable and melancholy, but with only one or two exceptions all seem merry and amused at the novelty of their situation though a greater confusion cannot well be imagined.

Friday, June 4th: More people arrive at the Depot. I think they cannot all be intending to go in one ship there are so many. One young woman was heard to say that she would not go although she has travelled a long distance with her luggage, and this morning she is nowhere to be found; she must have made her escape somehow during the evening. All the people have passed the doctor but one poor lad who has got an inflammation in his arm — he is not to go — and the poor lad has come from the other side of Dublin and has not a penny to take him back. Each person has two canvas bags given them and are told to put a month's clothes into them as all the boxes are to be put into the hold of the vessel today and only to be taken out once a month to get out another month's clothes and put our dirty ones away. I had been told they would keep us in the Depot a fortnight or more so that I am surprised to hear that we are to go on board tomorrow.

Saturday June 5th: . . . We all march on board with a canvas bag on each arm and nothing is allowed to go on board but what they will contain so that many of the people are obliged to leave sundry things behind, such as baskets and large jars. First the English go on board, then the Scotch; after them the Irish. Next come the married women who have children with them and are going out to their husbands; after them the married men and their wives and families, and last of all the single men. Nearly all the single women sit down and have a good cry the first thing, and I feel very much inclined to join them; but first ask myself what there is to cry about and as I cannot answer it to my own satisfaction, think it would be very foolish so begin to put things in order in our berths ... I am very glad that my berth is at the bottom of the main hatchway as we shall be all right for air in the hot weather, besides the nice light it gives. There are two persons in each berth [i.e. two women sharing a bed six feet by three feet]. I have got a very nice agreeable companion by the name of Miss Wellington, a native of Penzance in Cornwall. I am appointed captain of a mess; that is to make all the things ready for cooking for eight people and to attend at the storeroom when the stores are given out. In my Mess I have of course myself and Miss Wellington, two sisters likewise from Cornwall who are going out to be married, and one more Cornish girl who is going out to be married to a man she has never seen. She has been recommended by friends. And one little married woman with no children going out to her husband, and a young girl who is going out to her mother and stepfather who she has never seen. I hope they will all be agreeable and then we shall get along nicely ...

Tuesday June 8th: All in suspense expecting to sail and the day wears away but no Captain makes his appearance — we have not seen him yet.

Thursday June 10th: ... four o'clock in the afternoon a steamboat comes alongside with the Captain and soon all is hurry and bustle as the Captain has the old-fashioned superstition about it not being lucky to sail on a Friday so they fix the steamboat on to the ship and off we go ...

Saturday June 12: We went to bed expecting to have a good night's rest but about twelve o'clock we were awake with heavy peals of thunder and the lightning was very dreadful; they did not shut down the hatches as I had heard they did in bad weather. The wind rose very high and now began our troubles — the ship rolled and creaked and every mentionable article in the shape of water kegs, cans, teapots, buckets, with innumerable other things all pitched off the shelves and the tables onto the other side of the ship and then in a minute after the ship would roll over to the other side and all our things come back joined by all the articles from the other side of the ship with the most horrid noise as most of them were made of tin. We had to hold on to the sides of our berths to keep from joining the other articles on the floor. The people were all very much frightened and when we shipped a heavy sea they all began to shriek that we were sinking. The scene was one that cannot be described. In the morning the people are nearly all seasick but it is a fine day. [Diary is then misdated until Thursday 24 June.]

Sunday June 12: ... the wind rose very high and poor me, among the rest, began to feel very funny towards morning. It turns out that I am seasick; ... I am the only one except Miss Wellington out of twenty who is able to crawl out of bed in the course of the day long enough to get a cup of tea and then go to bed again. Some of the people are nearly dead with the seasickness, they reach so violently and with little intermission.

Monday June 13: All still very ill and the sailors are obliged to come down with buckets of water and mops and clean our apartment up as there is no one able to do the least thing but lay in bed and groan. I am much better and think I shall not be sick any more. The Doctor says if we can keep up we shall be much better, so I mean to try what I can do. The wind keeps very high.

Tuesday June 14: Of all the nights we have had yet, last night was the worst. The wind rose to a perfect hurricane; they fastened down the hatches but that did not prevent the water making its way down to us and, to make the matter worse, the ship began to leak in under the bottom berths under us and the carpenter had to be sent for in the middle of the night to stop it, and the waves washed over the deck the whole night. All at once there arose a cry that we were sinking and, of course, that added to the general confusion and many were on their knees praying who had perhaps never thought on the name of God before, and the Matron was as much frightened as the rest. She did so beg to be let out on deck. I suppose she thought she would be safer if the vessel went down up there. I don't know how it was that I was not at all frightened, but I felt that there was One able to calm the tempest and it seemed as if somebody whispered 'Fear not, for I am with thee; be not dismayed for I am thy God.' and I tried to comfort the others. About the height of the tempest we heard a rush of feet on deck and the cry of a man overboard. We all listened breathlessly but could hear no more.

Wednesday June 15: It was, alas, too true that a fine young man, one of the sailors, washed out of the rigging. They say he must have broken his back against the side of the vessel as he fell in the water; but it is so dreadful to think he cried out three times for the lifebuoy to be thrown out to him, but the tempest was so high that they could not make the least attempt to save him. It has cast a gloom over the whole ship. His chest has been taken to the Captain this morning and he had in it the likeness of his father, mother, and sweetheart. He seemed the most repectable man amongst all the sailors.

Thursday June 16: ... Many of the people keep very ill. I am allright again — it was a great mistake me being ill as I did not mean to be ...

Friday June 17: ... A girl ordered to keep below for a week for speaking to one of the sailors as it is against the rule.

Saturday June 18: Some of the people are a little better today but I hope they will not all get well at once as they are so hungry after it, that there will be a famine if they all get as hungry as me, for I can eat more than my share. A sailor sent up aloft all day for speaking to one of the young women.

Sunday June 19: ... Just as prayers were about to commence this morning one of the married women had a son and heir. He is to be called 'Conway' after the ship. They were all in high glee as they said it brings good luck and a fair wind to have a birth on board. We all laughed at the idea but it proved true for in the evening the wind changed and we had it much fairer than it has been since we sailed. The birth might not have had anything to do with it.

Thursday June 24: A very fine day — all on deck the whole of the day — everybody seems happy, and a more industrious set I never saw. There is enough embroidery in hand to stock all Melbourne. The days pass so fast and pleasantly it is like a dream. In the evening I generally read a long story to about a dozen whilst they work . . .

Monday June 28: Very hot — almost a calm — have an awning put up over the whole of the deck and stay on deck all day. It begins to turn the color of our skins — we shall all be black soon if the sun gets any hotter.

Wednesday June 30: All in a bustle as all the boxes that are marked 'wanted on the voyage' are brought out of the hold for us to put by our dirty clothes and get out clean ones for another month. We are not to have any dinner till we have finished and all the boxes put back in the hold . . .

Thursday July 1: . . . The wind has been fair for us ever since young Conway was born. A boy locked up for carrying messages from the sailors to the single women.

Friday July 2: . . . A boy had to stand sentry outside the Captain's door for four hours with a large piece of wood on his shoulders to imitate a musket for not keeping himself clean . . .

Monday July 5: . . . it is so hot downstairs that we are afraid to go to bed; however we do go about ten o'clock but we lay and toss about for hours with our clothes dripping wet with perspiration and of course cannot sleep. So at last I propose that we sit up in bed and have a gossip to tire us out. More than a dozen of us in adjoining berths sit up and each tell a story, and we find it a good plan for after that we all lay down and sleep soundly till six o'clock . . .

Friday July 9: A very calm day — too calm for our good. We shall never get to Melbourne till all our hair is grey if we go on at this rate . . .

Saturday July 10: Still a calm — we have only gone ninety miles since last Sunday.

Saturday July 17: Great excitement! We get sight of an island about twenty miles distant. It is a Portugese convict settlement called Fernando de Narnho [Fernando de Noronha — 225 miles north-east of Natal, Brazil] About dusk we see a large steamboat coming towards us showing three lights. It is soon passing us and we all think it the best sight we have seen since we left Birkenhead. It is so long since we saw anything but sea and sky.

Sunday July 18: Today after Morning Service we have notice that there will be a mail despatched to England at three o'clock tomorrow and of course we all think they are going to put into some port off the Brazils and so we are all very busy writing. At last to our no small amusement it comes out that they are to be packed up in tin boxes and put in a watertight cask with a broomstick driven through the bunghole and a small flag with a black ball in the middle on the top of it and to be put overboard. They expect it will float into the Brazils in two days.

Monday July 19: . . . Great excitement preparing the cask for the letters and putting new hoops on it to make it watertight. Having put all the letters in and mounted the flag, about three o'clock they lower it into the water over the stern of the vessel amidst three hearty cheers from the throats of between four and five hundred people and we all watched it out of sight.

Wednesday July 21: . . . Quarrels are quite the fashion, there is not an hour in the day but the Doctor is fetched to quell some riot. A young woman sentenced to stay downstairs till the Doctor gives her permission to come up for being insolent to the Matron. It comes on squally in the evening and we have to stay down for the first time since we came on board. No one that has never been in these regions ever saw such rain. It seems as we should all be drowned. They closed the hatches but we got a broomstick and hammered it till they came and opened it for it was so suffocating with the close air; we had it left open all night as it always is. I never saw such an advocate for fresh air as our Doctor is, and I do think that is the secret of all being in such good health. He will not let anybody stop down all day and woe to the unlucky one he catches in their berth in the daytime.

Friday July 23: . . . It would amuse anyone to be suddenly introduced onto our poop on a moonlight night — in one of the corners will be about two dozen singing, in another a lot talking scandal about everybody — how the captain of their mess makes one pot of tea stronger than the others for herself and 'they won't put up with it, that they won't' and lots more complaints that would make a cat laugh. In another place will be a lot of Scotch girls dancing with one of them imitating the bagpipes and not one of them with either shoes or stockings on; then the Irish will be squatting down under the boats talking over everybody's business but their own and vowing eternal hatred to the English, and even the children must have a game to themselves . . .

Saturday July 24: . . . All the single men have had a hearing before the Doctor and Captain for fighting last night and creating a riot . . .

Tuesday July 27: . . . Had one box up to get out another month's clothes. Nobody can form any idea of the bustle and confusion there is on these days, especially today for all the people have something spoiled with the damp, but in many cases it is their own fault for in one box a bottle of jam had burst and spoiled a new dress. In another it had spoiled two new bonnets, and can anyone pity them if people will be so careless as to pack jam and clothes together. And then several of the people changed their clothes at the Depot and put what they took off into their boxes all wet with perspiration. I am happy to say I had all my boxes up and none of my things were damp, perhaps that is owing to me not having any eatables of any sort. There are a great many wedding things on board which are anxiously thought of. I should tremble for a white bonnet here ...

Thursday July 29: ... Before we were up this morning there came down the news that [a] vessel we saw last night was close by and they had lowered a boat and were on their way to our ship. Up we all scampered on deck, some only half dressed, and hardly anybody got their hair done. The boat was soon alongside and the steps lowered and came up two young gentlemen and the mate of the other vessel which turns out to be the *Oliver Lang,* the same ship that Sarah went to Melbourne in — it seems like a relation to me. The visitors went into the Captain's cabin and then in a little time back to the boat, when it seemed as if they had come begging, for bucket after bucket was let down in the boat full of packets of candles and other stores ... At their going away all the people in our ship wanted to cheer them but our Doctor would not allow it, he said it was not respectable. Some of the girls had a good cry about it, it did seem hard that we should have been two months with nothing to look at but water and sky and then could not have a shout ...

Sunday August 1: ... Our Doctor keeps everyone well if he can, his whole study seems to be for our good; he goes and looks at our dinner to see that it is properly cooked, and tastes the soup ... We are much better off than we should be in a passenger ship for all is in such order. [This indicates that the *Conway* was not carrying fare-paying passengers.] On Saturdays after we have done all our scrubbing the Captain and Doctor come down to see who has done their part best ...

Friday August 6: Of all the days we have had for wind since we sailed this is decidedly the worst; it blows a perfect hurricane, we have only two sails up and the sea seems to move all in one huge mass. The Doctor told us we could crawl up and look if any of us felt inclined but to be sure and not stand up on deck, so two or three of the most courageous managed to crawl up with our clothes blowing over our heads, but we were soon satis-

fied to crawl back. The ship seems to lift right out of the water.
It is not a very cheering thing to think of that we are seven hundred miles from land ... The hospital is full of females. There
has been one taken up from the next berth to us today ... she
fell down with the rolling of the ship on Tuesday and knocked
several of her front teeth in, besides that she has been very weak
all the way ... The Matron is the most cowardly on board, she
has been so frightened that this is the first day this week that
she has been out of bed; she told me today that if they would
put her on shore and offer her two hundred pounds to go on
board again she should not think of it as she would never wish
anybody to go through the frights she has.

Sunday August 8: ... We had quite a Ball last night downstairs
[presumably without male partners] and a good many of the girls
afterwards recited some pieces. We can spend our evenings very
pleasantly if all make up their minds to agree as they generally
do as we are all locked down. There is one thing I am very glad
of; we see no more of the men than if there was none in the
ship, for the highest crime a girl can commit is to be seen speaking to one of them, and I think it is best so.

Monday August 9: A very cold day — all nearly frozen. Had a
grand dress ball in the evening. It gets people warm if it does
no other good, only some of them would come out in low necks
and short sleeves ...

Tuesday August 10: ... My cold still very bad today; one minute
I am shivering and the next shaking with cold.

Wednesday August 11: A very fine day but freezing cold, we cannot
even keep warm in bed ... They say we shall have it still colder.
We have got stoves, a sort of fire basket hung from the beams
by chains, put up this morning but they are no use to our part
except to smoke us out, blacker than the sun has made us. We
have another full dress ball this evening, all are making grand
preparations to out-do each other in the way of head-dress, some
of the Scotch girls dress in the [same] Highland costume as men.

It looks first-rate; a stranger introduced below at seven in the evening would wonder where he was, he would never believe he was on board a ship; but it is an early ball as it has to be over always by eight o'clock . . .

Friday August 13: We had a most fearful night, it has blown a perfect hurricane . . . Nearly every minute a large wave broke on our deck and the wind sounded fearfully. All we could hear besides was the Captain and mate shouting to the men all night. I wonder more and more every day how a man can be a sailor.

Saturday August 14: . . . it seems a little milder this morning. The Captain has caught another large cape hen. [He] wrote a label and fixed round its neck with a wire and set it swimming again. The Doctor in a great rage that there are so many girls shamming illness and threatens to stop their rations — if anything will rouse them, that will.

Sunday August 15: . . . There is only one invalid today where there was nine yesterday — the Doctor's threat had the desired effect.

Monday August 16: A more miserable day cannot well be imagined, we have been in bed all day to keep ourselves warm, only crawling out at meal times. The wind is right against us and the vessel rocks and creaks like an old wicker cradle. A boy came running calling for the Doctor saying that Mike had been getting into his hammock and it had given way and pitched him out head-first. 'And is he hurt much?' said the purser. 'Sure and he is' said the boy. 'Is he dead?' 'Ah, no, but he is kilt entirely'. We all had a good laugh at poor Mike's misfortune.

Tuesday August 17: Another very cold day, the wind cuts down our hatchway and nearly blows the hair off our heads and we are obliged to sit with a thick shawl on and even then we cannot keep a spark of warmth in us. My cold has left a sad weakness on my chest . . .

Sunday August 22: A very raw cold day and foggy; they tell us we shall only be two more Sundays on board. I hope it may

be correct for they must be getting anxious to hear of our safe
arrival at Melbourne . . .

Thursday August 26: It has been a most terrific night, such a one
as makes young people old in one night for it was a regular
night of horrors, the wind blew a perfect hurricane and every
now and then the ship seemed perfectly under water and it
poured down the hatchway in a perfect deluge. It is at such times
as that we feel the comfort of having a top berth for the people
in the bottom ones get washed out of their beds. The screams
of the people as each wave comes down the hatchway was
enough to make the stoutest heart to tremble. Many were fainting
away and the Matron was running about crying and, instead of
comforting people, making them more frightened. No one can
form any idea of the scene that have never been in a like predicament. I got up to try if I could get out to help anybody or bail
up the water, but my bed-fellow pulled me down again by main
force saying that she was sure that it would be nearly the death
of me if I got out in the wet as I have not got my chest strong
after my late severe cold. What will people in England think
when I tell them that in the month of August we have all our
feet covered with chilblains and many of them have broken ones
on their hands. The wind has kept up all day and we have been
obliged to have all our meals in our berths and cannot leave
anything standing by itself a minute for if we do and we look
round after, it has taken a spring to the other side of the ship
and we have hard work to keep from following it ourselves and
to hold on to the posts. The girls were giving cans of water and
dry oatmeal up the hatchway to have gruel made when the ship
gave a sudden lurch and down some of them went with both
oatmeal and water all over them. They had the gruel outside
instead of in and a pretty pickle they were in and some of them
rolled from side to side of the ship and could not stop themselves.
A poor woman who has laid in the hospital ever since we came
on board was confined this morning but the baby died as soon
as born; the mother is better than could be expected.

Friday August 27: The wind has abated a great deal and we have been able to take a little blowing on deck. It snowed very hard last night and I saw a large snowball brought down this morning . . .

Sunday August 29: It has been snowing all the morning, the snow is very deep on deck and it seems to get colder. Poor Mrs. Wilson who was confined on Thursday is not expected to live. They say we shall be in Melbourne in ten days.

Monday August 30: A very dull day, snowing at intervals. Poor Mrs. Wilson not expected to live the day out. One mess to have their rations stopped for not getting up in time.

Thursday September 2: Going a little steadier today but very fast. The Captain has been to the masthead twice today to catch the first sight of Western Australia but I do not think he has seen it and hope it will get warmer before we land as both our hands and feet are covered with chilblains and are very painful.

Saturday September 4: It blows a gale today but it is much warmer. Whilst they were busy scrubbing down in our place today a large wave came down the hatchway onto them and there was a pretty scene all at once for it fairly set the place in a float — the beds in the bottom berths were soaked out and Mrs. Usher was standing on a water keg balancing herself with the mop. I got upstairs as quick as possible for fear I should be drowned and there it was little better for the waves washed over the deck and soaked us. I have got another bad cold for the other night I got out of bed with no shoes and came down with my bare feet in a pond of water. My shoes had disappeared under one of the bottom berths and it was not till it got quite daylight that they could be found.

Thursday September 9: I have not been able to write any of my diary since last Saturday for it has been one continued hurricane. The Doctor and all who have been in the *Conway* seven years say that they never had such a bad passage. It has been fearful

— we are all totally worn out in mind and body and want of sleep ... We have had one of the boats washed to pieces that hung on the side of the ship and we are not able to have any sails up. Some of the ropes are like ragged lint where they have beaten against the mast. Still in the midst of it all we have much to thank God for; that we are all in good health and that the ship has not been disabled more, for we quite expected that we should lose our masts. It is almost a miracle that we have not. I had quite made up my mind when we went to bed last night that we should never behold the light of another day; it seemed to me impossible but still we are spared. I have not been well this week or more. I have got a severe cold again and no wonder, for we got to bed with beds wet through and it still keeps very cold.

Friday September 10: It is such a fine day that it has put fresh spirits in us. We are getting near the end of our voyage and all the sailors are very busy getting the ship ready.

This was Fanny Davis's last entry. On Sunday 12 September her fellow emigrant Anne Gratton wrote:

We were mustered on deck today. I never shall forget what poor sickly looking Creatures all looked when out in good daylight. I had no idea the cold weather and close confinement could have had such an effect ...

Diary of Dr H. M. Lightoller, 1878

Dr Henry Martin Lightoller was born near Manchester in 1851 and studied medicine there at Owen's College. In 1874 he qualified as a member of the Royal College of Surgeons and in the following year took the licentiate of the Royal College of Physicians, Edinburgh. After practising for two years in England, he emigrated to Australia at the age of twenty-seven. He sailed as surgeon-superintendent of the 816-ton iron barque *Scottish Bard* in 1878.

Soon after his arrival, Dr Lightoller took up practice in Ipswich, Queensland, and remained there for eighteen years. He returned to England to take out a doctorate of medicine at Durham University. On his return to Queensland he set up practice in Brisbane and remained there until his retirement in 1917. He was also a skilled artist in oils and water colours. He died in 1920.

His diary shows him as a man of strong nerve and a great sense of humour; one devoted to his charges, though often amused by their fervent calls on their Maker in their moments of distress. He refers to himself at times by his initials 'H.M.L.'

3rd July: Went on board. Ship lying in East India Dock. Inspected fittings, had some alterations made. Passengers came on board and are berthed.

4th July: Left the Dock at 2.30 a.m., in tow of tug. Arrived Gravesend. Had to undergo inspection by Government Officers. Took pilot on board.

6th July: Arrived opposite Beachy Head, where tug left us. Dropped one pilot and took on another, who is the Channel pilot.

9th July: Case of measles on board. Had him separated from the rest of passengers, and am taking all precautions to prevent infection.

10th July: A good deal of seasickness, wind still ahead. Pilot left us yesterday, off the Devonshire coast.

12th July: I find that I have a difficult part to play. I have to use the greatest strictness, amounting to what seems a severity, but I am obliged to do so, in order to preserve order. The ship is divided into three parts — first third, single men; middle third, married people; aft, single girls ... Blowing hard this evening. The amount of 'sicking' is prodigious, and I am running and scrambling all over the blessed ship looking after the 'sickers'.

15th July: Beautiful day, fair wind ... I have lots of work to do. I have most trouble with the single men and women. The married men are quiet enough, but there is an awful smell of babies, which I find almost impossible to do away with. Have had three confinements already ...

16th July: Have just been to see one of the girls who is very bad. She had just given me the benefit of part of the contents of her gastric organ, so I have just had a rattling good vomit myself. It is enough to make anyone laugh ... When any fresh sail is hoisted, the sailors sing a song and haul to the chorus; it sounds very jolly ... I appointed the schoolmaster, and we are making classes and Sunday School. 'It don't suit H.M.L.', but it has to be done ... Many trivial cases of illness, but I am getting them right.

18th July: Had concert last night. Went off very well. I gave a short address, and then we had a solo on the concertina, one on the flute, and some Lancashire readings by a man from Rockdale, which did my heart good, for when he finished I said, 'Good lad oud mon, tha's read it greadly well.' We then had several songs, one in Welsh, sung by a Welsh collier; it was what corresponds to our 'Home, Sweet Home'. All I can tell you is, that it was as much as many could do to keep from crying. We have a great many Welsh people on board, and there were certain parts where they all joined in. The song seemed to come from the fellow's soul, and it gave the impression that I have often imagined, of a number of people saying a last farewell to a dearly loved country ...

19th July: Two more cases of measles broke out today, one in a child 13 months old, the other in a single man. I expect that I shall have a nice time of it, for it is pretty certain that the disease will run through the ship. However, I must make the best of a bad job and do my bit. I hope I may get all well that take it ... When first we started out, I was awfully bothered with frequent applications for medicine and many cases not requiring any. I tried Epsom salts, but still the demand was excessive. Suddenly I bethought — one of H.M.L.'s 'early risers'; I called it 'Mist-Meribale', it is never known to fail. A person so far has never required a second dose ... Began giving stout, alias porter, to most of the married women.

21st July: Two fresh cases of measles, one of them a sailor ... I have all sorts of quarrels and complaints to see to, as well as other matters. Two women have called to tell me they think there are too many babies aboard. I asked them how many children they had themselves. One had six, the other five, 'Well,' I said, 'I only know of one plan to diminish the number on board.' They said they would like to know how it was to be done. I

replied, 'Drop a few of them overboard, and mind there are
no more additions before we reach Rockhampton' ... Temperature in the cabin at 8 p.m. — 85°F.

22nd July: Put one of the single men on half rations for disorderly
conduct ... I have now five cases of measles on my hands ...
Began to give out limejuice to passengers today. They like it
immensely ... We cannot put any letters on homeward bound
vessels whilst we have measles on board, as I should be liable
to imprisonment. There is a single man on board who will not
wash himself. I have told him if he does not, then I shall order
his companions to wash him in a tub on deck.

23rd July: Almost total calm, and a blazing hot sun. The temperature in the shade is 85°, but it seems as if it was over 100°.
Everyone is boiling with perspiration. The sky is very thick and
hazy. We should be somewhere not far from Cape Verde Islands,
but the atmosphere is too thick to see anything ... The only thing
I am afraid of in this vessel is fire. There are so many smokers
on board. No one is allowed to smoke between decks, and the
lamps are locked after they are lighted ...

25th July: Had all beds up on deck today and had a thorough
cleaning down ... Ship only going about 2½ knots, almost a flat
calm and very hot ... I think the best drink we have on board
is limejuice. Beer is much too heavy.

27th July: ... I am going to read prayers on the poop tomorrow.
Oh Henry, 'What wilt thou have me do next?' I am probably
going to baptize two kids sometime this week ... The noise these
blessed sailors make when they haul is at times amusing. For
instance, they are at the present time 'squaring the yards', and
are making noises after this fashion: 'Ya-ho-hup-la haul there-ha-
ho-now-ho-hup-yaho-hoy ye a-ohoo now Betsy-ya-ho.' It amuses
the single women immensely, they go into fits of laughter. There
is one man they always laugh at. He is a mulatto, about 6ft 4 in.
in his stockings. He is always getting his head in the way of
something or other and gets some awful knocks. Then we have

another sailor, a very active little fellow, but so short that he has to have a box to stand on at the wheel. It is fun to see the big fellow kick away the little fellow's box when he comes to relieve him at the wheel ... There is a family on board ... about 18 in [it], uncles, aunts, cousins, brothers, all going together as happy as the day. They come from Wales.

28th July: I read prayers on deck this morning to about 120 people. I would have given something to have got out of doing it, but as soon as I got fairly started I did not mind. We had three hymns and ended up with 'The Old Hundredth'. If the Yarrow people had seen the whole proceedings they would have all had fits — certain of it! Hang it! If I don't give them a 'blooming' sermon before long ... Distance for the day 78 miles.

29th July: Felt something tickling the end of my nose last night. Made a grab at my nose, and caught what do you think? Why, two cockroaches. Lord, didn't I jump! The animals were evidently having a day out at my expense. I nearly swallowed one in my coffee this morning.

30th July: I am very sick but don't know if it is sea sickness or not, but I feel awfully seedy ... Two fresh cases of measles broke out today ... Pouring with rain. I have just been on deck without my clothes (10.30 p.m.) having a fresh bath. It is delightful and I feel so comfortable after it.

1st August: One of the children died this morning from measles and chest affection. Myself and the purser went into my little dispensary (where the dead child had been put according to my instructions). I then read the burial service over it as it lay in its coffin. I took my dark lantern, called two hands to assist, and had the coffin carried to the aft quarter. We then lowered the body gently into the sea, which was no easy matter as it was blowing hard, and it was a dirty night. I said to the purser (as he lowered the coffin into the water), 'I hope you will deal as gently with me in case I have to be dropped before we reach Rockhampton.' 'I will sir,' he said. This little funeral had a somewhat depressing effect on myself and those who assisted me, for the rest of the evening ... I have been very seedy for the past 14 days. I cannot eat anything, and it makes me a bit weakish 'like' ...

6th August: The sickness is increasing. One of the children died today ... Blowing hard, very squally and wet. Most miserable state of things. I don't know what will become of the children. I am afraid the mortality will be awful ... Too busy to write more.

8th August: Had two deaths today ... The ship is like a steam bath. I have about thirty patients and a tremendous lot of bronchitis ... It was a nasty night last night. I feel almost knocked up myself. The anxiety is very trying when one does not feel well ...

9th August: The illness amongst the children is on the increase, bronchitis and a species of infantile cholera being very prevalent ... I was walking up the steps onto the poop this afternoon, when I suddenly heard a loud noise some distance off. I looked around and saw an immense body of water being thrown into the air. It was a whale spouting about 400 yards from the ship. The amount of water was much more than I thought possible for the animal to send up ...

12th August: One of the single men complained today about one of his comrades, who was in a filthy condition and never washed himself. I sent for the man, he was both lousy and filthy. I told him to go at once and wash himself in the tub near the forecastle. Ten minutes after he left, a man came to say that the fellow refused to wash himself. I ordered six men to strip him and wash him all over. Oh! It was most amusing to see the blessed fellow in the tub and the other fellows 'a-washing of him'. It is the only way to make them keep at all clean.

13th August: ... Three new cases of measles. Buried a child this morning ... We lost our little cat about a week ago. It somehow got its leg broken and one of the passengers threw it overboard. I and the captain were very angry and put out about it, for no doubt the fracture could have been fixed ...

14th August: ... We had a most trying night, hardly anyone got a single hour's rest, as the ship was rolling like the very deuce. It was as much as I could do to keep in my bed at times. She rolled her bulwarks right under water several times. I was up twice during the night, and it was lively work going along the deck at 3 a.m. ... The sickness amongst the children is fearful. I am at it all day, and at 6.30 p.m. I go and sit in my dispensary until 7.30 I then make another round and return to my little drug shop again, and am often there dealing out medicines or medicine comforts or making some little things in the shape of hot soup or sago pudding, by means of my spirit lamp, for the sick children. I do pity the poor little things at times. The condition below is something beyond description, even in fine weather they are awfully crowded at night, but just fancy when it is pouring with rain, water flying over the ship, all the people below, and the forward and middle hatch closed. Everything you can put your hand on, floor, bedding, is damp or wet, with an atmosphere like steam, scarcely any ventilation, and the ship rolling and pitching as if trying its best to add to the discomfiture. And the noise! What a clatter the pannikins make flying through the air like tambourines, with slop pails and buckets rolling and jumping all over, women groaning and screaming, babies yelling and some men crying!

15th August: Fine morning. The weather is becoming much colder, for which I am glad. Two children died last night. I am very much put out about it, but I have done all that is possible for them. I buried both the children. I always read the burial service ...

20th August: Had another confinement at 4 a.m. Both all right. I expect about five more before we arrive at Rockhampton. Another fresh case of measles. I don't swear as a rule, but I will, just upon this 'auspicious occasion' and say 'blast the measles' for they have been the means of spoiling my trip, and making a heavy death list.

23rd August: ... The single men are very much troubled by body lice or, as the sailors call them 'grey backs'. One sailor said he was up at the masthead yesterday, and he saw there one of the said grey back standing on its hind legs looking out for land. We have all kinds of jokes about them ... Should pass Goughs Island about midnight ...

27th August: Very cold. Temperature 44° ... You would be much amused if you could see me in my dispensary, or, as I call it, 'my old curiosity shop'. There I sit (surrounded by thousands of cockroaches) dealing out sugar, soup, tinned beef, wine, brandy, medicine, pills, flannel, et. After dealing out the above, I make my night round, find several people not so well, so up I go again, deal out some more medicine, and commence making sago puddings and gruel on an upturned empty porter barrel ... I have just seen the sailor who told me about the 'grey back' standing on the mast head. 'Well, J.,' said I, 'have you been aloft lately to see if the grey back is still there?' 'Yes sir,' he replied, 'but my old fellow is no longer on the mast head, there has been too much wind for him.' 'Oh then, he has been blown overboard?' I said. 'No, sir,' replied he, 'I found him taking a nap in one of the rope blocks, and he intends coming down tomorrow for something to eat amongst the single men, provided the weather is suitable for his journey.' 'Why don't you hold out your leg for him and give him a lie down?' I asked. 'I have as many as I can carry at present without taking an extra one in tow,' was the reply.

29th August: Blowing hard, and a heavy sea such as I have never seen in my life before. The water is coming over like the very deuce. None of your sprays, but green seas. We have nearly all the canvas taken in. Talk about shipping water! Solid water in great heavy masses every now and then comes over and fills her up to the bulwarks, and then swills and rushes about like a mill stream. I have just come up on the poop, where a heavy sea has struck the women's bath room, and broken it into small pieces like matchwood ... I just had time to get into my drug shop, and lock the door, as a heavy sea came on deck with a roar like thunder. I thought at first it was going to carry all before it, dispensary, H.M.L. and all. Everything shook and quivered like tinsel, and water came swilling in at the nicks of the doorway like so many little squirts. Up I jump on to my dispensary table for an instant, then back on my seat again and cock my legs up on the porter barrel to keep my feet out of the swill, for all is swimming on the floor. If I had been at the dispensary door when she shipped that sea, I fear H.M.L. would never have been able to write more in this book ... After having done my work amongst the drugs, I now have to go and make my round amongst the children, so I must make another dash forward again ... I got there all right. Lord, what a state of things below. Would that I had the power of description and a steady table to write on. 'Oh, ye gods' Fear has at last entered the hearts of the brave married men. 'Doctor, are we safe? Is there any danger?' The old salt, alias H.M.L., in sou'wester, sea boots and overcoat, answered, 'Oh dear no, there is no fear my good people. It is only a little spray coming over.' 'It is not for myself I am afraid' (says one brave looking fellow, with a face the colour of a dirty tablecloth), 'It is not for myself I care' (says he), 'but for my wife and family.' Now, thinks I to myself, here is a good chance of trying the fellow's pluck, so I said to him, 'Thomas, you had better come in about five minutes to my dispensary and I will give you a glass of brandy and water for your wife.' I had no sooner said it than it was as much as ever I could do to keep from roaring with laughing. I knew when I told him that he dare not come on deck for his own dear life. His reply was that he was sure that his wife would not take any wine or spirit tonight, or else he would be only too glad to fetch it for her ...

31st August: Began to worsen again last night, and has kept on worsening ever since. Talk about rolling, it is simply 'redickilous'. The captain and all the officers say they were never in a vessel that rolled so much. When on the poop you have often to hang on like 'grim death', or you would be shot overboard before you could say 'chopstick' ... I saw a fellow this evening who was carrying a can full of raisins in one hand, and a tin of flour in the other. The question arose in my mind, will that man arrive safe down stairs with his grub? My impression was 'certainly not'. No sooner thought than done. The ship gave a roll, over came a sea, flop went the man on his behind, and away he went for about ten yards before he can find his legs. (My dear friends, I nearly went overboard myself the other day through laughing at a circumstance similar to the above, but if I was to be drowned the next minute, I could not keep from laughing.) But let us get back to our friend who has now recovered his legs and is hanging on to a stanchion for dear life. 'Where are his tins of raisins and flour?' you ask. 'Ah, where are they? Ask of the winds which, far around with fragments, strew the sea.'

1st September: Still rolling like 'old Harry', but not much wind, and what we have is from the wrong quarter. The ship rolls me over in my bunk like a parcel of tobacco. I try all kinds of plans to wedge myself tight, but it is no go, and I get very little sleep ... I left the lid of a wine case on the top of my trunk which I have in my cabin. There are three nails in this lid, all pointing heavenward. The other evening, when I doffed my unmentionables, the ship gave a tremendous lurch, down sat Henry right on the points of the three nails. My friends, no doubt you have seen many conjuring tricks, but if you had seen me shoot out of my cabin with a piece of board firmly attached to that part of my person which bears the weight of my body while in a sitting position, you would have wondered how the trick was done ... Sixty-two days out from London, with goodness knows how many more days before we reach our destination ...

6th September: Blowing a gale of wind and a very heavy sea, wind abeam. I have just been to the middle of the ship and was on my way back to the poop when I saw a tremendous sea coming up. I rushed into the sailors' deck house just in time to save myself, when bang like a clap of thunder came the sea; the vessel shook and trembled as if she were coming to pieces and a solid mass of water came over, filling her decks up to the bulwarks, filled one of the ship's boats and nearly upset the others, ripped open the covering to the main hatch and sent gallons of water pouring down between decks. After it cleared away through the scuppers, I went on to the poop and met the captain. 'I have just been watching you,' he said. 'It was fortunate you missed that sea, or there is no telling what the consequence might have been, for very little more of it and our decks would have been clean swept fore and aft of everything except the masts.'

I never saw such a sea in my life, the water is sweeping clean over the vessel; we have only four sails set and it is as much as we can stagger under if this sort of thing goes on. The people below are in a deuce of a funk; singing hymns and praying is the order of the day.

4 p.m. I am dripping wet to the skin. I had to go to the forecastle and on my way back a sea caught me and sent me 'schooner rigged' for about 10 yards and nearly broke my back. How I have laughed this blessed day. Every now and then a sea strikes the cabin on deck and water comes pouring down the companion stairs into the cabin. The worst of it is that the weather is so bitterly cold. Old sailors who have been to sea for 15 years or so are pulling long faces today.

5 p.m.: Ship rolling very much, bulwarks under at each roll. Not quite so much wind and what there is is more aft. The captain has just come on the poop; he says he will try to see if she will stand her upper main topsail, and gives the order. Up it goes, but scarcely is it set than down comes a squall. You can see nothing; it is just as if the top of the water were bodily lifted up and carried in the air. The wind is howling through the rigging and the ship heeling over like a small boat. Crash! Bang! Away goes our upper main topsail — split to shreds. You could no more have stood on the poop than fly during that squall unless held fast with both hands ...

8th September: Fine morning, but very cold. Temp. 39°F. We had a smart snowstorm last night about 7 p.m.

Was up twice last night with one of the children. It is mighty cold going on deck in the middle of the night after one has been in bed. Nice breeze today.

1.30 p.m.: 'Land on the port beam'. Up we go like old hoots when we heard the third mate sing out the above, and sure enough there was the land (the Crozet Islands). We are a good deal out of our reckoning, as we are to the south of these islands and thought we were well north of them. We have not been able to get a sight of the sun at noon for some time, so that accounts for our position being rather out. It was on one of these islands that the *Strathmore* was wrecked, and if we had been about 15 miles more to the north and had come across them on a dark, thick night, most likely we should have struck them and gone down as well. However, we are clear of them now. Their appearance through the telescope shows them to be like so many large mountains. They are covered with snow on their tops and part of the way down . . .

9th September: . . .

Midnight: Blowing a gale of wind with a heavy sea running. A squall has just split the main topsail into shreds; it was a new sail, so you may imagine it is blowing. Water coming over freely, wind still increasing and simply howling through the rigging. We have only four sails set and she is going 10½ knots.

2 a.m.: Blowing harder than ever I have seen it. The sea is one mass of foam: I cannot get to sleep, too much noise, heavy water comes on board every now and then.

10th September: Running before the wind, but still with the same amount of canvas set. It is not blowing as hard as last night, but still a gale, with frequent squalls.

The sea is like so many immense mountains. At any one moment the water seems as if it were bound to tumble on the top of us, for when we are in the trough between the swells, the water is towering far above us. The top of the most of these immense swells breaks like an ordinary wave on the sea shore — it is a wild but magnificent sight . . .

6 p.m.: Heavy hail storm, the poop about 1½ inches deep. Made a few snowballs and went to tea.

7 p.m.: Wind increasing, we shall have a night like last night, I expect. The wind is howling and whistling through the rigging. I am going to make my night rounds.

10.30 p.m.: Blowing a hard gale, the sea one white sheet of foam. Every now and then an extra burst of wind in the shape of a violent squall makes everything tremble. Going 11½ knots. I did not think it possible for the water to be lifted with such tremendous swells, as we seem to be completely buried every two or three minutes. If the ship poops and one of these comes on board, it will make a clean sweep of everything, but she has not done so yet, though she has shipped some heavy seas on her quarter. Rain coming down in torrents every now and then, sometimes sleet or hail.

11 p.m.: Hard gale, the wind is blowing the top of the water bodily along. You cannot stand against the wind without holding on to something. If it suddenly fell calm with this tremendous sea on we should be certain to fall down.

11.30 p.m.: Just been on deck; it is blowing and hailing as hard as ever. Going to turn in. There is a deal of praying going on amongst the passengers just now.

13th September: p.m.: Beginning to rain. When shall we have some fine weather? Everything is very wet below, even in the cabin all is wet — clothes, bedding, etc. The sickness is beginning to increase again amongst the children. This is owing to the excessive damp and want of ventilation, for we cannot open the hatches or the people would be simply drowned. There is now about 5 in. depth of water in the married people's quarters on the lee side, and there are no scuppers to take it into the hold.

14th September: Moderately fine day. Had all the bedding, etc. up. The weather is beginning to get a little warmer. Temp. 57° below decks . . .

15th September: It is blowing a violent gale and has been all night. It blew harder last night than ever it has done since we started. The wind was terrific and every now and then a squall came enough to blow the teeth out of one's head. I could not go my night rounds; the vessel was one sheet of water from the forecastle to the break of the poop. She actually rolled her poop rails under water several times. The weather has been unusually heavy during the last 14 days, but last night the ship was simply buried in seas. We had only three sails set. Oh, Moses, you should have heard the praying! No one slept a wink that night. I tried my best, but I could not wedge myself tight enough in my bunk, so I rolled and jumped in my bed until every bone was as sore as a 'bile.'

18th September: ...

5.30 p.m.: Barometer falling suddenly and is very low. What can be the meaning of this sudden fall? ...

10.30 p.m.: I shall turn in, wind and sea still increasing. We are going to have a bad night of it.

19th September: I write this on the evening of the 20th September (I don't exaggerate this account). You will see that on the evening of the 18th at 10.30 I turned into bed — a gale of wind was blowing and a heavy sea running at the time. Well, I lay awake in my bed until eight bells (12 p.m.), then shortly after I fell asleep. I must have been asleep about an hour, when I was awakened by something striking the ship heavily, for she trembled like a bit of tin. Scarcely had I perceived this, when crash, like a load of bricks, goes something in the cabin, and water comes pouring down by thousands of gallons. I jumped out of my berth in an instant, and found myself up to my knees in water, the ship rolling and swilling this water from side to side. All was pitch dark, and it was evident that a sea must have struck our cabin skylight and broken it in, for the wind was simply screaming through a large opening somewhere in the roof. Scarcely was I out of bed, however, than I saw the captain dart towards the companion stairs. He had barely got there when a voice yelled out from the top, 'The wheel is washed away, sir.' Up rushed the captain, and then such a hullabaloo as never was. The wheel was smashed to atoms, the man at the wheel crashed to the main rail of the poop, while the first mate had been carried amidships. All he remembered was that heavy sea struck him, and when he picked himself up he was amidships with his arms round a capstan. How he missed going overboard was a miracle, for he was off his legs for half the length of the vessel, and the poop deck rather higher than the bulwarks of the main deck. All hands were aft in a very short time, ropes were soon fastened to a part of the rudder post made for the purpose, and ship was hove to the wind. Fortunately the rudder was left, or I am afraid these lines would never have reach *Yarrow*. She came up to the wind well and behaved excellently during this trying time. The wind and sea were something beyond description: one had to shout at the top of one's voice to be heard at all, the sea seemed like one immense mass of large mountains with long, sweeping valleys between them, both perfectly white with foam. If the top of one of these seas had come on board it would have smashed everything, and then all our hatches would have gone and we should have been swamped, but as I said before, the *Scottish Bard* hove to well and, although the decks were filled with water, no very heavy seas came on board.

A covering board was now placed over the hole in the skylight (there would be about 12 sq. feet of a hole), and all the sail taken off except the two small sails which kept her hove to.

I went on deck and it was as much as ever I could do to stand holding on as hard as I could to the rigging. You should have heard the wind; it was like one tremendous roar of thunder with every now and then a sharp, high note like a train whistle, as it rushed through the rigging. The poop rail and bulwarks aft are all smashed to bits; to add to all this it is pitch dark. Everything in my cabin wet through and as cold as winter.

The captain has come down and says, 'Thank God! It is no worse, we have had the rudder and steering gear aft and she is lying well.'

In the middle of all this, one of the single men ran below and shouted out, 'The vessel is going down, and they are getting out the life boats.' You may just imagine the effect this produced. They were coming out by swarms, so we got all below that we could and then lashed down the hatches to prevent them coming up again until all the uproar was over. The people were all in a terrible fright, and no wonder.

Two or three of the sailors were in as big a funk as anyone. Although we were lying-to still, we ran a great risk of a heavy sea coming on board and sweeping away the aft deckhouse. If it had done so, the risk of foundering would have been very great indeed, for in the centre of one of these houses runs a large air shaft, some 30 squ. feet of an opening, and, as there is no combing round this, it is doubtful if it could have been closed in time. The main hatch, too, is a dangerous arrangement. It is only a temporary thing for the passage, constructed of common deal wood, and if one sea caught it, it would be smashed to match wood, leaving a square opening half the width of the vessel. One or two seas down this would swamp us. We were hove to all night, so no one went to bed until about 6 a.m. I got the first mate to bed and did all I could for him. I am glad to say he is all right again at the time I write this, with the exception of a general soreness from bruises and the shaking he got. We were hove to all day until about 6 p.m., as the sea was too heavy to run before it. It blew a hard gale all day.

A temporary wheel has been made out of capstan bars, et., and at about 6 p.m. we start on our course again, although there is still a very heavy sea running. She only took one sea on board as she got under way, and that did no damage.

20th September: Fine morning, fair wind, not very much sea on now. If it was not for the accident yesterday and we had been able to run, we should have made over 300 miles in the 24 hours, but as it is we have lost about 17 hours or so.

Our temporary wheel looks a proper caution, something like an old cart wheel.

I hear one of the sailors say today 'any man that would go to sea for pleasure would go to hell for a pastime'...

Sunday, 22nd September: Services as usual. Fine, dry day, next to no wind at all... We should be in the meridian of Cape Leeuwin tomorrow evening if we can get a fairly strong breeze.

24th Sept.: ... Had another confinement; this makes seven since the commencement of the voyage...

25th Sept.: ... I am too busy to write much in my notes as I have a great deal of work to do in the shape of reports, lists, etc., to be ready for the authorities at Rockhampton.

27th Sept.: ... I am beginning to wish the voyage was at an end, as I have much trouble with some of the married people at times. They seem to think I have nothing else to do but look after them alone.

29th Sept.: Fine morning, much warmer than we have had it for some time. Temperature 50°. I think the captain intends going through Bass Strait.

30th Sept.: Fine day, not much wind; sighted King's Island and the mainland this morning. Had a general cleaning down today...

1st Oct.: Beautifully fine day and fair wind. The purser came to my bed this morning at 4.30 a.m. and said that we were passing through the straits, so up I jumped and a more beautiful sight you could not wish to see. The sea was as smooth as a mill pond, but we had a nice breeze taking us at the rate of 8 knots. Islands and rocks on every side of us, but they are all of them in such deep water that it would be quite possible to run the ship close enough for anyone to jump from her deck on to the island. Gradually we came up abreast of Wilson's Promontory, where there is a fine lighthouse. We hoisted our signals and they were answered by the man in charge of the lighthouse. This is our first communication with the mainland of Australia. The coast is very pretty indeed and reminds me of the Welsh coast.

2nd Oct.: ... We can see the coast very plainly as we are pretty close in. It seems very hilly, and all the mountains covered with timber up to their very tops, but the trees have not that fresh green look that they have at home. They look a faded sort of green, as if scorched ...

7th Oct.: ... The wind is chopping round from every point of the compass in the space of an hour. We are going to have some nasty weather again. We lost 30 miles last night and I never saw the sky look so bad as it does tonight.

11 p.m.: Every part of the sky except just where the moon is shining through, is as black as ink. There is hardly a breath of wind, but a low moaning kind of sound through the rigging bodes no good. The clouds up above are flying at a tremendous rate. There is evidently a battle amongst the winds, and we shall catch it soon.

8th Oct.: ...

4 p.m.: Blowing a tremendous gale and right ahead, all down the coast there is a rapid current from N. to S. We must be losing ground dreadfully.

9 p.m.: Blowing a hard gale, shipping some very heavy seas aft and we are rolling and pitching fearfully. I am wet through to the skin. There will be no sleep for anyone tonight.

11 p.m.: Ship labouring heavily. She keeps breaking off every now and then. Every time she does so, of course, her way through the water is almost stopped and she gets the seas broadside on. Oh, Moses, she does kick up old Dido at these times! It is very hard to write under these circumstances, I can tell you. We all sat down to tea this evening at 6 p.m., but no sooner had we got ourselves in position than we all felt a very heavy sea strike the vessel. She trembled and heeled over terribly. The next instant hundreds of gallons of water poured in through the cabin skylight, washing everything off the table and drenching us all to the skin. It is wretched work this beating against a gale of wind.

9th Oct.: Blowing hard, head wind. This is very trying . . .

10th Oct.: Still blowing a gale of wind. We are losing ground instead of gaining.

11th Oct.: Had a very uneasy night. The ship rolled dreadfully. All the officers were afraid she would lose her masts, every instant. She rolls to the rails under water, one at each roll.

13th Oct.: Fair wind, but not much of it. We are afraid of the 'backstays' going if the vessel rolls again as she has been doing. If they do go, our masts are bound to go, nothing can stop them.

14th Oct.: Fine day, head wind, blowing hard. Disinfected the ship today.

16th Oct.: Fine day. Fair wind; we are now close to our destination . . .

18th Oct.: 6 a.m. Pilot came on board.

11 a.m.: Anchored in Keppel Bay. The country looks lovely; the banks of the river are wooded down to the very edge. The captain and I are to go on shore to the Quarantine Station and telegraph to Rockhampton that we are here. Rockhampton is 40 miles down the river.

We have been 106 days from London.

Notes

Chapter 1 The Perils

1. Extrapolated from statistics given by Charles Bateson in *The Convict Ships 1787-1868*, A. H. & A. W. Reed, Sydney, 1974, appendix vii, pp. 378-96.

2. ibid, appendix vii, pp. 378-96.

3. For data on *Tayleur, Northfleet, British Navy* and *Strathmore*, see, 'Wrecks and Shipping Disaster' in Alec H. Chisholm (ed.) and others, *Australian Encyclopaedia*, The Grolier Society of Australia, Sydney, 1965, vol. x, pp. 5-31.

4. Victoria, Legislative Assembly, Immigration Officer, Report of the Immigration Officer (Charles Strutt) on the *Guiding Star*, 9 January 1855.

5. Ewan Corlett states that the American ship *Salem* reported this island of ice on reaching Australia. See Ewan Corlett, *The Iron Ship: The History and Significance of Brunel's Great Britain*, Moonraker Press, Bradford-on-Avon, Wilts., 1975, p. 158.

6. Nathaniel Levi, diary on *Matilda Wattenbach*, Liverpool for Melbourne, 1853-4, MS 8021, La Trobe Collection, State Library of Victoria. Levi was elected to the Victorian Legislative Assembly in 1860 and remained in politics for ten years. He was one of the main movers in the opening of the Wonthaggi coalfields, one of the founders of the Melbourne Chamber of Manufactures, and President of the Hebrew Congregation of Melbourne. He died in 1903.

7. Mary Anne Bedford, diary on *Champion of the Seas*, Liverpool for Melbourne, 1864.

8. Georgiana McCrae, diary on *Argyle*, London for Melbourne, 1840-1, in Hugh McCrae (ed.), *Georgiana's Journal*, Angus & Robertson, Sydney, 1966, p. 16.

9. See 'Wrecks and Shipping Disasters', (n.a.) in Alec H. Chisholm (ed.), *Australian Encyclopaedia*, 1965, vol. x, p. 28.

10. John Dill, account of emigration with brother on *Monarch of the Seas*, attached to the Shipping List of 1857 for *Monarch of the Seas* in Victorian Public Record Office.

11. Charles Bateson, *Australian Shipwrecks*, vol. 1, 1622-1850, A. H. & A. W. Reed, Sydney, 1974, p. 150.

12. Basil Lubbock, *The Colonial Clippers*, Brown, Son & Ferguson, Glasgow, 1968, pp. 296-8.

13. Letter from Thomas Guthrey attached to *Reports and Correspondence Respecting the Loss of Emigrant Ship Cataraqui(e) in Bass's Straights*, ordered by the H.C. to be printed, 27 March 1846.

14. Captain A. G. Course, *The Merchant Navy: A Social History*, Frederick Muller, London, 1963, p. 200.

15. Terry Coleman, *Passage to America: A History of Emigrants from Great Britain and Ireland to America in the mid-nineteenth Century*, Hutchinson, London, 1972, p. 151.

16. Testimony by Francis Spaight on Colonization from Ireland,

1847, given before the Select Committee of House of Lords in Charlotte Erickson, *Emigration from Europe, 1815-1914*, A. & C. Black, London, 1976, p. 35.
17. United Kingdom, House of Commons, *Parliamentary Paper: A Report to the Secretary of State for the Colonies from the Agent-General for Emigration from the United Kingdom*, 28 April 1838.
18. Geoffrey Blainey, *The Tyranny of Distance*, Sun Books, Melbourne, 1966, p. 158.

Chapter 2 The Route

1. Paul Hasluck, address on 'The Voyage of the *Ivy*', 1871, to Western Australian Historical Society, 31 July 1931, in *Western Australian Historical Society, Journal and Proceedings*, vol. 1, part X, 1931.
2. Jack Loney, *Australian Shipwrecks*, vol. 2, 1851-1971, A. H. & A. W. Reed, Sydney, 1980, p. 25.
3. T. Skinner Prout, 'Emigration — A Voyage to Australia' in *Illustrated London News*, 20 January 1849.
4. Bateson in *The Convict Ships 1787-1868* gives the route of the First Fleet, pp. 102-13. In his *Explanations and Sailing Directions to Accompany the Wind and Current Chart* (published on the authority of the Secretary of the Navy, Washington, 1853.), Maury stated after his visit to England in 1853 that this was still the 'Admiralty Route', pp. 588, 595.
5. John Thomas Towson, *Tables to Facilitate the Practice of Great Circle Sailing and Determination of Azimuths*, 5th edition, printed for the Hydrographic Office, Admiralty, 1854, *passim*.
6. Ltnt M. F. Maury, *The Physical Geography of the Sea*, Thomas Nelson & Sons, London, 1881, p.iii of the introduction to first edition (1855) was repeated in a later edition in 1881.
7. Maury, *Explanations and Sailing Directions*, p. 591.
8. ibid, p. 595.
9. ibid, p. 588.
10. ibid, p. 588.
11. 'Testimonial to Mr. Towson', in *The Times*, 27 September 1854.
12. Maury, *Explanations and Sailing Directions*, pp. 587-8.
13. Maury, *The Physical Geography of the Sea*, p. 249.
14. Robert Mitchell, recollections on *Malabar*, Glasgow for Melbourne, 1852, in Castlemaine Association of Pioneers and Old Residents (compilers), *Records of the Castlemaine Pioneers*, Rigby, Adelaide, 1972, p. 30.
15. William John Adams, twenty-two-year-old son of an English nurseryman, emigrating with his wife, diary on *Victory*, Southampton for Sydney, 1855, MSS 1068, Mitchell Library, Sydney.
16. William Scoresby, Master Mariner and son of a whaling captain, carried out a survey of 400 miles of the Greenland coast, as well as studies of development of waves. In 1856 at the age of sixty-seven he travelled to Melbourne on the first voyage of auxiliary ship *Royal Charter* as an expert on effects of iron hulls on ships' compasses. His exertions during this voyage led to his death soon after his return to England. See Robert Edmund Scoresby-Jackson, *The Life of William Scoresby*, Thomas Nelson, London, 1861, pp. 372-5.
17. Moses Melchior, diary on *Gauntlet*, London for Melbourne, 1853, in the *Annual Dog Watch*, Melbourne, No. 30, 1973.
18. Charles Scott, diary on *Annie Wilson*, Liverpool for Sydney, 1859, MSS 599, Mitchell Library, Sydney.
19. R. H. Dana, jnr, *Two Years Before the Mast, or a Sailor's Life at Sea*, Hutchinson & Co., London, no date, pp. 255-6. Richard Henry Dana (1815-82) was born in Massachusetts and interrupted his studies to go to sea in 1834. *Two Years Before the Mast* was published in the 1840s. Dana later became a US jurist and politician.
20. Antoine Fauchery, *Letters from a Miner in Australia*, 1957, tr. Professor A. R. Chisholm, Georgian House, Melbourne, 1965, p. 6. Fauchery became well known as a goldfields photographer.

Chapter 3 The Ships

1. Bateson, *The Convict Ships 1787-1868*, p. 83.
2. Lubbock, *The Colonial Clippers*, p. 2.
3. Extrapolated from the appendices to *The Convict Ships 1787-1868* by Bateson, appendix 1, pp. 337-77.
4. Basil Greenhill and Ann Giffard, *Travelling by Sea in the Nineteenth Century*, A. & C. Black, London, 1972, p. 11.
5. Peter Kemp (ed.), *Oxford Companion to the Sea and Ships*, Oxford University Press, London, 1976, p. 172.
6. Douglas Lobley, *Ships Through the Ages*, Octopus Press, London, 1972, pp. 63-6.
7. Quoted by Lubbock in *The Colonial Clippers*, p. 22.
8. Alexander Laing, *Seafaring America*, American Heritage Publishing Company, New York, 1974, pp. 276-7.

9. George Campbell, *China Tea Clippers*, Adlard Coles, London, 1974, pp. 20-21.
10. Michael Stammers, *The Passage Makers*, Teredo Books, Brighton, Sussex, 1978, p. 84.
11. Don Charlwood, *Wrecks and Reputations: Loss of the Schomberg and Loch Ard*, Angus & Robertson, Sydney, 1977, pp. 48-51.
12. From a roller-blind scroll covering the years 1855-63, the latitude and longitude for 300 passages is given for each of the voyages. Held at The Royal Historical Society of Victoria.
13. Lubbock, *The Colonial Clippers*, p. 164.
14. William Scoresby, 'Variation of the Compass in Iron Ships', report of paper given before the British Association at Liverpool, *The Times*, 27 September 1854.
15. Scoresby-Jackson, *The Life of William Scoresby*, pp. 385-92.
16. For more information on the *Great Britain* see: (i) Victoria Wegg-Prosser (comp.). *S.S. 'Great Britain*; (ii) Corlett, *The Iron Ship; The History and Significance of Brunel's Great Britain*; (iii) C. Smith Cuttings (Shipping), The Royal Historical Society of Victoria; (iv) Victorian Public Record Office, Passenger list of *Great Britain*, Liverpool for Melbourne, February 1857, no. 5638/74.
17. The C. Smith Cuttings (Shipping) held at The Royal Historical Society of Victoria.
18. Rachel Henning, *The Letters of Rachel Henning*, Angus & Robertson, Sydney, 1963, p. 59.
19. Robert Saddington, diary on *Great Britain*, Liverpool for Melbourne, 1853, MSS 1271, Mitchell Library, Sydney.
20. Victoria, Legislative Council,

Submission by George Verdon, Agent-General for Victoria, Parl. Paper A, no. 21, 1869.
21. William McFee, *Law of the Sea*, Faber & Faber, London, 1951, pp. 207-36.
22. Course, *The Merchant Navy*, pp. 229-39.
23. ibid. pp. 229-39.

Chapter 4 Life at Home

1. Sidney Smith, *Whether to Go and Whither?*, John Kendrick, London, 1849, p. 46.
2. Greenhill and Giffard, *Travelling by Sea in the Nineteenth Century*, p. 17.
3. Dorothy Wilkinson, *The Dinton-Dalwood Letters* from 1827 to 1853, privately printed, 1964.
4. Walter Allen (selector), *Transatlantic Crossing; American Visitors to Britain and British Visitors to America in the Nineteenth Century*, Heinemann, London, 1971, pp. 94-5, 102.
5. Samuel Warren, 'A Press-Room Sketch', *Blackwood's Magazine*, Edinburgh, April 1837 (reprinted 1977).
6. Howard Clayton, *Cathedral City: A Look at Victorian Lichfield*, published by the author at the Benhill Press, Rugely, 1977, p. 88.
7. Ronald Blythe quoting a Suffolk farmer in *Akenfield*, Allen Lane, London, 1969, p. 36.
8. John Prebble, *The Highland Clearances*, Penguin Books, Harmondsworth, 1977, p. 183.
9. Either Christine or Mary McRitchie, sisters, diary on *William Stewart*, London for Melbourne, 1848, MS 10233, La Trobe Collection, State Library of Victoria.

Chapter 5 Decision and Preparation

1. 'The Emigrant Ship', *Illustrated*

London News, 15 November 1851. Poet identified only as 'W'.
2. *The Young Englishwoman*, a magazine published by S. O. Beeton, London, vol. 111, 30 December 1865 to 23 June 1866.
3. Thomas Coggan, recollections of voyage to Melbourne, 1857, in Castlemaine Association of Pioneers and Old Residents (compilers), *Records of the Castlemaine Pioneers*, p. 72.
4. Letter from Edward Parry to John Marshall, Agent to the Emigration Committee, dated 11 August 1835 at Norwich, Australian Pamphlets XVII, La Trobe Collection, State Library of Victoria, quoting Anne and John Loomes.
5. Margaret Kiddle, *Caroline Chisholm*, Melbourne University Press, Melbourne, 1969, appendix B, statement 5 – Ellen W. London.
6. Mrs Charles Clacy, *A Lady's Visit to the Gold Diggings of Australia, 1852-53*, Lansdowne Press, Melbourne, 1963, p. 151.
7. Letter from J. A. Rochlitz, quoted in Dr Egon Kunz, *Blood and Gold: Hungarians in Australia*, Cheshire, Melbourne, 1969, p. 60.
8. Letter from Sophy Taylor (Mrs Edward Cooke) to her sister, quoted in Irene C. Taylor, *Sophy under Sail*, Hodder & Stoughton, Sydney, 1969, pp. 158-60.
9. Letter from John Smith to mother, 3 March 1856, in *Templestowe Community News*, Victoria, September, 1978.
10. Verses from the papers of Arthur Charlwood, bookseller and printer, Melbourne, 1851, author unknown.
11. Mrs Thomas Hinshelwood, diary and notes on *Nebo*, Glasgow for Rockhampton, 1853, in *Port of Melbourne Quarterly*, October-

December 1963, January–March 1964.

12. Letter from J. B. Hack, Esq., Launceston, January 1837, in Henry Watson, *A Lecture on South Australia; including letters from J. B. Hack, Esq. and other Emigrants*, 2nd ed., Gliddon, London, 1838, appendix 1, p. 24.

13. G. Butler Earp, *The Gold Colonies of Australia*, Geo. Routledge & Co., London, 1852, p. 7. La Trobe Library, Australian Pamphlets, vol. xxxiv.

14. Arthur Hodgson, *Emigration to the Australian Settlements*, Trelawney Saunders, London, 1849, p. 5.

15. Samuel and John Sidney (editors), *Sidney's Emigrant's Journal*, vol. 1, no. 19, 8 February 1849, W. S. Orr & Co., London, 1849. La Trobe Collection, Rare Books, State Library of Victoria.

16. D. J. Golding (ed.), *The Emigrant's Guide to Australia in the Eighteen Fifties*, The Hawthorn Press, Melbourne, 1973, pp. 7 and 12. Originally written by John Capper as *Philips' Emigrant's Guide to Australia*, George Philip and Son, Liverpool, 1856.

17. Mr. Sydney, 'Three Colonies of Australia' in Golding (ed.), *The Emigrant's Guide to Australia in the Eighteen Fifties*, p. 18. (No other reference to 'Mr. Sydney' could be found.)

18. Golding (ed.), *The Emigrant's Guide to Australia in the Eighteen Fifties*, pp. 24-5.

19. ibid, p. 26. 20. ibid, pp. 36-7.

21. Samuel and John Sidney (editors), *Sidney's Emigrant's Journal*, vol. 1, no. 3, 19 October 1848.

22. ibid, vol. 1, no. 3, 19 October 1848.

23. Coleman, *Passage to America*, p. 67.

24. ibid, quotes Sir George Stephen, Liverpool barrister and philanthropist, p. 73.

25. Earp, *The Gold Colonies of Australia*, p. 211.

26. William H. G. Kingston, *The Emigrant Voyager's Manual*, Trelawney Saunders, London, 1850, p. 7.

27. Henry Capper, *The Australian Colonies: Where they are and How to get there*, Groombridge and Sons, London, 1855, pp. 55-6. La Trobe Library, Australian Pamphlets, vol. xxxiv.

28. Letter from James Henty to father from Swan River Settlement, 1829, ML 7810, La Trobe Collections, State Library of Victoria.

29. Each of these impending departures was advertised in *The Times*, 9 January 1855.

30. E. Cuzens, 'Voyage in the Early Days' in Melbourne *Argus*, 31 December 1921 as quoted in W. E. Masters, *Our Centenary*, privately published, 1949. By courtesy Mrs W. S. C. Hare, Melbourne.

Chapter 6 The Departure

1. Anonymous poet quoted in the *Illustrated London News*, 6 July 1850.

2. Dr R. Scot Skirving, also Master Mariner, Surgeon-superintendent on *Palomar* (the fictitious name for the *Ellora*), Plymouth for Sydney, 1883, in *Medical Journal of Australia*, vol. 1, no. 26, 27 June 1942. Dr Skirving, who became superintendent of Prince Alfred Hospital in Sydney, was a noted practitioner until his death in 1956 at the age of ninety-seven.

3. J. F. Hughes, recollections of a voyage, Liverpool for Melbourne, 1852, in Castlemaine Association of Pioneers and Old Residents (compilers), *Records of the Castlemaine Pioneers*, p. 1.

4. Coleman quoting evidence of John Bramley Moore before the Commons Committee of 1851 on docks, in *Passage to America*, p. 195.

5. Joseph Tarry, diary on *Ghenghis Khan*, Liverpool for Melbourne, 1853. By courtesy W. Tarry, Melbourne.

6. Robert Beckett, diary on *Underly*, Liverpool for Sydney, 1866-7. By courtesy Mrs E. Walker, Melbourne.

7. Robert Corkhill, diary on *British Trident*, Liverpool for Melbourne, 1855, published in *Digger*, February and March 1974.

8. Charles Dickens, *David Copperfield*, The Thames Publishing Co., London, no date, pp. 455-7.

9. John Sayers, diary on *Osyth*, London for Melbourne, 1875, MST 1917, Public Record Office, Northern Ireland.

10. William Rayment, diary on *Himalaya*, London for Melbourne, 1852, MS 4471, La Trobe Collection, State Library of Victoria.

11. 'Departure of the *Hercules*' in the *Illustrated London News*, 15 January 1853.

12. Victoria, Legislative Assembly, *Report of the Immigration Officer (Edward Grimes) on the* Hercules, 9 June 1853.

13. For a description of the *Indus* departing for Brisbane see 'Outward Bound', *Graphic*, London, vol. v, no. 135, 29 June 1872.

14. Coleman, quoting *Ballou's Pictorial*, Boston, January-June 1855, vol. 8, in *Passage to America*, p. 82.

15. Fauchery, *Letters from a Miner in Australia*, pp. 4-5.
16. Edward Snell, diary on *Bolton*, London for Melbourne, 1849, MS 8970, La Trobe Collection, State Library of Victoria.
17. Robert C. Leslie, *Old Sea Wings Ways and Words in the Days of Oak and Hemp*, Chapman & Hall, London, 1890, pp. 235-7.
18. F. W. Leighton, diary on *Bloomer*, Liverpool for Melbourne, 1853, MS 10461, La Trobe Collection, State Library of Victoria.
19. Article covering the departure of *Schomberg*, Liverpool for Melbourne, 1855 in *The Forget-Me-Not; or, Last Hours on the Mersey*, Liverpool Seamen's and Bethel Union, Liverpool, no. 50, 1855.
20. William Harbottle, diary on *Scotia*, London for Sydney, 1849, MS 160, National Library of Australia, Canberra.
21. Thomas Small, diary on *Donald Mackay*, Liverpool for Melbourne, 1863, MS 8406, La Trobe Collection, State Library of Victoria.
22. E. Lloyd, *A Visit to the Antipodes*, Smith, Elder & Co., London, 1846, p. 2.
23. Clacy, *A Lady's Visit to the Gold Diggings of Australia*, pp. 10-11.
24. Henry McIntosh, diary on *Overtes*, Plymouth for Melbourne, 1852. By courtesy Mrs Dorothy Smith, Melbourne.
25. Samuel Shaw, diary on *Tyburnia*, London for Sydney, 1877, MS T/1923/1, Public Record Office, Northern Ireland.
26. Lloyd, *A Visit to the Antipodes*, p. 7.
27. Letters from Joseph Beale on *Sarah Sands*, Cork for Melbourne, 1853, MSS 1083, Mitchell Library, Sydney.
28. Mrs Charles Meredith, *Notes and Sketches of New South Wales*, John Murray, London, 1844, p. 19.

Chapter 7 Accommodation

1. Henning, *The Letters of Rachel Henning*, pp. 18-9, 50.
2. William Thompson, diary on *Meteor*, Glasgow for Melbourne, 1854, MS 9085, La Trobe Collection, State Library of Victoria.
3. William Johnstone, diary on *Arab*, bound for Launceston, 1841-2, quoted in Greenhill and Gifford, *Travelling by Sea in the Nineteenth Century*. p. 16.
4. Coleman, quoting evidence of Thomas William Clinton Murdoch to 1854 Select Committee on the Passengers' Acts, in *Passage to America*, p. 112.
5. Jessie Campbell, diary on *Blenheim*, bound for New Zealand, 1840, quoted in Greenhill and Gifford, *Women under Sail*, p. 55.
6. Article on accommodation on *St Vincent* in the *Illustrated London News*, 13 April 1844.
7. The Melbourne *Argus*, 6 October 1855, quoting *Aberdeen Reporter* of unspecified date.
8. *White Star Journal*, 20 April to 17 July 1855, published on voyage of *White Star* to Australia.
9. W. Shaw, *Land of Promise; or my Impressions of Australia*, Simpkin, Marshall & Co., London, 1854, pp. 321-3.
10. *White Star Journal*, voyage newspaper, 1859.
11. Robert Poynter, diary on *Cornelis Gips*, London for Melbourne, 1854. By courtesy Professor J. R. Poynter, Melbourne.
12. Meredith, *Notes and Sketches of New South Wales*, p. 2.
13. Article on accommodation on *St Vincent* in the *Illustrated London News*, 13 April 1844.
14. Coleman, *Passage to America*, p. 110.
15. Bateson, *The Convict Ships 1787-1868*, p. 69.
16. Alexander Laing, *Seafaring America*, p. 230.
17. United Kingdom, House of Commons, *Parliamentary Paper: Reports and Correspondence Respecting Emigration to the Colonies*, No. 16, 'Extracts of a letter from Lieutenant Lean, Emigration Agent at the Port of London', 1839.
18. ibid.
19. Victoria, Legislative Council, *Report of the Health Officer (A. Robertson MD), Return of Diseases*, six months ending 31 December 1855.
20. W. H. Leigh, *Reconnoitring Voyages and Travels with Adventures in the New Colonies of South Australia*, Smith, Elder & Co., London, 1839, p. 13.
21. R. Scott Skirving, recollections in the *Medical Journal of Australia*, 27 June 1942.
22. Unidentified newspaper in the C. Smith Cuttings (Shipping), held by The Royal Historical Society of Victoria.
23. George Tucker, diary on *Northumberland*, Plymouth for Melbourne, 1876. By courtesy Mrs D. W. Cruickshank, Melbourne.
24. New South Wales, Legislative Council, *Report from the Select Committee of the Legislative Council to Inquire into the Present System of German Immigration into this Colony*, Government Printer, Sydney, 11 August 1858.
25. 'Female Emigration' in London *Morning Herald*, 11 July 1834.

26. Caroline Chisholm [identified as Secretary to the Sydney Immigrants' Home], *Female Immigration considered in a Brief Account of the Sydney Immigrants' Home*, James Tegg, Sydney, 1842, p. 30.

27. W. E. Masters, *Our Centenary*, privately published, 1949. By courtesy Mrs W. S. C. Hare, Melbourne.

28. Kiddle, *Caroline Chisholm*, p. 117.

29. Mark T. Amos, recollections on voyage from Liverpool to Melbourne, 1852, in Castlemaine Association of Pioneers and Old Residents (compilers), *Records of the Castlemaine Pioneers*, p. 179.

30. John Fitch Clark, diary on *Nepaul*, London for Geelong, 1852, 2627A. By courtesy of the Battye Library.

Chapter 8 The Crew

1. Bateson, *The Convict Ships 1787-1868*, p. 86.

2. Dana, *Two Years Before the Mast*, p. 16.

3. William Culshaw Greenhalgh, diary on *Marco Polo*, Liverpool for Melbourne, 1853, Merseyside County Museums, Liverpool.

4. Arthur Wilcox Manning, diary on *Earl Grey*, Plymouth for Sydney, 1839-40, MS 289, National Library of Australia, Canberra.

5. Thomas Herbert Boykett, letter to Dr H. G. Bunn telling of voyage on *The Gypsy*, Southampton for Adelaide, 1853. By courtesy Mrs J. E. Nilsson, Melbourne.

6. Lloyd, *A Visit to the Antipodes*, pp. 71-2.

7. Charlotte Haldane, *Daughter of Paris*, biography of Celeste de Chabrillan based in part on Celeste de Chabrillan's autobiographical works, Hutchinson, London, 1961, p. 124.

8. ibid, p. 156.

9. Captain George Calcutt, *Voyage of the Loch Tay*, 1892, Maritime Historical Productions, Melbourne, 1965, p. 12.

10. Lloyd, *A Visit to the Antipodes*, p. 11.

11. Dana, *Two Years before the Mast*, p. 215.

12. Lloyd, *A Visit to the Antipodes*, p. 60.

13. John Ramsay, diary on *Loch Sunart*, Glasgow for Melbourne, 1878. By courtesy Mrs Edith M. Ramsay, Melbourne.

14. Lloyd, *A Visit to the Antipodes*, p. 26.

15. Dr Francis Workman, letter to Reading Pathological Society, 1884, after his arrival in Melbourne as Surgeon-superintendent on *Sobraon*. Printed for the society as a pamphlet: 'The Ocean as a Health Resort'. See Australian Medical Association Library, Melbourne.

16. Francis Maybury journal, probably based on diary first kept on *Kochinor*, Liverpool for Cape Town, then on *Cheapside*, Cape Town for Melbourne, after loss of *Kochinor* by fire, 1856, MSS 73, Mitchell Library, Sydney.

17. Captain James Gaby, *Mate in Sail*, Antipodean Publishers, Artarmon, NSW, 1974, p. 151.

18. 'Shalimar' [Captain F. C. Hendry], 'Stern First', *Blackwood's Magazine*, October 1931.

19. 'By A Passenger', *Narrative of a Voyage from England to Australia in the S.S. "Somersetshire" 1879-80 with Notes on Ship Life*, Walker, May & Co., Melbourne, 1880, Petherick Collection, National Library of Australia, Canberra.

20. Lubbock, *The Colonial Clippers*, p. 199.

21. Scoresby-Jackson, *The Life of William Scoresby*, pp. 377-8.

22. Aleck Gibson, diary on *Stebonheath*, London for Melbourne, 1855, Aleck Gibson papers, H 15943, La Trobe Collection, State Library of Victoria.

23. A. G. Harvie, diary on *Scottish Wizard*, London for Brisbane, 1892. By courtesy late Mrs J. L. Potter, Adelaide.

24. Dana, *Two Years Before the Mast*, p. 37.

25. Calcutt, *Voyage of the Loch Tay*, p. 41.

26. John Fenwick, diary on *Lightning*, Liverpool for Melbourne, 1854, published as *The Lightning Diary of John Fenwick*, The Geelong Historical Society, Geelong, Vic., 1969.

27. Diary of Mary Thomas en route London for Adelaide, 1836, quoted in Penelope Hope, *The Voyage of the Africaine*, Heinemann, London, 1968, p. 65.

28. Captain A. W. Pearse, *Windward Ho!*, John Andrew & Co., Sydney, 1932, p. 15.

29. Letter from Aitken Lilburn & Co., London, to Stan McPhee, Warrnambool, Victoria, 8 September 1964.

30. Dana, *Two Years Before the Mast*, footnote on p. 243.

31. Havelock Wilson, quoted by Ronald Hope, 'Those Good Old Days', *5000 Weeks of Fairplay*, 28 June 1979.

32. Dana, *Two Years Before the Mast*, footnote on p. 309.

33. Anne Drysdale, diary on *Indus*, London for Melbourne, 1839, MS 9249, La Trobe Collection, State Library of Victoria.

34. William Howitt, diary on *Kent*, Plymouth for Melbourne, 1852, MS 9356, La Trobe Collection, State Library of Victoria.

35. Victoria, Supreme Court, Criminal Session, *Report on the stranding of the* United, 1853, no. 1/252/13, Victorian Public Record Office.

36. Sir Charles Gavan Duffy, *My Life in Two Hemispheres*, T. Fisher Unwin, London, 1898, p. 130.
37. Havelock Wilson quoted by Ronald Hope, 'Those Good Old Days', *5000 Weeks of Fairplay*, 28 June 1979.

Chapter 9 Surgeons and Health

1. Dr Murray Verso, 'Peripatetic Doctors', *Victorian Historical Journal*, vol. 49, no. 1, February 1978.
2. Bateson, *The Convict Ships 1787-1868*, p. 52.
3. United Kingdom, Secretary of State for the Colonies, *Instructions for Surgeons-superintendent of Government Ships going to New South Wales*, 'Enclosure No. 6 to Copies or Extracts of Correspondence between the Secretary of State for the Colonies and the Governor of the Australian Colonies, respecting Emigration', 14 May 1838.
4. Victorian Public Record Office, Instructions for Surgeon of *Georgiana*, signed 'Wm. Smith & Sons', Liverpool 22 September 1840, File no. 41/383A, Box 19. Contained in Superintendent La Trobe's Inward Correspondence received on arrival of *Georgiana* in Port Phillip, 25 February 1841. Attached to ship's papers.
5. Chisholm, *Female Immigration Considered in a Brief Account of the Sydney Immigrants' Home*, p. 26.
6. Coleman, quoting Tenth Annual Report of the Colonial Land and Emigration Commissioners, H.C., 1850, vol. 23, p. 59, in *Passage to America*, p. 115.
7. William Merifield, diary on *Lincolnshire*, London for Melbourne, 1858, MS 8044, La Trobe Collection, State Library of Victoria.
8. George Verdon, Agent-General for Victoria, *Instructions to Surgeons-superintendent of Victorian Government Emigrant Ships*, Spottiswoode & Co., London, 1871.
9. New South Wales, Legislative Council, *Report from the Select Committee of the Legislative Council to Inquire into the Present System of German Immigration into this Colony*, Government Printer, Sydney, 11 August 1858.
10. Dr R. Scott Skirving recollections.
11. F. W. C. Beavan, report by Surgeon-superintendent on emigrant ship *Kate*, 1854. Manuscript in the Australian Medical Association Library, Melbourne.
12. Jean M. Manning, Ph.C., Melbourne, notes to author.
13. Coleman, quoting *Medical Hints for Emigrants*, vol. 9 of *Emigrant Tracts*, London, Society for Promoting Christian Knowledge. 1850-2, in *Passage to America*, p. 138.
14. R. S. Allison, *Sea Diseases*, John Bale Medical Publications Ltd., London, 1943, p. 88.
15. ibid, p. 89.
16. Bryn Thomas and Byron Gandevia, 'Dr Francis Workman, Emigrant, and the History of Taking the Cure for Consumption in the Australian Colonies', *Medical Journal of Australia*, vol. 2, 4 July 1959, p. 2.
17. Dr Francis Workman, *The Ocean as a Health Resort*, Reading Pathological Society, England, 1884, p. 1.
18. Greenhill and Giffard, *Travelling by Sea in the Nineteenth Century*, p. 14.
19. Dr R. Scott Skirving recollections.
20. Rosamund Duruz, 'What Wonders Behind Walls', *Parade Magazine*, Southdown Press, Melbourne, December 1973.
21. Oswald Bloxome, diary on *Florentia*, Plymouth for Sydney, 1838, MS 336, National Library of Australia, Canberra.
22. Frances Thomson (wife of James Thomson, voyage surgeon-superintendent) diary on *Selkirkshire*, Glasgow for Rockhampton, 1882, MS 1025, National Library of Australia, Canberra.
23. Sarah Docker, diary on *Adams*, London for Sydney, 1828, MS 10437, La Trobe Collection, State Library of Victoria.
24. Dr R. Scott Skirving recollections.
25. Thomas Wilmot, diary as surgeon-superintendent on *Irene*, Liverpool for Sydney, 1852, MSS 559, Mitchell Library, Sydney.
26. Victoria, Legislative Council, *Report of the Health Officer*, 'Return of Diseases most Prevalant on Board Ships Performing Quarantine', during the half-year ending 31 December 1852.
27. Major J. H. Welch, *From the HELL of the Fever Ships to HEALTH*, Nepean Historical Society, 1969, p. 17. (This book appears as Book 2 of *The Peninsula Story*).
28. ibid, report on *Ticonderoga*, 25 January 1853, p. 28.
29. ibid, p. 29.
30. ibid, quotes Ltnt Governor La Trobe's despatch on the *Ticonderoga*, p. 29.
31. Victoria, Legislative Assembly, *Report of the Chief Medical Officer (Dr W. McCrae) on the Report of the Board Appointed to Enquire into the Quarantine Regulations and in Regard to the "Golden Empire"*, Paper A, no. 35, July 1865.
32. Coleman, *Passage to America*, p. 140.
33. Greenhill and Giffard, *Women Under Sail*, pp. 58-9.

34. Sarah Allingham, diary on *Marco Polo*, Liverpool for Melbourne, 1855, MS 9409, La Trobe Collection, State Library of Victoria.
35. H. F. Leader, diary on *John Mitchell*, London for Adelaide, 1849, D 4779(L), State Library of South Australia.
36. New South Wales, Legislative Council, *Report from the Select Committee of the Legislative Council to Inquire into the Present System of German Immigration into this Colony*, Government Printer, Sydney, 11 August 1858. Mr Otto Sutor, witness called and examined.

Chapter 10 Messing and Dining

1. Bateson, *The Convict Ships 1787-1868*, pp. 66-7.
2. ibid, p. 266.
3. Captain S. B. Sandford, 'Salt-Beef and Biscuits' in *Nautical Magazine*, Glasgow, vol. 222, no. 1, July 1979.
4. Bateson, *The Convict Ships 1787-1868*, p. 52.
5. United Kingdom, Secretary of State for the Colonies, *Instructions for the Surgeons-superintendent of Government Ships going to New South Wales*, 'Enclosure No. 6 to Copies or Extracts of Correspondence between the Secretary of State for the Colonies and the Governors of the Australian Colonies, respecting Emigration', 14 May 1838.
6. E. Cuzens, 'Voyage in the Early Days', account of emigration on *Travancore*, 1849, in Melbourne *Argus*, 31 December 1921.
7. Fauchery, *Letters from a Miner in Australia*, p. 8.
8. John MacKenzie, diary on *Robert Benn*, Glasgow for Melbourne, 1841, MS 685, National Library of Australia, Canberra.
9. Edward Stamp, 'London Towards Port Phillip', diary on

Tasman, 1849, MS 29, National Library of Australia, Canberra.
10. Letter from John Hatfield to mother dated 14.10.1857 at Collingwood, Victoria, soon after his arrival, MS 8172, Box 964/3D, La Trobe Collection, State Library of Victoria.
11. Fauchery, *Letters from a Miner in Australia*, p. 8.
12. New South Wales, Legislative Council, *Votes and Proceedings*, 'Immigration Despatch from Secretary of State to Governor Fitzroy', No. 16, 31 January 1848.
13. United Kingdom, *Passenger Act*, 1849, Amendments of 1852.
14. Henry Nicholls, diary on *Norway*, London for Melbourne, 1853, A 4070, Mitchell Library, Sydney.
15. Edwin Bird, diary on *Marco Polo*, Liverpool for Melbourne, 1853, MS 6069, National Library of Australia, Canberra.
16. Lubbock quoting 'Rules and Customs aboard the *Eagle*, 1853', in *The Colonial Clippers*, p. 127.
17. Letter of Mr Tait, dated 12 June 1837 on *North Briton*, Firth of Forth for Sydney, MS 1412, National Library of Australia, Canberra.
18. Unidentified passenger of 1842 is quoted in Helen M. Simpson, 'The Women of New Zealand', *Historical Publications*, Department of Internal Affairs, Wellington, 1940, p. 38.
19. Lloyd, *A Visit to the Antipodes*, p. 41.
20. Anonymous diarist on *Asiatic*, London for Sydney, 1852. By courtesy Mrs Warren Perry, Melbourne.
21. William Deakin, diary on *Samuel Boddington*, London for Adelaide, 1849-50, MS 1540/19/357, National Library of Australia, Canberra.
22. Bateson, *The Convict Ships 1787-1868*, p. 68.
23. Leigh, *Reconnoitring Voyages and Travels with Adventures in the*

New Colonies of South Australia, pp. 55-6.
24. Allison, *Sea Diseases*, p. 143.
25. Fauchery, *Letters from a Miner in Australia*, p. 7.
26. E. Cuzens, 'Voyage in the Early Days' in Melbourne *Argus*, 31 December 1921, quoted in W. E. Masters, *Our Centenary*.
27. Greenhill and Giffard, *Women Under Sail*, p. 80.
28. Herman Melville, *Redburn: His First Voyage*, Jonathan Cape, London, 1924.
29. Mark Amos recollections.
30. New South Wales, Legislative Council, *Report from the Select Committee of the Legislative Council to Inquire into the Present System of German Immigration into this Colony*, Government Printer, Sydney, 11 August 1858.

Chapter 11 Pastimes and Consolations

1. Anne Gratton, diary on *Conway*, Liverpool for Melbourne, 1858, MS 9367, La Trobe Collection, State Library of Victoria.
2. James Robertson, recollections of voyage Liverpool to Melbourne, 1852, in Castlemaine Association of Pioneers and Old Residents (compilers), *Records of the Castlemaine Pioneers, 1880-1927*, pp. 43-44.
3. Kingston, *The Emigrant Voyager's Manual*, pp. 23, 27, 38.
4. Anonymous diarist from Ireland, 1842. (In author's keeping.)
5. Joseph Tarry diary.
6. Duffy, *My Life in Two Hemispheres*, p. 131.
7. The 'Father of Sandridge', Wilbraham Liardet, was left £30,000, but, with nine children and being a free spender, he was obliged to emigrate to Sydney. It was typical of his impetuosity that he decided to leave the *William Metcalfe* at Melbourne. He established

a ferry to Liardet's Beach, now Port Melbourne, and also had a hotel there.

8. J. B. Were, diary on *William Metcalfe*, Plymouth for Melbourne, 1839, published for clients of J. B. Were & Son, 1964.

9. Taylor, *Sophy Under Sail*, p. 57.

10. *White Star Journal*, voyage newspaper, 20 April to 17 July 1855.

11. Robert Main Abbott, diary on *James L. Bogart*, London for Melbourne, 1852-3, The Royal Historical Society of Victoria.

12. Report of protest meeting following Captain Forbes' loss of *Schomberg*, in Melbourne *Argus*, 5 January 1856.

13. Leigh, *Reconnoitring Voyages and Travels with Adventures in the New Colonies of South Australia*, p. 17.

14. Meredith, *Notes and Sketches of New South Wales*, p. 25.

15. Robert Mitchell recollections in Castlemaine Association of Pioneers and Old Residents (compilers), *Records of the Castlemaine Pioneers*, pp. 30-1.

16. George Tucker diary.

17. Lubbock, *The Colonial Clippers*, p. 84.

18. ibid, p. 83.

19. Lloyd, *A Visit to the Antipodes*, p. 28.

20. Clacy, *A Lady's Visit to the Gold Diggings of Australia*, p. 12.

21. Letter written by Mrs Hugh Martin en route to Plymouth, New Zealand, 1843-4, to her sister, AM 143, Mitchell Library, Sydney.

22. Letter from Leonardo Pozzi on unidentified ship, Hamburg for Melbourne, 1855. By courtesy Ms Glen Tomasetti.

23. Henry McIntosh diary.

24. Robert Corkhill diary.

Chapter 12 The New Shore

1. Text of the last sermon on an unidentified emigrant ship, Liverpool for Melbourne, 1852, recorded by Mark Amos who could 'well remember the effect this address appeared to have on those who heard it', in Castlemaine Association of Pioneers and Old Residents (compilers), *Records of the Castlemaine Pioneers*, p. 180.

2. Blainey, *The Tyranny of Distance*, p. 161.

3. Mrs C. Gill (probably), journal of a voyage to Australia Felix in the *Caledonia*, 1842, MS 4053, National Library of Australia, Canberra.

4. *Lincolnshire Observer*, voyage newspaper, 1866.

5. William Howitt, *Land, Labour and Gold, or Two Years in Victoria with Visits to Sydney and Van Diemen's Land*, 1855; Facsimile edition, Sydney University Press, Sydney, 1972, p. 1.

6. James Robertson recollections in Castlemaine Association of Pioneers and Old Residents (compilers), *Records of the Castlemaine Pioneers*, p. 44.

7. Samuel Rawson, diary on *Florentia*, Plymouth for Sydney, 1838, MS 204, National Library of Australia, Canberra.

8. Howitt, *Land, Labour and Gold, or Two Years in Victoria with Visits to Sydney and Van Diemen's Land*, pp. 1-2.

9. Mitchell recollections, in Castlemaine Association of Pioneers and Old Residents (compilers), *Records of the Castlemaine Pioneers*, p. 32.

10. *Netherby Gazette*, newspaper of 1866 voyage of Black Ball clipper *Netherby*. Copies were taken ashore when the ship was wrecked on King Island. The account of rescue and removal to Melbourne was added by H. D. Vincent, one of its editors. The whole account published by W. B. Stephens of Melbourne.

11. Lloyd, *A Visit to the Antipodes*, p. 68.

12. Howitt, *Land, Labour and Gold, or Two Years in Victoria with Visits to Sydney and Van Diemen's Land*, pp. 2-3.

13. Clacy, *A Lady's Visit to the Gold Diggings of Australia*, p. 17.

14. William Rayment diary.

15. Kunz, *Blood and Gold: Hungarians in Australia*, p. 61.

16. Thomas Sutcliffe Mort, diary on *Superb*, Liverpool for Sydney, 1837, MS 3308, National Library of Australia, Sydney.

17. Lloyd, *A Visit to the Antipodes*, p. 69.

18. Fanny L. Bussell, diary on *Cygnet*, Portsmouth for Swan River Settlement, 1832-3, MS 1415A, Battye Library, Perth.

19. Mary Ann Friend, diary on *Wanstead*, Portsmouth for Swan River Settlement, 1829-30, on ship commanded by her husband, Commander Matthew Friend, in *Western Australian Historical Society, Journal and Proceedings*, vol. 1, part x, 1931.

20. Richard Watt, diary on *Young Australia*, London for Brisbane, 1864, in *Sea Breezes*, Charles Birchall & Sons Ltd., Liverpool, vol. 22, July-August 1956.

21. Edward Webster, diary on *White Eagle*, Glasgow for Melbourne, 1856-7, MSS 302, Mitchell Library, Sydney.

Bibliography

Books, Pamphlets and Articles

ALLEN, Walter (selector), *Transatlantic Crossing: American Visitors to Britain and British Visitors to America in the Nineteenth Century*, Heinemann, London, 1971.
ALLISON, R. S., *Sea Diseases,* John Bale, Medical Publications Limited, London, 1943.
ANON. 'By a Passenger', *Narrative of a Voyage from England to Australia in the S.S. ''Somersetshire'', 1879-80 with Notes on Ship Life*, Walker, May & Co., Melbourne, 1880. Petherick Collection, National Library of Australia.

BATESON, Charles, *Australian Shipwrecks*, Vol. 1, 1622-1850, A. H. & A. W. Reed, Sydney, 1974.
— , *The Convict Ships 1787-1868*, A. H. & A. W. Reed, Sydney, 1974.
BEAGLEHOLE, J. C., *The Life of Captain James Cook*, A. & C. Black, London, 1974.
BEAVAN, F. W. C., Report by

Surgeon-superintendent on emigrant ship *Kate*, 1854. Manuscript in Australian Medical Association Library, Melbourne.
BLAINEY, Geoffrey, *The Tyranny of Distance*, Sun Books, Melbourne, 1966.
BLYTHE, Ronald, *Akenfield*, Penguin Books, Harmondsworth, 1977.

CALCUTT, Captain George, *Voyage of the Loch Tay*, Maritime Historical Productions, Melbourne, 1965.
CAMPBELL, George, *China Tea Clippers*, Adlard Coles, London, 1974.
CAPPER, Henry, *The Australian Colonies: Where they are and How to get there*, Groombridge and Sons, London, 1855. La Trobe Library, Australian Pamphlets, vol. xxxiv.
CAPPER, John, *Philips' Emigrant's Guide to Australia*, George Philip and Son, Liverpool, 1856.
CASTLEMAINE ASSOCIATION OF PIONEERS AND OLD RESIDENTS

(compilers), *Records of the Castlemaine Pioneers*, 1880-1927, Rigby, Adelaide, 1972.
CHARLWOOD, Don, *Wrecks and Reputations: Loss of the Schomberg and Loch Ard*, Angus & Robertson, Sydney, 1977.
CHISHOLM, Alec H. and others (editors), *Australian Encyclopaedia*, The Grolier Society of Australia, Sydney, 1965.
CHISHOLM, Caroline [identified as Secretary to the Sydney Immigrants' Home], *Female Immigration Considered in a Brief Account of the Sydney Immigrants' Home*, James Tegg, Sydney, 1842.
CLACY, Mrs Charles, *A Lady's Visit to the Gold Diggings of Australia, 1852-3*, Lansdowne Press, Melbourne, 1963.
CLARK, C. M. H., *Select Documents in Australian History*, Angus & Robertson, Sydney, 1950.
CLAYTON, Howard, *Cathedral City, A Look at Victorian Lichfield*, published by the author at The Benhill Press, Rugely, 1977.
COLEMAN, Terry, *Passage to*

America: A History of Emigrants from Great Britain and Ireland to America in the mid-nineteenth Century, Hutchinson, London, 1972.
COLERIDGE, Samuel Taylor, *The Rime of the Ancient Mariner*, in E. W. Parker (selector), *The Poet's Way*, Longman's Green & Co., London, 1938.
CORLETT, Ewan, *The Iron Ship: The History and Significance of Brunel's Great Britain*, Moonraker Press, Bradford-on-Avon, Wilts., 1975.
COURSE, Captain A. G., *The Merchant Navy: A Social History*, Frederick Muller, London, 1963.
CUZENS, E., 'Voyage in the Early Days', *Argus*, Melbourne, 31 December 1921.

DANA, Richard, *Two Years Before the Mast or A Sailor's Life at Sea*, Hutchinson & Co., London, [1946].
DICKENS, Charles, *David Copperfield*, The Thames Publishing Co., London, no date.
DUFFY, Sir Charles Gavan, *My Life in Two Hemispheres*, T. Fisher Unwin, London, 1898.
DURUZ, Rosamund, 'What Wonders behind Walls', *Parade Magazine*, Southdown Press, Melbourne, December 1973.

EARP, G. Butler, *The Gold Colonies of Australia*, Geo. Routledge & Co., London, 1852. La Trobe Library, Australian Pamphlets, vol. xxxiv.
ERICKSON, Charlotte, *Emigration from Europe 1815-1914*, Series: *Documents in Economic History*, A. & C. Black, London, 1976.

FAUCHERY, Antoine, *Letters from a Miner in Australia*, 1857, tr.

Professor A. R. Chisholm, Georgian House, Melbourne, 1965.

GABY, Captain James, *Mate in Sail*, Antipodean Publishers, Artarmon, New South Wales, 1974.
'GARRYOWEN' [Edmund Finn], *The Chronicles of Early Melbourne, 1835 to 1852 Historical, Anecdotal and Personal*, 2 vols, originally published, Fergusson & Mitchell, Melbourne, 1888; facsimile edition published by Heritage Publications, Melbourne, 1976.
GOLDING, D. J. (ed.), *The Emigrant's Guide to Australia in the Eighteen Fifties*, The Hawthorn Press, Melbourne, 1973, originally written by John Capper as *Philip's Emigrant's Guide to Australia*, George Philip and Son, Liverpool, 1856.
GOULD, Ltnt Commdr Rupert Thomas, *The Marine Chronometer: Its History and Development*, J. D. Potter, London, 1923.
GREENHILL, Basil and Giffard, Ann, *Travelling by Sea in the Nineteenth Century*, A. & C. Black, London, 1972.
— , *Women under Sail*, Davies & Charles, Newton Abbot, England, [1970].

HALDANE, Charlotte, *Daughter of Paris*, Hutchinson, London, 1961.
HASLUCK, Mr Paul, address on 'The Voyage of the *Ivy*', *Western Australian Historical Society, Journal and Proceedings*, vol. 1, part X, 1931.
HENDRY, Captain F. C. [pseudonym 'Shalimar'], 'Stern First', *Blackwood's Magazine*, Edinburgh, October 1931.
HENNING, Rachel, *The Letters of Rachel Henning*, Angus & Robertson, Sydney, 1963.

HODGSON, Arthur, *Emigration to the Australian Settlements*, Trelawney Saunders, London, 1849.
HOPE, Penelope, *The Voyage of the Africaine*, Heinemann, London, 1968.
HOPE, Ronald, 'Those Good Old Days', *5000 Weeks of Fairplay*, supplement to *Fairplay: Weekly Shipping Journal*, 28 June 1979.
HOWITT, William, *Land, Labour and Gold, or Two Years in Victoria with Visits to Sydney and Van Diemen's Land*, first published Longman, Brown, Green & Longmans, London, 1855; facsimile edition, Sydney University Press, Sydney, 1972.

KEMP, Peter (ed.), *Oxford Companion to the Sea and Ships*, Oxford University Press, London, 1976.
KIDDLE, Margaret, *Caroline Chisholm*, Melbourne University Press, Melbourne, 1950.
KINGSTON, William H. G., *The Emigrant Voyager's Manual*, Trelawney Saunders, London, 1850.
KUNZ, Dr Egon, *Blood and Gold: Hungarians in Australia*, Cheshire, Melbourne, 1969.

LAING, Alexander, *The Sea Witch, A Narrative of the Experiences of Captain Roger Murray and others in an American Clipper Ship during the Years 1846 to 1856*, Thornton Butterworth, London, 1933.
— , *Seafaring America*, American Heritage Publishing, New York, 1974.
LEIGH, W. H., *Reconnoitring Voyages and Travels with Adventures in the New Colonies of South Australia*, Smith, Elder & Co., London, 1839.
LESLIE, Robert C., *Old Sea Wings*

Ways and Words, in the Days of Oak and Hemp, Chapman & Hall, London, 1890.

LEWIS, Charles Lee, *Matthew Fontaine Maury, the Pathfinder of the Seas*, AMS Press, New York, 1927, republished same publisher, 1969.

[LLOYD, E.] 'By a Squatter', *A Visit to the Antipodes*, Smith, Elder & Co., London, 1846.

LOBLEY, Douglas, *Ships Through the Ages*, Octopus Press, London, 1972.

LONEY, Jack, *Australian Shipwrecks, 1851-1971*, vol. 2, A. H. & A. W. Reed, Sydney, 1980.

LUBBOCK, Basil, *The Colonial Clippers*, Brown, Son & Ferguson, Glasgow, 1968.

McCRAE, Hugh (ed.), *Georgiana's Journal*, Angus & Robertson, Sydney, 1966.

McFEE, W. *Law of the Sea*, Faber & Faber, London, 1951.

MARRIOTT, Mrs Ida, *The Voyage of the Caroline*, Longman Green, London, 1927.

MASTERS, W. E., *Our Centenary*, privately printed, Melbourne, 1949. By courtesy Mrs W. S. C. Hare, Melbourne.

MAURY, Ltnt M. F., *Explanations and Sailing Directions to Accompany the Wind and Current Chart*, published by authority Secretary of the Navy, C. Alexander, Printer, Washington, 1853.

— , *The Physical Geography of the Sea*, Thomas Nelson & Sons, London, 1881.

MELVILLE, Herman, *Redburn: His First Voyage*, Jonathan Cape, London, 1924.

MEREDITH, Mrs Charles, *Notes and Sketches of New South Wales: Account of Voyage on Letita,*

London for Sydney, 1839, John Murray, London, 1844; Penguin Colonial Facsimiles, Melbourne, 1973.

MORGAN, Marjorie, 'The First Hundred Years of Migration to Australasia', in B. R. Blaze (ed.), *Genealogy in a Changing Society*, Australian Institute of Genealogical Studies, Melbourne, 1980.

PEARSE, Captain A. W., *Windward Ho!*, John Andrew & Co., Sydney, 1932.

PREBBLE, John, *The Highland Clearances*, Penguin Books, Harmondsworth, 1975.

ROBERTS, Jane, *Two Years at Sea: the Narrative of a Voyage to the Swan River and Van Dieman's (sic) Land, during the Years 1829, 30, 31*, Richard Bentley, London, 1834.

SANDFORD, Captain S. B., 'Salt-Beef and Biscuits', *Nautical Magazine*, Glasgow, vol. 222, no. 1, July 1979.

SAYERS, C. E. (ed.), *Historical Records of Port Phillip*, Heinemann, Melbourne, 1972.

SCHILDER, Gunter, *Australia Unveiled, the Share of the Dutch Navigators in the Discovery of Australia*, tr. Olaf Richter, Theatrum Orbis Terrarum Ltd, Amsterdam, 1976.

SCORESBY, William, 'Variation of the Compass in Iron Ships', paper given before the British Association, Liverpool, see *The Times*, 27 September 1874.

SCORESBY-JACKSON, Robert Edmund, *The Life of William Scoresby*, Thomas Nelson and Sons, London, 1861.

SCOTT, J. W. Robertson, *The Day before Yesterday*, Methuen,

London, 1951.

SERLE, Geoffrey, *The Golden Age*, Melbourne University Press, Melbourne, 1963.

SHAW, W., *Land of Promise; or my Impressions of Australia*, Simpkin, Marshall & Co., London, 1854.

SIDNEY, Samuel and John (editors), *Sidney's Emigrant's Journal*, W. S. Orr & C., London, 1849. La Trobe Collection, Rare Books, State Library of Victoria.

SIMPSON, Helen M. *The Women of New Zealand*, Historical Publications, Department of Internal Affairs, Wellington, 1940.

SMITH, Sidney, *Whether to Go and Whither?*, John Kendrick, London, 1849.

STAMMERS, Michael, *The Passage Makers*, Teredo Books, Brighton, Sussex, 1978.

TAYLOR, Irene C., *Sophy under Sail*, Hodder & Stoughton, Sydney, 1969.

THOMAS, Bryn and GANDEVIA, Bryon, 'Dr. Francis Workman, Emigrant, and the History of Taking the Cure for Consumption in the Australian Colonies', *Medical Journal of Australia*, vol. 2, 4 July 1959.

TOWSON, John Thomas, *Tables to Facilitate the Practice of Great Circle Sailing and Determination of Azimuths*, published by order of the Lords Commissioners of the Admiralty, 15th edition, London, 1854.

VAN LOON, Hendrick Willem, *Ships and How They Sailed the Seven Seas*, G. Harrap & Co., London, 1935.

VERDON, George, Agent-General for Victoria, *Instructions to Surgeons-superintendent of Victorian Government Emigrant*

Ships, Spottiswoode & Co., London, 1871.
VERSO, Dr Murray, 'Peripatetic Doctors', *The Victorian Historical Journal*, vol. 49, no.1, February 1978.
VILLIERS, Captain Alan, *The War with Cape Horn*, Scribner, New York, 1971.

WARD, Russel, *The Australian Legend*, Oxford University Press, Melbourne, 1958.
WARREN, Samuel (Pegsworth pseud.), 'Press-room Sketch', *Blackwood's Magazine*, Edinburgh, April 1837 (reprinted 1977).
WATSON, Henry, *A Lecture on South Australia; including letters from J. B. Hack, Esq. and other Emigrants*, 2nd ed., Gliddon, London, 1838.
WEGG-PROSSER, Victoria (comp.), *S.S. 'Great Britain'*, The Illustrated London News, with the co-operation of the s.s. *'Great Britain'* Project, no date.
WELCH, Major J. H., *From the HELL of the Fever Ships to HEALTH* (Book 2 of *The Peninsula Story*), Nepean Historical Society, Victoria, 1969.
WORKMAN, Dr Francis, 'The Ocean as a Health Resort', pamphlet printed by Reading Pathological Society in the Medical Association of Australia Library, Melbourne. (First written as a letter in 1884.)
WYND, I. (ed.), *The Lightning Diary of John Fenwick 1854*, Geelong Historical Society, Geelong, Victoria, 1969.

Diaries and Recollections

ABBOTT, Robert Main, diary on *James L. Bogart*, London for
Melbourne, 1852-3, Royal Historical Society of Victoria.
ADAMS, William John, diary on *Victory*, Southampton for Sydney, 1855, MSS 1068, Mitchell Library, Sydney.
ALLINGHAM, Sarah, diary on *Marco Polo*, Liverpool for Melbourne, 1855, MS 9409, La Trobe Collection, State Library of Victoria. By courtesy Mrs A. R. Allingham, Melbourne.
AMOS, Mark T., recollections of a voyage from Liverpool to Melbourne, 1852, in Castlemaine Association of Pioneers and Old Residents (compilers), *Records of the Castlemaine Pioneers*.
Anonymous diarist from Ireland, 1842, diary in author's keeping.
Anonymous diarist on *Asiatic*, London for Sydney, 1852. By courtesy Mrs Warren Perry, Melbourne.

BECKETT, Robert, diary on *Underly*, Liverpool for Sydney, 1866-7. By courtesy Mrs E. Walker, Melbourne.
BEDFORD, Mary Anne, diary on *Champion of the Seas*, Liverpool for Melbourne, 1864. By courtesy Miss D. Nicholls, Melbourne.
BIRD, Edwin, diary on *Marco Polo*, Liverpool for Melbourne, 1853, MS 6064, National Library of Australia, Canberra.
BLOXOME, Oswald, diary on *Florentia*, Plymouth for Sydney, 1838, MS 336, National Library of Australia, Canberra.
BUSSELL, Bessie, diary on *Cygnet*, Portsmouth for Swan River Settlement, 1832-3, 1415A, J. S. Battye Library, Perth.
BUSSELL, Fanny L., diary on *Cygnet*, Portsmouth for Swan River Settlement, 1832-3, MS 337A, J. S. Battye Library, Perth.

CAMPBELL, Jessie, diary on *Blenheim* bound for New Zealand, 1840, quoted by Greenhill and Giffard in *Women under Sail*.
CLARK, John Fitch, diary on *Nepaul*, London for Geelong, 1852, 2627 A, J. S. Battye Library, Perth.
COGGAN, Thomas, recollections of voyage to Melbourne, 1857, in Castlemaine Association of Pioneers and Old Residents (compilers), *Records of the Castlemaine Pioneers*.
CORKHILL, Robert, diary on *British Trident*, Liverpool for Melbourne, 1855, in *Digger*, February and March 1974.

DAVIS, Fanny, diary on *Conway*, Liverpool for Melbourne, 1858, MS 10509, La Trobe Collection, State Library of Victoria. By courtesy Miss Ella B. Jones, Melbourne.
DEAKIN, William, diary on *Samuel Boddington*, London for Adelaide, 1849-50, MS 1540/19/357, National Library of Australia, Canberra.
DILL, John, account of emigration with brother on *Monarch of the Seas*, 1857, attached to Shipping List of *Monarch of the Seas*, 1857 in Public Record Office, Victoria.
DOCKER, Sarah, diary on *Adams*, London for Sydney 1828, MS 10437, La Trobe Collection, State Library of Victoria.
DRYSDALE, Anne, diary on *Indus*, London for Melbourne, 1839, MS 9249, La Trobe Collection, State Library of Victoria. By courtesy Mrs K. D. den Hollander, Surrey, England.

FRIEND, Mary Ann, diary on *Wanstead*, Portsmouth for Swan River Settlement, 1829-30, on ship commanded by her husband, Commander Matthew Friend, in *Western Australian Historical Society, Journal and Proceedings*, vol. 1, part 10, 1931.

GIBSON, Aleck, diary on *Stebonheath*, London for Melbourne, 1855, Aleck Gibson papers, H 15943, La Trobe Collection, State Library of Victoria.
GILL, Mrs [probably], *Journal of a Voyage to Australia Felix in 1842*, on *Caledonia*, MS 4053, National Library of Australia, Canberra.
GRATTON, Anne, diary on *Conway*, Liverpool for Melbourne, 1858, MS 9367, La Trobe Collection, State Library of Victoria.
GREENHALGH, William Culshaw, diary on *Marco Polo*, Liverpool for Melbourne, 1853, Merseyside County Museums, Liverpool.

HARBOTTLE, William, diary on *Scotia*, London for Sydney, 1849, MS 160, National Library of Australia, Canberra.
HARVIE, A. G., diary on *Scottish Wizard*, London for Brisbane, 1892. By courtesy late Mrs J. L. Potter, Adelaide.
HINSHELWOOD, Mrs Thomas, diary and notes on *Nebo*, Glasgow for Rockhampton, 1883, in *Port of Melbourne Quarterly*, Oct-Dec 1963, Jan-Mar 1964.
HOWITT, William, diary on *Kent*, Plymouth for Melbourne, 1852, MS 9356, La Trobe Collection, State Library of Victoria.
HUGHES, J. F., recollections of a voyage, Liverpool for Melbourne, 1852, in Castlemaine Association of Pioneers and Old Residents (compilers), *Records of the Castlemaine Pioneers*.

JOHNSTONE, William, diary on

Arab, bound for Launceston, 1841-2, quoted by Greenhill and Giffard in *Travelling by Sea in the Nineteenth Century*.

LEADER, H. F., diary on *John Mitchell*, London for Adelaide, 1849, D 4779(L), State Library of South Australia, Archives.
LEIGHTON, F. W., diary on *Bloomer*, Liverpool for Melbourne, 1853, MS 10461, La Trobe Collection, State Library of Victoria.
LEVI, Nathaniel, diary on *Matilda Wattenbach*, Liverpool for Melbourne, 1853-4, MS 8021, La Trobe Collection, State Library of Victoria. By courtesy Rabbi John Levi, Melbourne.
LIGHTOLLER, Dr Henry Martin, diary on *Scottish Bard*, London for Rockhampton, 1878, in *Annual Dog Watch*, No. 20, 1963 and No. 21, 1964. (By permission of the editor.)

McINTOSH, Henry, diary on *Overtes*, Plymouth for Melbourne, 1852. By courtesy Mrs Dorothy Smith, Melbourne.
MacKENZIE, John, diary on *Robert Benn*, Glasgow for Melbourne, 1841, MS 685, National Library of Australia, Canberra.
McRITCHIE, Christine or Mary, sisters, diary on *William Stewart*, London for Melbourne, 1848, MS 10233, La Trobe Collection, State Library of Victoria.
MANNING, Arthur Wilcox, diary on *Earl Grey*, 1843-4, included in [E. Lloyd], 'by a Squatter', *A Visit to the Antipodes*.
MAYBURY, Francis, journal, probably based on diary kept first on *Kochinor*, Liverpool for Cape Town, then *Cheapside*, Cape Town for Melbourne, after loss of *Kochinor* by fire, 1856, MMS 73,

Mitchell Library, Sydney.
MELCHIOR, Moses, diary on *Gauntlet*, London for Melbourne. 1853, in *Annual Dog Watch*, No. 30 1973. By courtesy Mr Sven Tvermoes, Denmark.
MERIFIELD, William, diary on *Lincolnshire*, London for Melbourne, 1858, MS 8044, La Trobe Collection, State Library of Victoria. By courtesy Mrs Patricia Excell, Melbourne.
Mr A., diary on *Clifton*, Liverpool for Launceston, 1837-8, MS 1540/19/357, National Library of Australia, Canberra.
MITCHELL, Robert, recollections of voyage on *Malabar*, Glasgow for Melbourne, 1852, in Castlemaine Association of Pioneers and Old Residents (compilers), *Records of the Castlemaine Pioneers*.
MORT, Thomas Sutcliffe, diary on *Superb*, Liverpool for Sydney, 1837, MS 3308, National Library of Australia, Canberra.

NICHOLLS, Henry, diary on *Norway*, London for Melbourne, 1853, A 4070, Mitchell Library, Sydney. By courtesy D. M. Nicholls, Hobart.

POYNTER, Robert, diary on *Cornelis Gips*, London for Melbourne, 1854. By courtesy Professor J. R. Poynter, Melbourne.

RAMSAY, John, diary on *Loch Sunart*, Glasgow for Melbourne, 1878. By courtesy Mrs Edith M. Ramsay, Melbourne.
RAWSON, Samuel, diary on *Florentia*, Plymouth for Sydney, 1838, MS 204, National Library of Australia, Canberra.
RAYMENT, William, diary on *Himalaya*, London for Melbourne,

1852, MS 4471, La Trobe Collection, State Library of Victoria.
RENSHAW, David, diary on *Ocean Chief*, Liverpool for Melbourne, 1858-9. By courtesy Mr W. F. Renshaw, Melbourne.
ROBERTSON, James, recollections of a voyage, Liverpool to Melbourne, 1852, in Castlemaine Association of Pioneers and Old Residents (compilers), *Records of the Castlemaine Pioneers*.
RODDAN, Jane, diary on *Queen of the East*, Liverpool for Melbourne, 1857, MS 7620 La Trobe Collection, State Library of Victoria.

SADDINGTON, Robert, diary on *Great Britain*, Liverpool for Melbourne, 1853, MSS 1271, Mitchell Library, Sydney.
SAYERS, John, diary on *Osyth*, London for Melbourne, 1875, MS T/1917, Public Record Office, Northern Ireland.
SCOTT, Charles, diary on *Annie Wilson*, Liverpool for Sydney, 1859, MSS 599, Mitchell Library, Sydney.
SHAW, Samuel, diary on *Tyburnia*, London for Sydney, 1877, MS T/1923/1, Public Record Office, Northern Ireland.
SKIRVING, R. Scot, recollections of a voyage on *Ellora*, Plymouth for Sydney, 1883, *Medical Journal of Australia*, 27 June 1942.
SMALL, Thomas, diary on *Donald Mackay*, Liverpool for Melbourne, 1863, MS 8406, La Trobe Collection, State Library of Victoria.
SNELL, Edward, diary on *Bolton*, London for Melbourne, 1849, MS 8970, La Trobe Collection, State Library of Victoria.
STAMP, Edward, 'London Towards Port Phillip', diary on *Tasman*, 1849, MS 29, National Library of Australia, Canberra.

TARRY, Joseph, diary on *Ghenghis Khan*, Liverpool for Melbourne, 1853. By courtesy W. Tarry, Melbourne.
THOMAS, Mary, diary en route London for Adelaide, 1836, in Penelope Hope, *The Voyage of the Africaine*.
THOMPSON, William, diary on *Meteor*, Glasgow for Melbourne, 1854, MS 9085, La Trobe Collection, State Library of Victoria.
THOMSON, Frances (wife of James Thomson, voyage surgeon-superintendent), diary on *Selkirkshire*, Glasgow for Rockhampton, 1882, MS 1025, National Library of Australia, Canberra.
TUCKER, George, diary on *Northumberland*, Plymouth for Melbourne, 1876. By courtesy Mrs D. W. Cruickshank, Melbourne.

WATT, Richard, diary on *Young Australia*, London for Brisbane, 1864, in *Sea Breezes*, vol. 22, July-August 1956, Liverpool.
WEBSTER, Edward, diary on *White Eagle*, Glasgow for Melbourne, 1856-7, MSS 1302, Mitchell Library, Sydney.
WERE, J. B., diary on *William Metcalfe*, Plymouth for Melbourne, 1839, published for clients of J. B. Were & Son, Melbourne, 1964. By courtesy J. B. Were & Son, Melbourne.
WILMOT, Thomas, diary as surgeon-superintendent on *Irene*, Liverpool for Sydney, 1852, MSS 559, Mitchell Library, Sydney.

Letters

AITKEN, Lilburn & Co., letter to Stan McPhee, Warrnambool, Victoria, 8 September 1964.

BEALE, Joseph, letters on *Sarah Sands*, Cork for Melbourne, 1853, MSS 1083, Mitchell Library, Sydney.
BOYKETT, Thomas Herbert, letter to Dr H. G. Bunn telling of voyage on *The Gypsy*, Southampton for Adelaide, 1853. By courtesy Mrs J. E. Nilsson, Melbourne.

GUTHREY, Thomas, letter attached to Reports and Correspondence Respecting the Loss of Emigrant Ship *Cataraqui*(e) in Bass's Straights, ordered by the H.C. to be printed, 27 March 1846.

HACK, Mr S., letter from Launceston, January 1837, in Henry Watson, *A Lecture on South Australia; including letters from J. B. Hack, Esq. and other Emigrants*.
HATFIELD, John, letter to mother dated 14.10.1857 at Collingwood, Victoria, soon after his arrival, MS 8172, Box 964/3D, La Trobe Collection, State Library of Victoria.
HENTY, James, letter to father from Swan River Settlement, 1829, ML 7810, La Trobe Collection, State Library of Victoria.

McSPARRAN, Oliver, letter to parents in Northern Ireland, 4 February 1860, MS T/2743/1, Public Record Office, Northern Ireland.
MARTIN, Mrs Hugh, shipboard letter written en route to Plymouth, New Zealand, 1843-4, to her sister, AM 143, Mitchell Library, Sydney.

PARRY, Edward, letter to John Marshall, Agent to the Emigration Committee, 11 August 1835 at Norwich. Australian Pamphlets

XVII, La Trobe Collection, State
Library of Victoria.
POZZI, Leonardo, letter on
unidentified ship, Hamburg for
Melbourne, 1855. By courtesy Ms
Glen Tomasetti, Melbourne.

SMITH, John, letter to his mother,
3 March 1856, published in
Templestowe Community News,
Victoria, September 1978. By
courtesy William Ross, Melbourne.

TAIT, Mr, letter dated 12 June
1837 on *North Briton*, Firth of
Forth for Sydney, MS 1412,
National Library of Australia,
Canberra.
TOWNSEND, H. S., captain's clerk
on *York*, letter written to father
between 24 June and 30 August
1825, MS 112, National Library of
Australia, Canberra.

WALCOT, S., Land and Emigration
Commission, letter to *Inquirer*,
4 July 1845, C.O. 386/38, Public
Record Office, London.
WILKINSON, Dorothy Edith, *The
Dinton-Dalwood Letters* from 1827
to 1853, privately printed, 1964. By
courtesy The Reverend Philip
Newman, Melbourne.

Newspapers, Periodicals

Age (Melbourne), 17 October
1854.
Annual Dog Watch (Journal of Ship
Lovers' Society of Victoria,
Melbourne), No. 20, 1963, No. 21,
1964, No. 30, 1973.
Argus (Melbourne), 6 October
1855, 4 January 1856, 31
December 1921.

Blackwood's Magazine
(Edinburgh), April 1837, October
1931.

Digger (Melbourne), February and
March, 1974.

Fairplay: Weekly Shipping Journal,
supplement, *5000 Weeks of
Fairplay*, 28 June 1979.
*Forget-Me-Not; or, Last Hours on
the Mersey*, Liverpool Seamen's
Friend Society and Bethel Union,
No. 50, 1855.

*Graphic, an Illustrated Weekly
Newspaper* (London), vol. v, no.
135, 29 June 1872.

Illustrated London News, 13 April
1844, 20 January 1849, 6 July
1850, 15 November 1851, 15
January 1853.

Lady Jocelyn Weekly Mail (voyage
newspaper), 1869.
Lincolnshire Observer (voyage
newspaper), 1866.

Marco Polo Chronicle (voyage
newspaper), 1854.
Medical Journal of Australia, vol. 1,
27 June 1942, vol. 2, 4 July 1959.
Morning Herald (London), 11 July
1834.

Nautical Magazine (Glasgow), vol.
222, no. 1, July 1979.
Netherby Gazette (voyage
newspaper), 1866.

Parade Magazine (Melbourne),
December 1973.
Port of Melbourne Quarterly,
October-December 1963, January-
March 1964.

Sea Breezes (Liverpool), vol. 22
July-August 1956.

Templestowe Community News
(Victoria), September 1978.
The Times (London),

27 September 1854, 9 January
1855.

Victorian Historical Journal
(Melbourne), vol. 49, no. 1,
February 1978.

*Western Australian Historical
Society, Journal and Proceedings*,
vol. 1, part 10, 1931.
White Star Journal (voyage
newspaper), April 20 to July 17,
1855.

*The Young Englishwoman, A
Magazine of Fiction and
Entertainment, Literature, Music,
Poetry, Fine Arts, Fashions and
Useful and Ornamental
Needlework* (London), 30
December 1865-23 June 1866.

Documents

PARLIAMENTARY
New South Wales, Legislative
Council, *Report from the Select
Committee of the Legislative
Council to Inquire into the Present
System of German Immigration into
this Colony*, Government Printer,
Sydney, 11 August 1858.
New South Wales, Legislative
Council, *Votes and Proceedings*,
'Immigration Despatch from the
Secretary of State to Governor
Fitzroy', No. 16, 31 January 1848.

United Kingdom, House of
Commons, *Parliamentary Paper: A
Report to the Secretary of State for
the Colonies from the Agent-
General for Emigration from the
United Kingdom*, 28 April 1838.
United Kingdom, House of
Commons, *Parliamentary Paper:
Reports and Correspondence
Respecting Emigration to the
Colonies*, No. 16, 'Extract of a

letter from Lieutenant Lean, Emigration Agent at the Port of London', 1839.

United Kingdom, *Passenger Act*, 1849, Amendments of 1852.

United Kingdom, Secretary of State for the Colonies, *Instructions for Surgeons-superintendent of Government Ships going to New South Wales*, 'Enclosure No. 6 to Copies or Extracts of Correspondence between the Secretary of State for the Colonies and the Governors of the Australian Colonies, respecting Emigration', 14 May 1838.

Victoria, Legislative Assembly, *Report of the Agent-General and Correspondence on the Subject of Immigration*, 8 June 1869.

Victoria, Legislative Assembly, *Report of the Chief Medical Officer (Dr W. McCrae) on the Report of the Board Appointed to Enquire into the Quarantine Regulations and in Regard to the "Golden Empire"*, Paper A, no. 35, July 1865.

Victoria, Legislative Assembly, *Report of the Immigration Officer (Charles Strutt) on the* Guiding Star, 1855.

Victoria, Legislative Assembly, Immigration Officer, *Report of the Immigration Officer (Edward Grimes), on the* Hercules, 9 June 1853.

Victoria, Legislative Council, *Report of the Health Officer*, 'Return of Diseases most Prevalent on Board Ships Performing Quarantine', during the half year ending the 31 December 1852.

Victoria, Legislative Council, *Report of the Health Officer (A. Robertson MD)*, 'Return of Diseases', six months ending 31 December 1855.

Victoria, Legislative Council, *Submission by George Verdon, Agent-General for Victoria*, Parl. Paper A., no. 21, 1869.

VICTORIAN PUBLIC RECORD OFFICE

Report on the Stranding of the United, no. 1/252/13, 1853.

Superintendent La Trobe, Inward Correspondence, Instructions for Surgeon of *Georgiana* signed 'Wm. Smith & Sons', Liverpool, 22 September 1840, File no. 41/383A, Box 19. Attached to ship's papers.

Passenger list of *Great Britain*, 1857, no. 5638/74.

OTHER

The C. Smith Cuttings (Shipping) held at The Royal Historical Society of Victoria.

A roller-blind scroll covering the years 1855-63, the latitude and longitude for 300 passages is given for each of the voyages. Held at The Royal Historical Society of Victoria.

Acknowledgements

The author wishes to thank those
organizations and people who
provided illustrations, especially
Helen Semmler, of Penguin
Australia, for her line drawings and
maps, which have been based on
material from various sources.
Acknowledgements by reference
to page numbers follow:

part I
La Trobe Collection, State Library
of Victoria.
page
1 *Illustrated Australian News*,
15 June 1874, National
Library of Australia, Canberra.
3 *Illustrated Sydney News*,
13 July 1878, La Trobe
Collection, State Library of
Victoria.
4 A. D. Edwardes Collection,
State Library of South
Australia.
7 Photographs by author.
9 Coppin Collection, La Trobe
Collection, State Library of
Victoria.
10 (top) A. D. Edwardes Collec-
tion, State Library of South
Australia.
10 (bottom) A. D. Edwardes
Collection, State Library of
South Australia.
13 A. D. Edwardes Collection,
State Library of South
Australia.
14 *Mate in Sail* by Captain James
Gaby. By permission of
photographer.
16 Painting by Jack Spurling.
Reproduced by permission of
Calendars of Distinction
Limited, London.
18 (margin) *San Francisco:
Historic Ships*, publication of
Golden Gate Recreation Area,
San Francisco, USA.
18 (bottom) *The Wonder Book of
Ships*, edited by H. Golding,
fourteenth edition, Ward, Lock
& Co., Limited, London.
19 Science Museum of Victoria.
21 (bottom) Cook Collection,
Valentine Museum, Richmond,
Virgina, USA.
24 Photographs by Ken Stepnell,
Warrnambool.
26 A. D. Edwardes Collection,
State Library of South
Australia.
28 Rex Nan Kivell Collection,
National Library of Australia,
Canberra.
30 A. D. Edwardes Collection,
State Library of South
Australia.
31 A. D. Edwardes Collection,
State Library of South
Australia.
32 (top) Metropolitan Museum of
Art, New York, N.Y., Gift of I.N.
Phelps Stokes, Edward S.
Hawes, Alice Mary Hawes,
Marion Augusta Hawes, 1937.
32 (bottom) *The Colonial Clippers*
by Basil Lubbock.
33 *Illustrated London News*,
19 February 1853, La Trobe
Collection, State Library of
Victoria.
40 *Illustrated London News*,
3 April 1852, La Trobe Collec-
tion, State Library of Victoria.
43 *Oxford Illustrated Dictionary*,
Oxford University Press,
London, 1962.

45 Peter Williams Collection, Melbourne, Victoria.

48 Merseyside County Museums, Liverpool, UK.

51 (top) *Illustrated London News*, 15 January 1853, La Trobe Collection, State Library of Victoria.

51 (bottom) *Illustrated London News*, 15 January 1853, La Trobe Collection, State Library of Victoria.

53 *Graphic*, 10 October 1855, Illustrated London News Picture Library, London.

54 Merseyside County Museums, Liverpool, UK.

56 Merseyside County Museums, Liverpool, UK.

59 Merseyside County Museums, Liverpool, UK.

60 Merseyside County Museums, Liverpool, UK.

61 Merseyside County Museums, Liverpool, UK.

62 *Illustrated London News*, 21 December 1844, La Trobe Collection, State Library of Victoria.

65 National Library of Australia, Canberra.

66 Mansell Collection, London.

69 National Library of Australia, Canberra.

72 Mitchell Collection, State Library of New South Wales.

75 Lithograph by A. C. Hayter, Rex Nan Kivell Collection, National Library of Australia, Canberra.

79 National Library of Australia, Canberra.

80 *Illustrated London News*, 17 March 1849, La Trobe Collection, State Library of Victoria.

82 *Australasian Sketcher*, 18 December 1880, National Library of Australia, Canberra.

85 *Illustrated London News*, 10 July 1852, La Trobe Collection, State Library of Victoria.

86 (top) *Illustrated London News*, 10 July 1852, La Trobe Collection, State Library of Victoria.

86 (bottom) *Illustrated London News*, 12 March 1853, La Trobe Collection, State Library of Victoria.

88 Victorian Public Record Office, Microfilm Reel 9, December 1856.

89 Birmingham Museums and Art Gallery, UK.

90 *Illustrated London News*, 6 July 1850, La Trobe Collection, State Library of Victoria.

91 *Illustrated Australian News*, 24 March 1875, National Library of Australia, Canberra.

93 Australian National Library, Canberra.

96 *Illustrated London News*, 7 July 1859, La Trobe Collection, State Library of Victoria.

98 Photograph by Barney Roberts, Flowerdale, Tasmania; chest in possession of Mr and Mrs R. Lewis, Wynyard, Tasmania.

101 *Illustrated London News*, 19 July 1852, Illustrated London News Picture Library, London.

102 Part of undated coloured lithograph, *Emigrants going to Australia*, by C. J. Stanisland, Rex Nan Kivell Collection, National Library of Australia, Canberra.

104 South Australian Archives, Document number D3062/17.

108 *Illustrated London News*, 13 April 1844, La Trobe Collection, State Library of Victoria.

110 National Maritime Museum, Greenwich, UK.

113 Merseyside County Museums, Liverpool, UK.

114 *Illustrated London News*, 10 July 1852, La Trobe Collection, State Library of Victoria.

116 From the ship *Charles W. Morgan*, Mystic Seaport, Connecticut, USA.

119 *Illustrated London News*, 10 May 1851, National Library of Australia, Canberra.

120 *Illustrated London News*, 17 August 1850, La Trobe Collection, State Library of Victoria.

121 *Queenslander* supplement, 14 July 1877, National Library of Australia, Canberra.

126 *Illustrated Australian News*, 24 March 1875, National Library of Australia, Canberra.

127 *Illustrated London News*, 17 August 1850, La Trobe Collection, State Library of Victoria.

130 *Illustrated London News*, 13 April 1844, La Trobe Collection, State Library of Victoria.

132 Peter Williams Collection, Melbourne, Victoria.

136 *China Tea Clippers* by George Campbell.

139 *China Tea Clippers* by George Campbell.

142 A. D. Edwardes Collection, State Library of South Australia.

143 National Maritime Museum, Greenwich, UK.

144 *Illustrated Australian News*, 24 March 1875, National Library of Australia, Canberra.

146 (top) National Maritime Museum, Greenwich, UK.

146 (bottom) *Mate in Sail* by

Captain James Gaby. By permission of photographer.

148 A. D. Edwardes Collection, State Library of South Australia.

149 A. D. Edwardes Collection, State Library of South Australia.

156 *Australasian Sketcher*, November 1880, La Trobe Collection, State Library of Victoria.

161 (top and bottom) *Surgical Instrument Catalogue*, Arnold & Sons, 1885, University of Melbourne Medical Museum.

165 *Illustrated Australian News*, 24 March 1873, National Library of Australia, Canberra.

168 *Surgical Instrument Catalogue*, Arnold & Sons, 1885, University of Melbourne Medical Museum.

173 *Surgical Instrument Catalogue*, Arnold & Sons, 1885, University of Melbourne Medical Museum.

174 Australian Medical Association Library, Melbourne.

177 Australian Medical Association Library, Melbourne.

178 *Surgical Instrument Catalogue*, Arnold & Sons, 1885, University of Melbourne Medical Museum.

179 Edward Snell, diary on *Bolton*, 1849, La Trobe Collection, State Library of Victoria.

183 *Surgical Instrument Cata-*

logue, Arnold & Sons, 1885, University of Melbourne Medical Museum.

185 A. D. Edwardes Collection, State Library of South Australia.

186 *Surgical Instrument Catalogue*, Arnold & Sons, 1885, University of Melbourne Medical Museum.

190 *Surgical Instrument Catalogue*, Arnold & Sons, 1885, University of Melbourne Medical Museum.

192 *Illustrated London News*, 12 February 1887, Illustrated London News Picture Library, London.

195 Mitchell Collection, State Library of New South Wales.

198 *Graphic*, 29 June 1853, La Trobe Collection, State Library of Victoria.

200 Edward Snell, diary on *Bolton*, 1849, La Trobe Collection, State Library of Victoria.

203 *Graphic*, 29 June 1853, La Trobe Collection, State Library of Victoria.

206 *Illustrated London News*, 20 January 1849, La Trobe Collection, State Library of Victoria.

211 *Illustrated London News*, 20 January 1849, La Trobe Collection, State Library of Victoria.

214 *Illustrated London News*,

20 January 1849, La Trobe Collection, State Library of Victoria.

216 *Illustrated London News*, 6 July 1850, Illustrated London News Picture Library, London.

224 *Graphic*, 29 June 1853, La Trobe Collection, State Library of Victoria.

229 *Illustrated London News*, 20 January 1849, La Trobe Collection, State Library of Victoria.

235 Painting by T. Kirby. National Library of Australia, Canberra.

238 A. D. Edwardes Collection, State Library of South Australia.

243 *Illustrated Sydney News*, 25 July 1874, National Library of Australia, Canberra.

246 A. D. Edwardes Collection, State Library of South Australia.

250 A. D. Edwardes Collection, State Library of South Australia.

part II

Edward Snell, diary on *Bolton*, 1849, La Trobe Collection, State Library of Victoria.

253 Edward Snell, diary on *Bolton*, 1849, La Trobe Collection, State Library of Victoria.

277 Miss Ella Jones, Melbourne.

Index